center for contemporary art, Rotterdam

Witte de With

October, 1996

CAHIER #5

Richter Verlag, Düsseldorf

01 HYDE PARK

02 STILL/ A NOVEL

03 VOORWERK 5

01 HYDE PARK

The work of Brandt Junceau was shown in the exhibition Hyde Park at Witte de With from 28 October until 24 December 1995. In the exhibition, Junceau created a meeting place for the studio of Elie Nadelman and the presidential library site of Franklin Delano Roosevelt. The exhibition was accompanied by two illustrated essays by the artist, 'The Late Style of Elie Nadelman' and 'The Franklin Delano Roosevelt Library,' published in Witte de With – Cahier # 4.

Thomas Sokolowski

View of Nadelman studio, 1948 ›

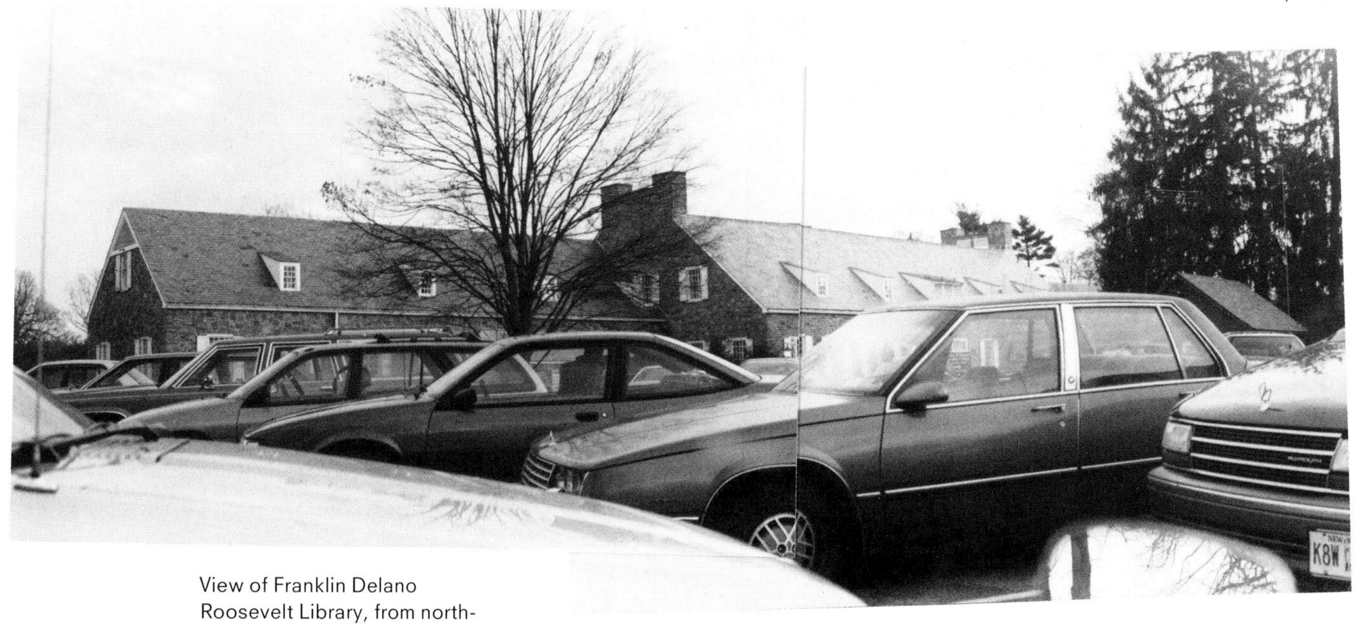

View of Franklin Delano Roosevelt Library, from north-west parking lot, 1995

Conjuring American Res Gestae

'The old people in a new world, the new people made out of the old,
that is the story that I mean to tell, for that is what really is and what I really know.'
Gertrude Stein, The Making of Americans

As I polish off this set of comments about Brandt Junceau's exhibition Hyde Park, I am struck by the symbolic implications of today's date, '4 July 1996,' the 220th anniversary of America's Declaration of Independence from the Old World, from the old ways of doing things, in an endeavor to create something better, something brighter, something newer, something fashioned according to a new, indigenous design in order to provide a better fit! While the language of the declaration is intentionally rebarbative, its formal carapace is enduringly, nay, lovingly, graceful, its architects savvy to the wallop which its measured elegance would impact. Similarly, Hyde Park, in its quirky and quintessentially late-twentieth-century American way, also employs the rhetorical devices of the ancients. Synecdoche selects the constituent parts, supplies the aggregate associations, and feeds an emblematic taxonomy that renders a symbolic coup de grace in something very like the language of the American myth-making machine, now more than two centuries old. Recent works by other New World artists such as the Americans Fred Wilson, Allan McCollum, and Mike Kelley, as well as their Antipodean colleague Narelle Jubelin, have trafficked in revisionist, de-constructions of the museum and all that it has come to signify.

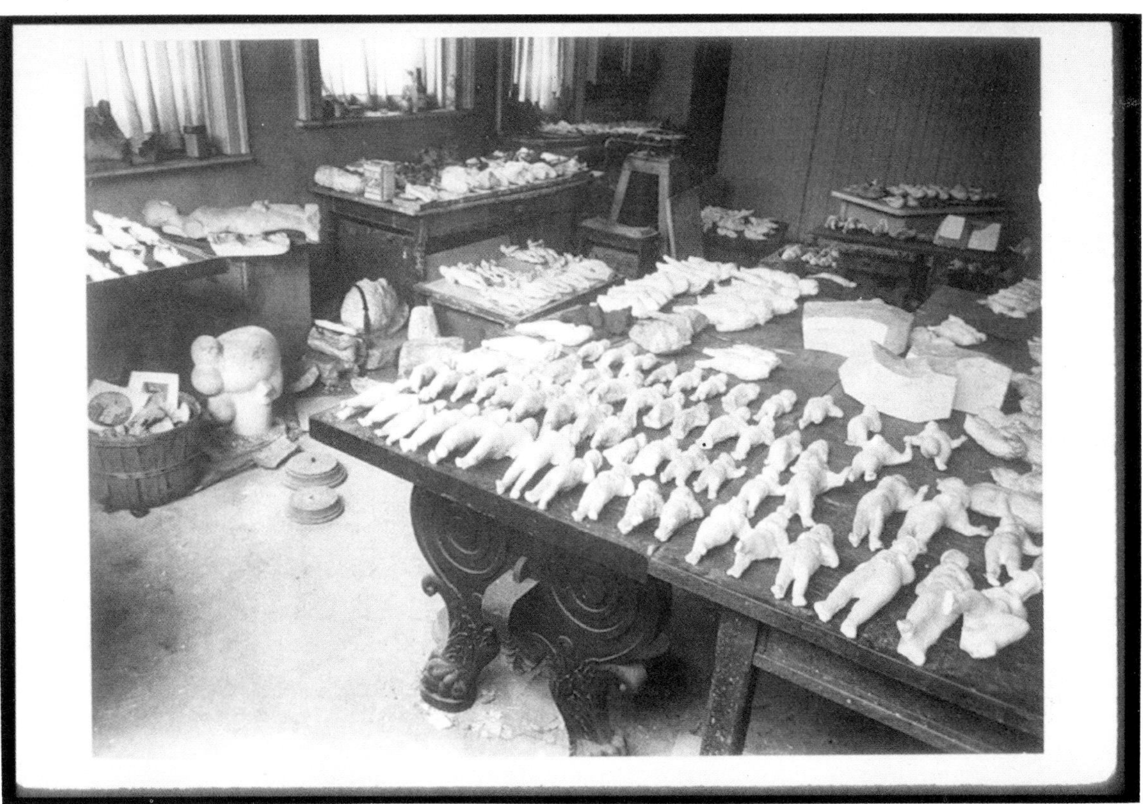

Brandt Junceau has done something decidedly more clever, recalling both Renaissance cosmographies and twentieth-century American history simultaneously. As a serious student of history, he realized that half of the story is in the telling.

Others have chosen to tell America's story. Gertrude Stein's self-styled 'long book,' The Making of Americans, published in 1925, was her first attempt at literary writing. Begun in 1902 as a thirty-five page essay entitled 'The Making of Americans, Being the History of a Family's Progress,' the piece opens with the statement

'It has always seemed to me a rare privilege this of being an American, a real American and yet one whose tradition has taken scarcely sixty years to create.'

Throughout the literary convolutions of her 925 succeeding pages, Stein makes the case for a truly American Tree of Jesse, yet one which seemed to happen in an almost Big Bang-like fashion rather than by means of a multi-generational evolutionary process. If placed against the four-hundred-plus 'Screen Test' 16mm film portraits which Andy Warhol produced at The Factory during the seminal years of the sixties, it is clear that Steinian genealogy has metamorphosed into a much more anthropological mode of description. Lasting only three minutes a piece, these black-and-white capsules of celluloid fame constitute a chilling, yet poignant, commentary on America during one of its greatest cultural heydays. Run end-to-end and taken as a whole, as one might well do, with the approximately five thousand, forty-inch-square portraits which Warhol made during his lifetime, a remarkably pellucid visual American family tree appears. If Stein conjured the dynamics of the 'making' of Americans, Warhol then catalogued them, clearly and succinctly, and perhaps

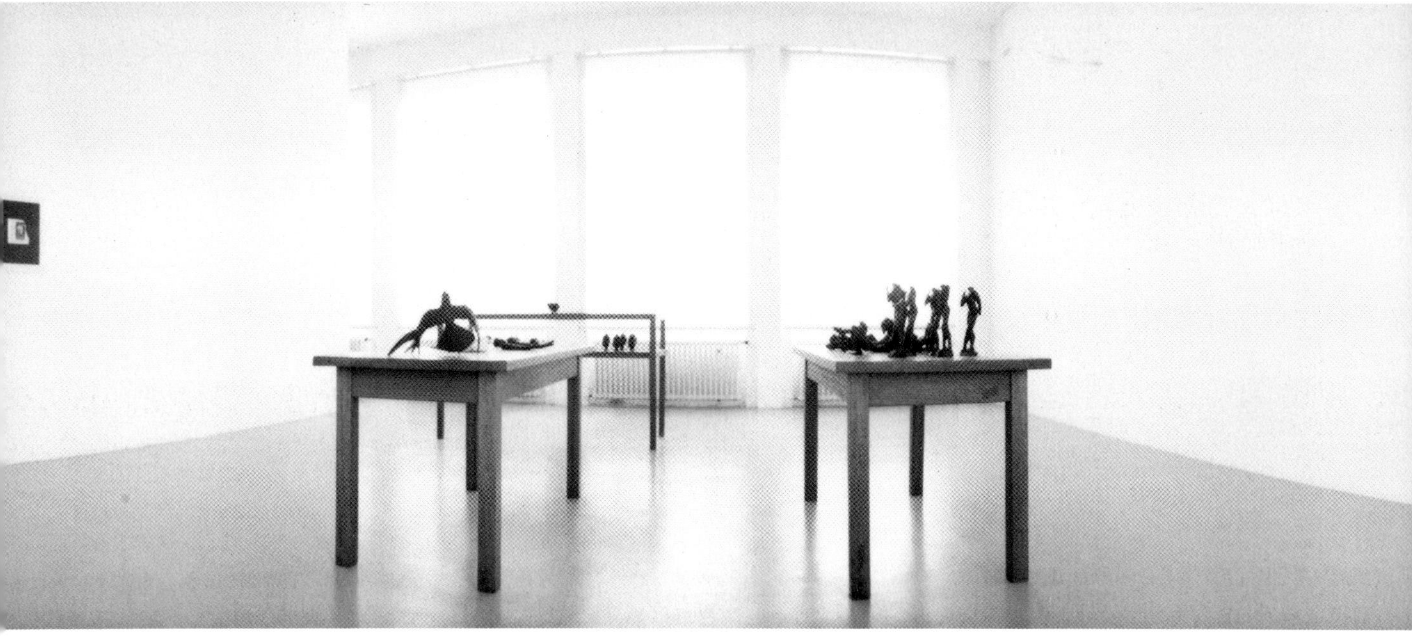

Hyde Park, installation views at Witte de With

prophesied their eventual unmaking. Where Stein exposed the warts over and over again in her tumbling prose, Warhol performed supreme acts of cosmetic surgery on his subjects, including Stein herself, before hanging them before the public eye, each resultant eponym-image brilliantly and uniquely glamorous, yet blandly the same. 'Are we all the same?' both Stein and Warhol ask, and 'if so, then what?'

In the previous century, the poet Walt Whitman (Junceau wove the reference into both the Nadelman and Roosevelt texts) conjured up this same American connective tissue

'I celebrate myself
And what I assume you shall assume
For every atom belonging to me as good belongs to you.'

And later on, referring to the long-poem's eponymous Leaves of Grass,

'Or I guess it is the handkerchief of the Lord
A scented gift and remembrancer designedly dropped,
Bearing the owner's name someway in the corners, that we see and remark,
And say Whose?'

Both Stein and Warhol seem to have operated according to a bowdlerization of the biblical dictum: 'by their [faces] you shall know them' Brandt Junceau and the two subjects of Hyde Park, Elie Nadelman and Franklin Delano Roosevelt, stick to the original text, since it is indeed around the proverbial 'fruits of their labors' that Hyde Park deftly revolves.

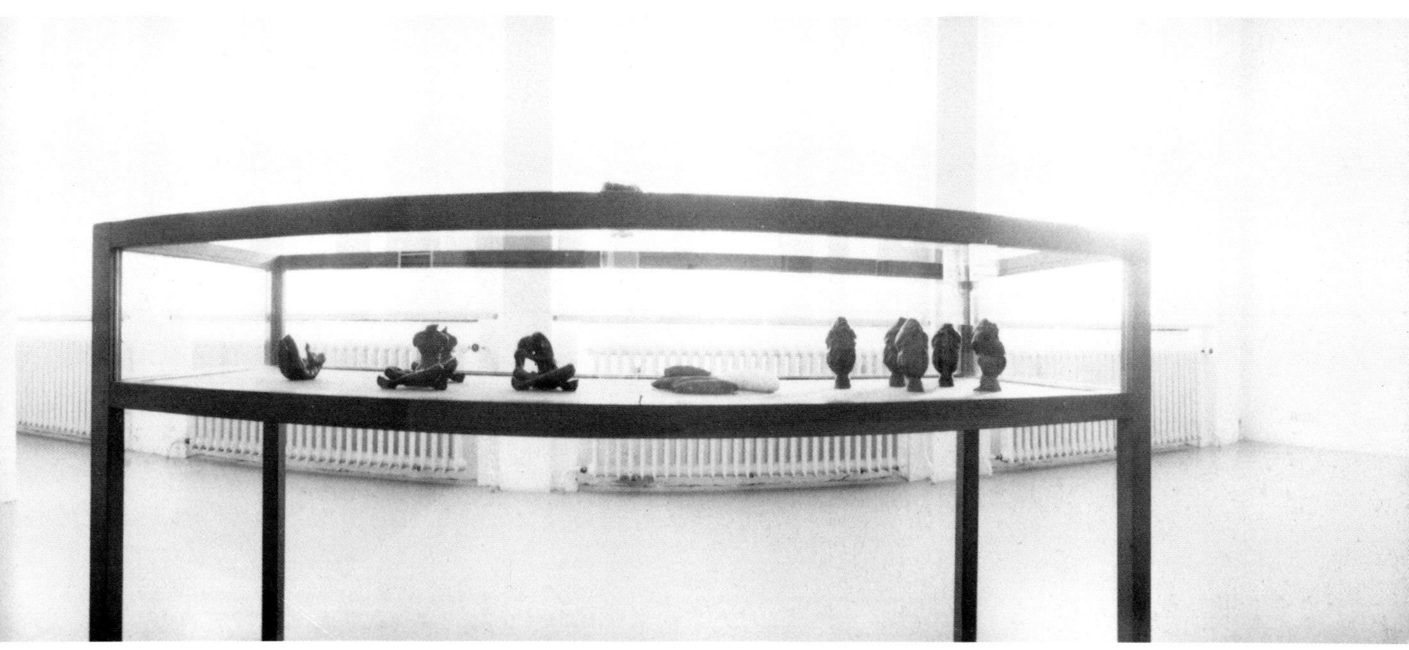

Junceau's essays (Witte de With – Cahier # 4, pp. 103-137) presented a necessary prolegomenon to a proper viewing of Hyde Park. Though the essays are matter-of-fact in style and self-contained in subject, a diligent reader quickly becomes aware that, while investigating the work of others, the author has set his own stage pictures. Deep within his detailed texts he has inserted two crucial phrases 'original conception' and a pet expression of the former president: 'you're not in the game unless you're doing at least two things at once.' As he tells his story in an ostensibly American plainspoken manner, Junceau is setting up the reader, readying him for the experience of the actual artwork, in short, directing him towards the precise intellectual belvedere from which the installation can best be seen. This is Junceau's original conception, and in a prodigious feat of prestidigitation he juggles the lives of Nadelman and Roosevelt before us in order to show us something very different and of far more consequence, if only we are quick enough to detect the sleight of hand.

Conjurers were a common part of the American scene, especially during the latter half of the nineteenth and early twentieth centuries. Nadelman and Roosevelt were two of the best. However, rather than selling flasks of bogus snake oil remedies to unsuspecting chumps along the carny circuit, each in his own way chose to perpetuate a version of history upon an adoring public which showcased the conjurers themselves. Not surprisingly, like their nineteenth-century primogenitors, both Nadelman and Roosevelt chose rustic suburbia as the locale for their stagecraft/statecraft. In addition, the pastoral settings in the Hudson Valley provided each with

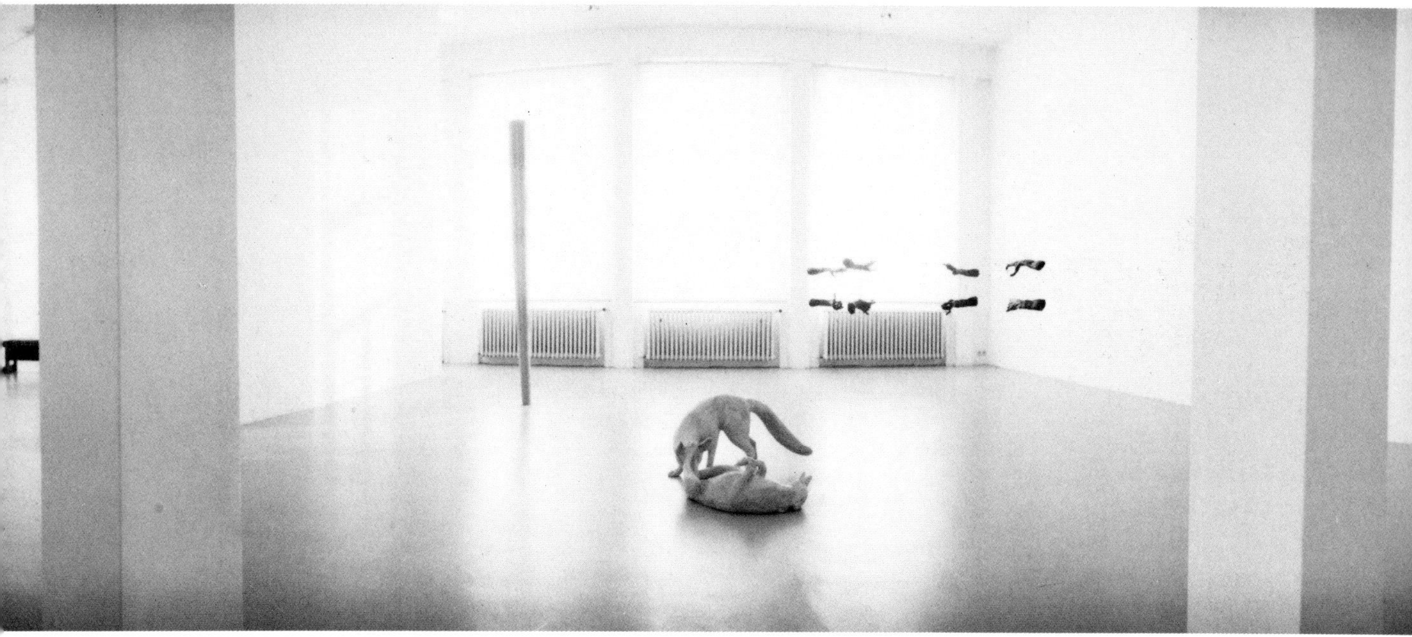

a quiet repose and informality as similar settings had done for the Emperor Hadrian in his villa at Tivoli near Rome; for Grand Duke Cosimo I de Medici at his Villa at Castello all' Olmo outside of Florence; and for president Thomas Jefferson at his home Monticello near Chalottesville, Virginia. Eschewing the constraints and decorum of urban society, suburbia allows for the projection and creation of personal cosmographies which may be merely illusory or cleverly propagandistic. For each, the setting and the contents within became synonymous with the architect/keeper/lord of the manor. While none of the aforementioned rural estates rivaled the horrific splendor of the Villa at Bomarzo, complete with its funhouse tricks and grottos, each programmatically arranged not only the stones and mortar, but the flora and fauna as well, to metaphorically reflect the prime inhabitant of the villa. In some cases, the game plan was clear. For others, especially as in the work of Brandt Junceau, the entire piece becomes a grandiloquent rebus of sorts. Hyde Park was not, however, without clues.

The floor plan of the third-floor gallery of Witte de With immediately recalls the ground plan of a typical Renaissance villa (Agostino Chigi's Villa Farnesina in Rome, for example), an analogy which has not gone unnoticed by the artist. Mounting the grand staircase, the visitor has the choice to move either to the front or to the rear of the gallery, the former fronting on the street, thus the formal or 'urban' half of the villa, the latter fronting on the back or the 'garden' side, the suburban end of the villa. In the suburban, rear space, Junceau placed two sculptural groups, making up a bucolic grove with grazing deer, and children at play. The front parlor housed

numerous vitrines which enshrined bits of nature or art, keeping it at one remove from our touch. While Roosevelt, as Junceau informs us, chose to reflect the architectural style of early America, he did so in a manner not unlike the antique referencing of his Renaissance forbears, each seeking justification and credence by association with the past; form following mythic fiction in each case rather than adhering to mere quotidian function. In Hyde Park, the binary references continued as each room served as a meeting place twixt the Nadelman studio and the Roosevelt library. Just as the architectonics of the galleries gave rise to the displacement of the objects within, so too did the presence of the flocks of birds that alit and swept down upon the vitrines of the installation. Black common swifts and yellow warblers co-existed in the galleries, a condition unreplicated in nature, where swifts thrive in urban conditions and warblers eschew the city for the countryside. In the words of the artist, the birds are 'radically mobile and pedestal-less ... visitors who come and go according to no plan, and leave without a trace.' In their wild flight they obstructed certain views without impeding the progress of the visitor through the exhibition.

Despite the potentially imperial ambitions of president Roosevelt which might be suggested in the layout and construction of the original buildings at Hyde Park, the entire revetment suggests the lair of a wise and able leader, one unfettered by doubt or frailty. Given his paraplegic condition, brought on by a case of polio as a young adult, Junceau's use of swifts as a metaphor for Roosevelt himself is made clear when it is explained that swallows cannot walk, but only perch upon walls. News-

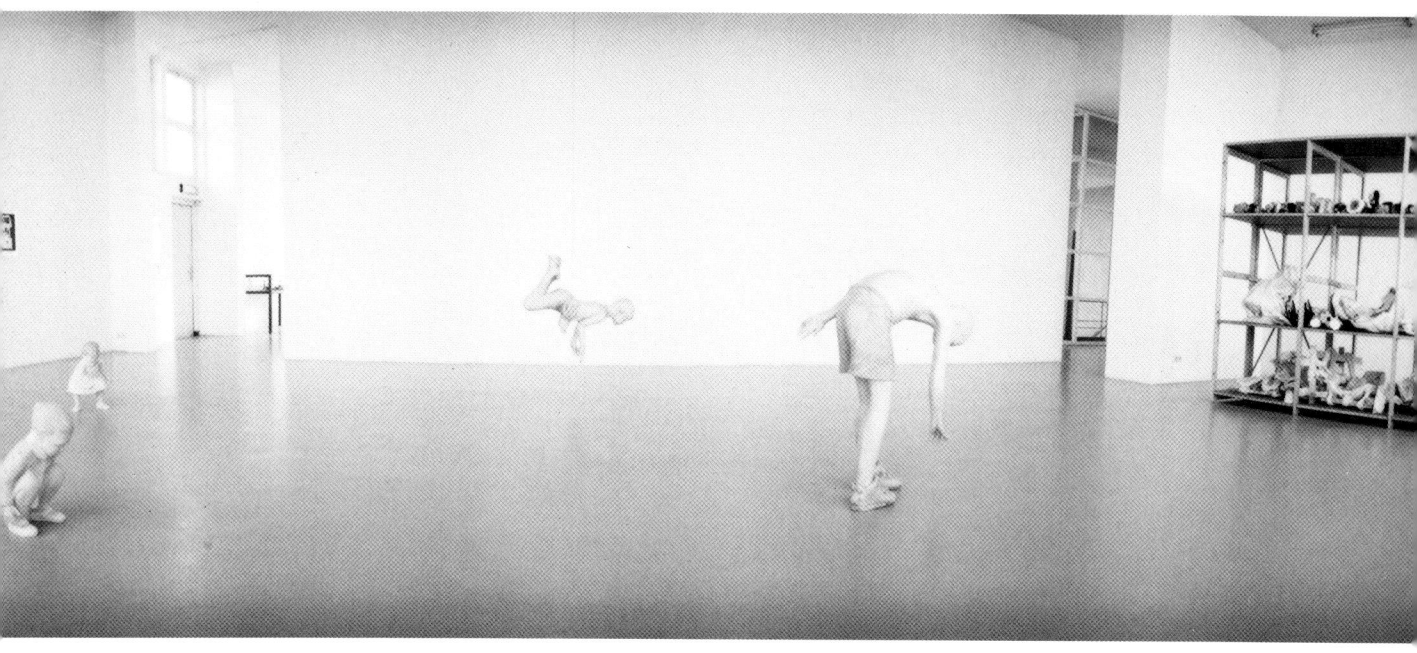

reels and home movies taken during the period of the library's construction, depict Roosevelt as pre-eminently able under the watchful eye of the camera. Suffice it to say that, like the library complex itself and the tightly controlled media campaign during the years of his three-term presidency, myth overrode the fact in the eyes of a knowing and adoring citizenry. Like the black swallows of Junceau's installation, in flight Roosevelt was omnipotent.

Nadelman's late work, a collection of figurines predicated upon ancient sources and transmogrified by contemporary culture, were displayed throughout the 'urban' installation without hierarchy of structure and without apparent hierarchy of purpose. Quoting the early museologist and classical aesthetician, Johann Joachim Winckelmann (1717-68) at the entrance to the installation, Junceau evoked the scholar's belief in ancient Greek culture as the epitome of civilization in both style and spirit. Junceau placed Winckelmann's excavation of the ancients in parallel to the practice of Nadelman and Roosevelt, noting that Winckelmann's conception of the ancients is in fact 'a self-portrait, and his speculative ancient world a picture of his own imagination.' In Hyde Park, nothing was what it seemed to be, but then again, it was only the country.

Hyde Park became, at base, a simulacrum for America, a terrarium of the American Dream, and a template for American ambition. Coopting the lives of a famous president and a lesser known artist of the first half of the century and placing the resulting admixture within the confines of a suburban villa, the site for contemplation and retreat, Brandt Junceau, recreated history within his own waxworks. Without

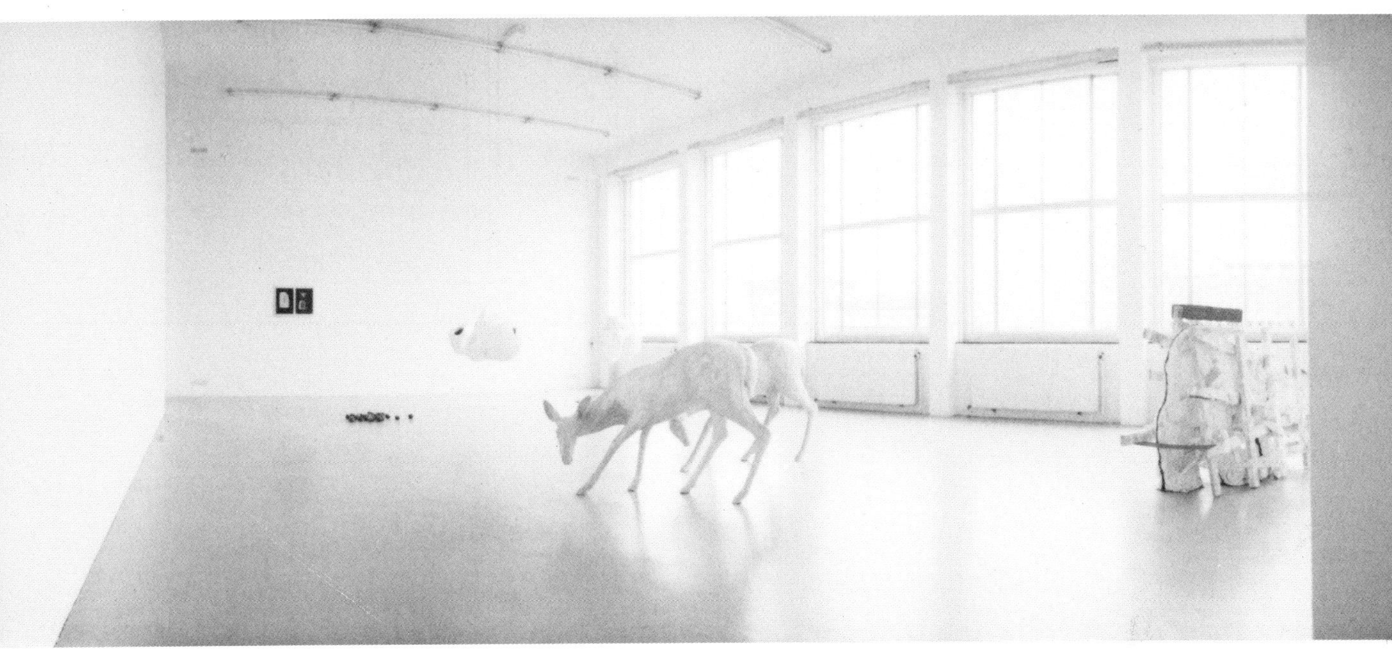

a docent to lead us along the way, we were encouraged to abandon the high street for the footpath and there, search for ourselves. In the words of the artist:

> 'I like for the visitor to have all the references I had, for him to see the archival materials as I saw them, and to test what I made by what it comes from. The visitor ought to have all the information necessary and available, to reach his own conclusions. I love to speculate for myself, but I do not interpret for others.'

The facts are there. Perhaps only for fifteen minutes and not in perpetuity. Take your pick, follow your path. Incredibly democratic, especially on the Fourth of July. How American!

02 STILL / A NOV

Eadweard Muyb

Jan Dibbets

Carl Andre

Marcel Broodth

Chris Dercon

dge

ers

Still/A Novel was a two-part project: An exhibition with works by Eadweard Muybridge and Jan Dibbets, as well as homages to Muybridge by Carl Andre and Marcel Broodthaers, at Witte de With from 13 January until 10 March 1996; and a documentary, made by Chris Dercon for Dutch television (VPRO), on the history and the future of cinema.

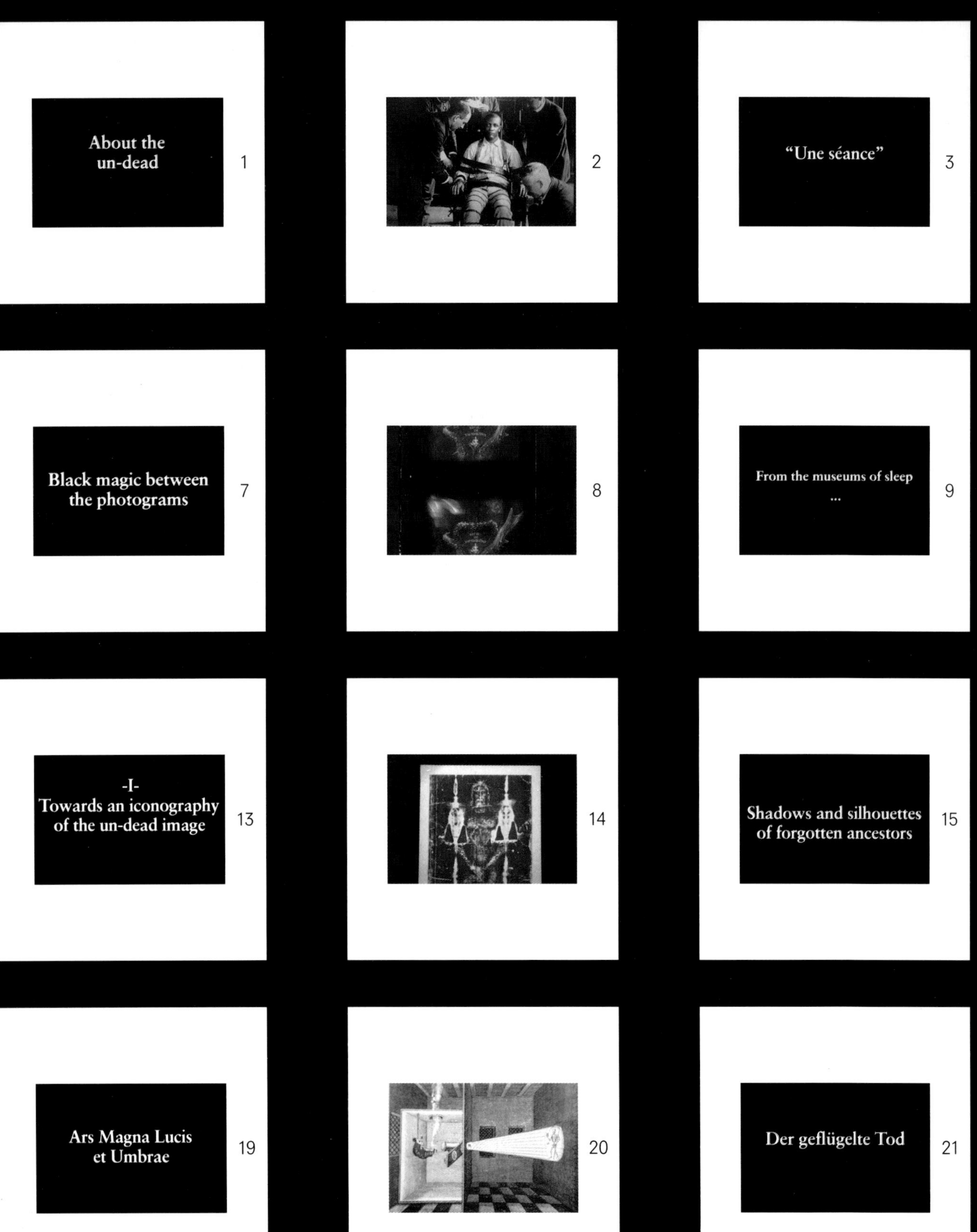

This sequence of images was conceived as a slide presentation for a program entitled Cinemagie at the Zaal de Unie, in Rotterdam on 24

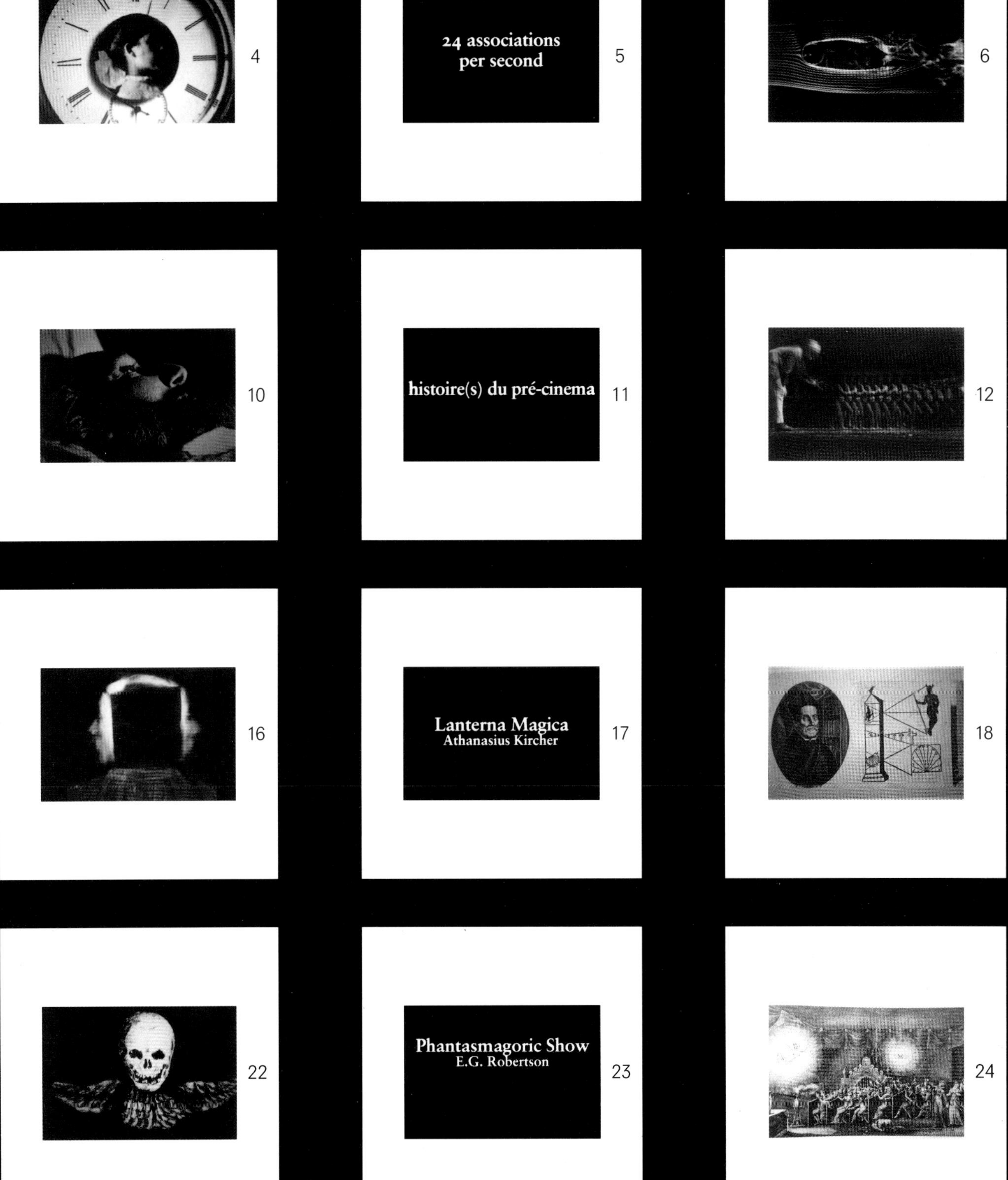

. The evening's program covered magic in the electronic media and

was part of a series organized by the Unie on 'Magic and Art.'

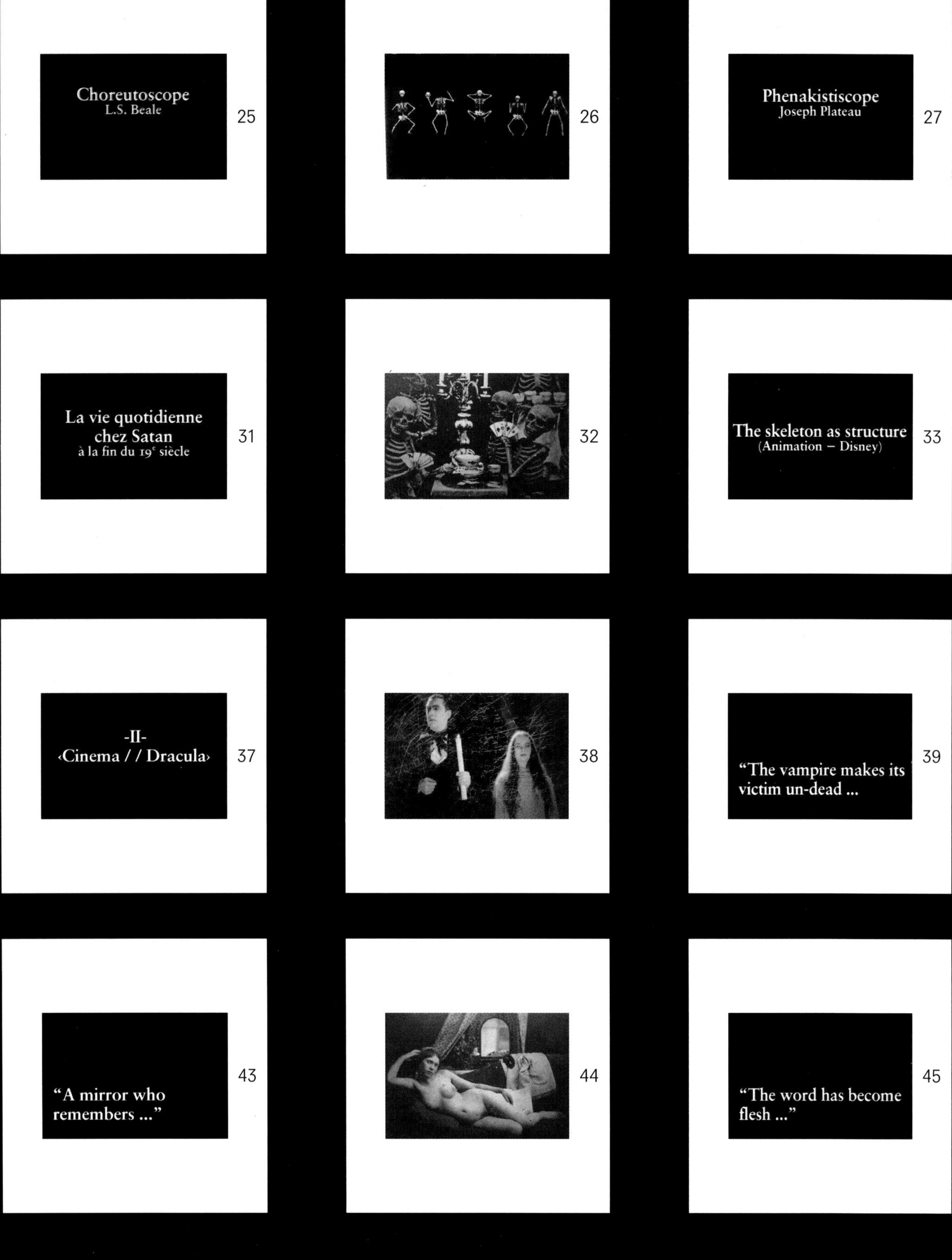
Choreutoscope
L.S. Beale
25
26
Phenakistiscope
Joseph Plateau
27
La vie quotidienne
chez Satan
à la fin du 19e siècle
31
32
The skeleton as structure
(Animation – Disney)
33
-II-
‹Cinema / / Dracula›
37
38
"The vampire makes its
victim un-dead ...
39
"A mirror who
remembers ..."
43
44
"The word has become
flesh ..."
45

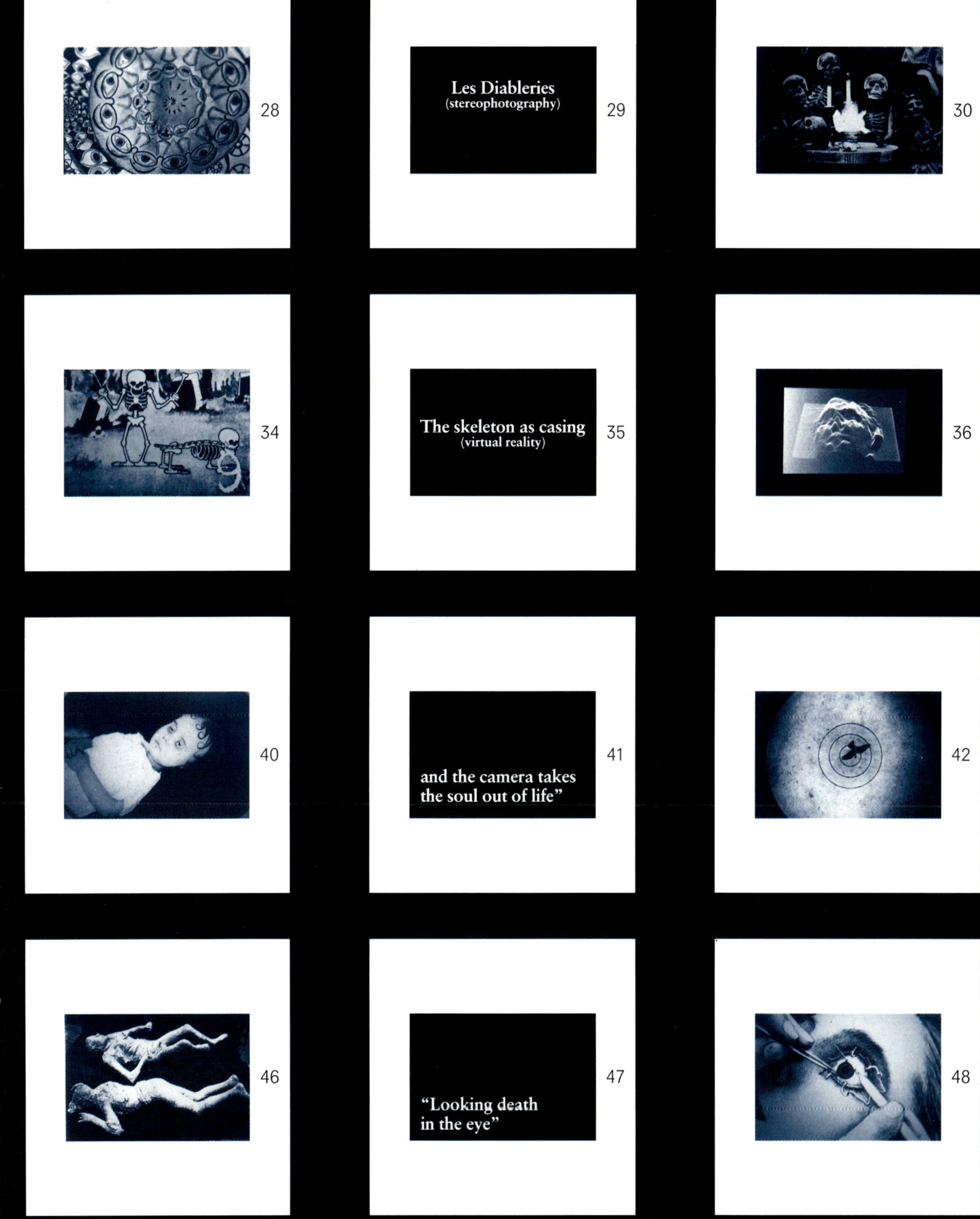
28
Les Diableries
(stereophotography)
29
30
34
The skeleton as casing
(virtual reality)
35
36
40
41
and the camera takes
the soul out of life"
42
46
47
"Looking death
in the eye"
48

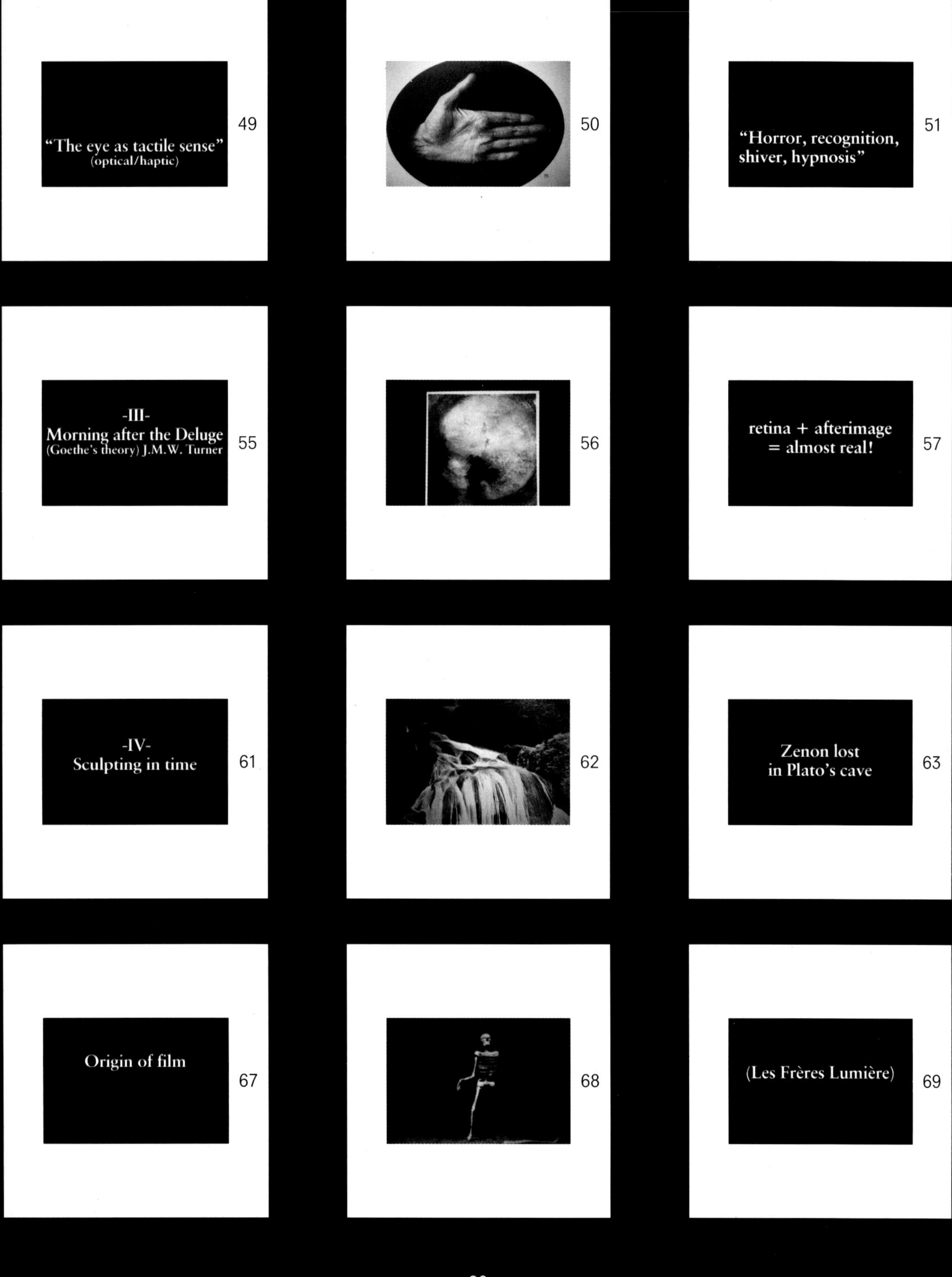
"The eye as tactile sense"
(optical/haptic)
49
50
"Horror, recognition,
shiver, hypnosis"
51
-III-
Morning after the Deluge
(Goethe's theory) J.M.W. Turner
55
56
retina + afterimage
= almost real!
57
-IV-
Sculpting in time
61
62
Zenon lost
in Plato's cave
63
Origin of film
67
68
(Les Frères Lumière)
69

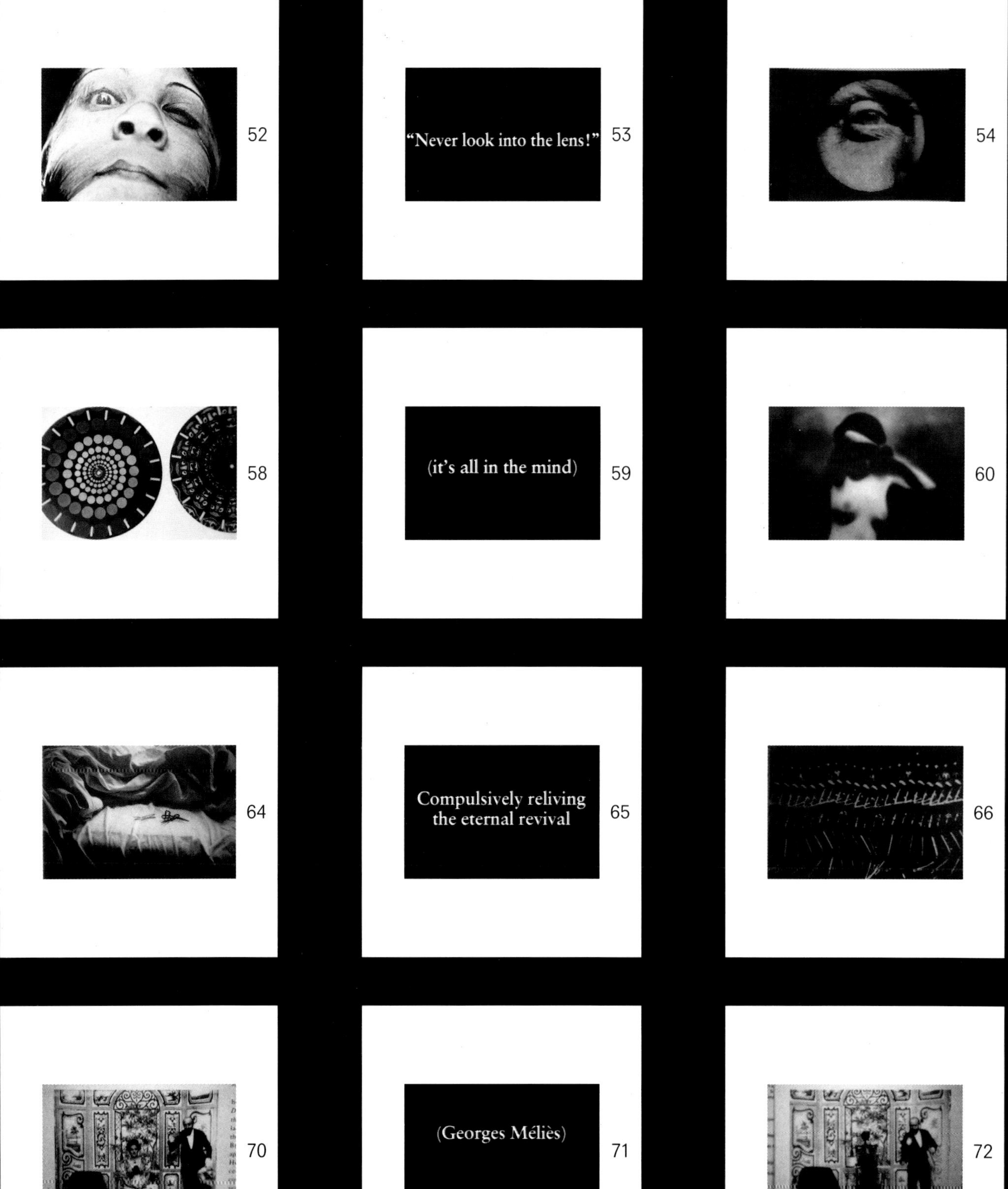
52
"Never look into the lens!"
53
54
58
(it's all in the mind)
59
60
64
Compulsively reliving
the eternal revival
65
66
70
(Georges Méliès)
71
72

Origin of film form

73

74

-V-
memento mori

75

image: Edwin Carels
sound: Wolfgang Zeller

79

FIN

80

References

2
William van der Weyde, Man in the Electric Chair, c. 1900 (detail), in Photodiscovery - Masterworks of Photography 1840-1940 (1980).

4
Anonymous, Woman's Face Superimposed on Clock, c. 1890 (detail), in Sleeping Beauty - Memorial Photography in America (1990).

6
Étienne-Jules Marey, Movement of Air (Smoke Currents) against a Bullet, 1900 (detail), in Étienne-Jules Marey (1984).

8
The Brothers Quay, photogram from Stille Nacht III, 1992.

10
Étienne Carjat, Léon Gambetta on His Deathbed, 1882, in Photodiscovery - Masterworks of Photography 1840-1940 (1980).

12
Étienne-Jules Marey, Nude Child Walking, after 1886, in Étienne-Jules Marey (1984).

14
Devotional picture of the Shroud of Turin.

16
Étienne-Jules Marey, Articulated Movement. Lateral rotation of the head seen from behind; registrated in seated position. 1894, in Étienne-Jules Marey (1984).

18
Portrait gravure in Athanasius Kircher, Ars Magnae Lucis et Umbrae, 1643 reprinted in Archeology of the Cinema (1965).

20
Gravure of demonstration of Lanterna Magica in Athanasius Kircher, Ars Magnae Lucis et Umbrae, 1643, reprinted in Archeology of the Cinema (1965).

22
Der Geflügelte Tod, in Buñuel - Auge des Jahrhunderts (1994).

24
Étienne Gaspard Robertson, Gravure of a phantasmagoric performance, in Archeology of the Cinema (1965).

26
L.S. Beale's choreutoscope, 1866, in Archeology of the Cinema (1965).

28
Joseph Plateau's Phenakistiscope-disk, c. 1832 (detail), in Archeology of the Cinema (1965).

30
New Year's Day in Hell (detail), in Diableries - la vie quotidienne chez Satan à la fin du 19e siècle (1978).

32
Game Room at Satan's (detail), in Diableries - la vie quotidienne chez Satan à la fin du 19e siècle (1978).

34
Walt Disney Productions, The Skeleton Dance, 1929, in J'aime le dessin animé (1962).

36
In Tech Images Internationales (September/October, 1992).

38
Bela Lugosi in Tod Browning's Dracula, 1931 (detail), cover illustration of Bram Stoker - Biographie (1989).

40
Anonymous, Girl with Ring Curls - Neillie, c. 1844 (detail), in Sleeping Beauty - Memorial Photography in America (1990).

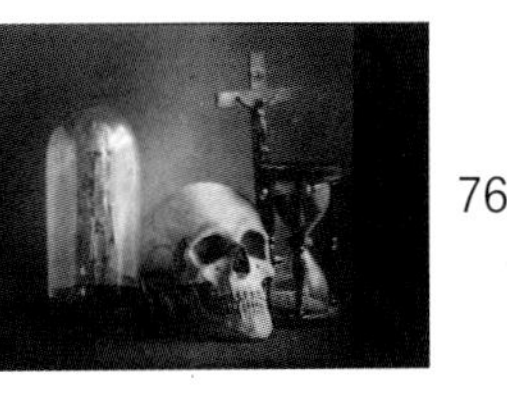

76

credit/genesis

77

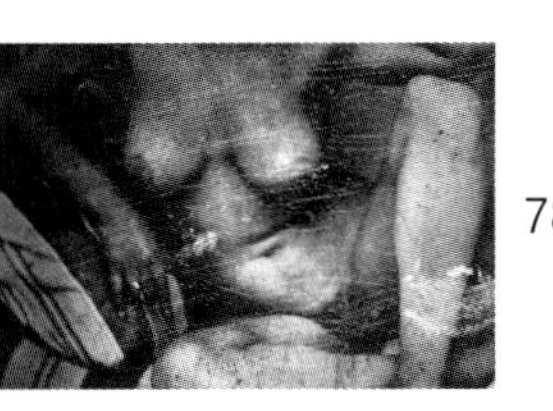

78

42
Étienne-Jules Marey, Instantaneous Photograph of a Bird, Made by a Single Shot Photographic Gun, 1882, in Étienne-Jules Marey (1984).

44
Anonymous, in Die Erotische Daguerreotypie - Sammlung Uwe Scheid (1990).

46
Giorgio Sommer, Pompei, Human Casts c. 1878, in Photographies (September 1985).

48
Dr. A. de Montmeja, Linear Incision of the Eye, 1871 (detail), in Photodiscovery - Masterworks of Photography 1840-1940 (1980).

50
Nadar (Gaspard Félix Tournachon), Hand of M.D. Banker, c. 1860, in Photodiscovery - Masterworks of Photography 1840-1940 (1980).

52
Henri Cartier-Bresson, Face with Stocking Mask, c. 1931 (detail), in Photodiscovery - Masterworks of Photography 1840-1940 (1980).

54
George Albert Smith, Grandma's Reading Glass, 1990 (film still), cover illustration of G.A. Smiths's Life to Those Shadows (1990).

56
J.M.W. Turner, Light and Colour (Goethe's Theory) - The Morning after the Deluge, 1843.

58
Source unknown.

60
Thomas Mistiaen, Untitled, 1993 (detail), after Nadar's Musette, c. 1858.

62
Robert Macpherson, The Falls of the Terni, before 1867 (detail), in Photodiscovery - Masterworks of Photography 1840-1940 (1980).

64
Imogen Cunningham, Unmade Bed, 1957 (detail), in Photography as Fine Art - The Library of World Photography (1987).

66
Étienne-Jules Marey, Joinville Soldier Walking, 1883 (detail), in Picturing Time - The Work of Étienne-Jules Marey (1830-1904) (1992).

68
Source unknown.

70
Georges Meliès, Dodging of a Lady at Robert Houdini's, 1986 (film still), in Georges Meliès, Father of Film Fantasy (1993).

72
Georges Meliès, Dodging of a Lady at Robert Houdini's, 1986 (film still), in Georges Meliès, Father of Film Fantasy (1993).

74
Edwin Porter, The Great Train Robbery, 1903 (film still), in Discovering the Movies - An Illustrated Introduction to the Motion Pictures (1972).

76
Duboscq-Soleil, daguerreotype Memento Mori, after 1854, in Photodiscovery - Masterworks of Photography 1840-1940 (1980).

78
Anonymous, daguerreotype Nude Woman with Cushion, c. 1855 (detail), in The Art of the Daguerreotype (1989).

80
Final image, in Diableries - la vie quotidienne chez Satan à la fin du 19e siècle (1978).

Edwin Carels

The Cinema and Its Afterimage Projection and Hindsight in Still/A Novel

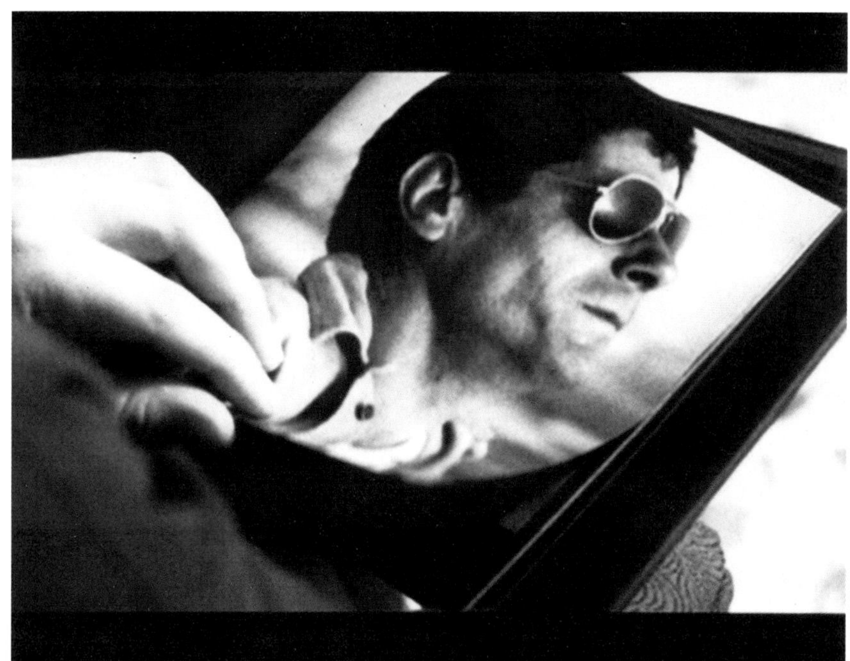

Bruce Mau with Chris Marker's La jetée, ciné-roman, 1995

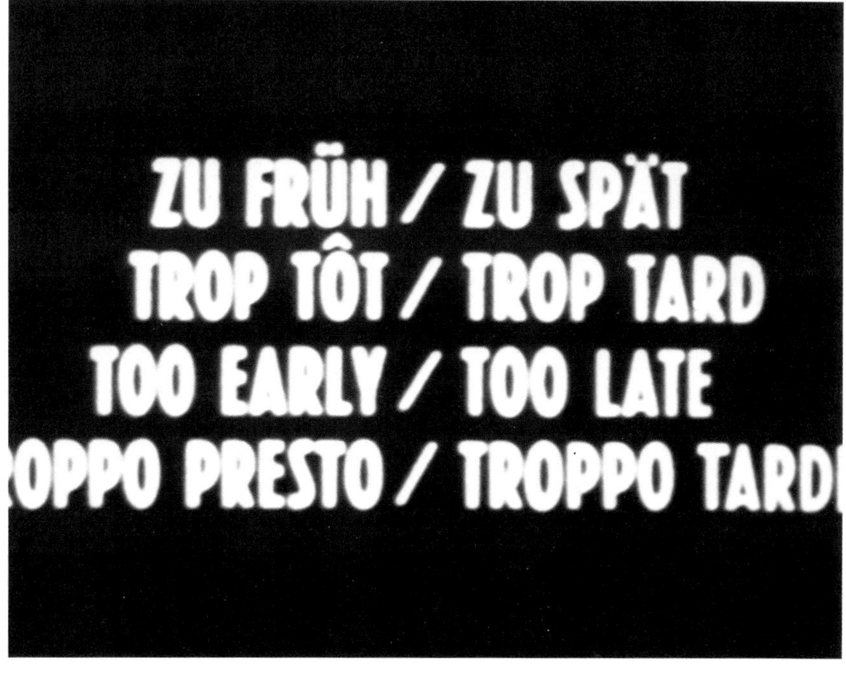

Jean-Marie Straub & Danièle Huillet Trop tôt, trop tard, 1981

Can the cinema still make images on behalf of our civilization? Is film the *Gesamtkunstwerk* of the twentieth century? Is the cinema still the pre-eminent twentieth-century art? Do we really need the cinema?
With such questions in his luggage, curator Chris Dercon set off on a journey to speak with scores of theoreticians, filmmakers, visual artists and even a typographer. Time and again, the encounters primarily provided him with new questions: Was the cinema perhaps born too early or too late? How did the cinema succeed in recent years to win over the museums of visual arts? Is the cinema retreating from fear of the new media? Ought the cinema recognize itself as 'the art by the grace of the other arts'?
The viewer, after watching both parts of the documentary *Still/A Novel*, is not left in his armchair with an unambiguous conclusion or a set of clear answers. In a third part, which is to be appended to the project in the fall of 1996, Dercon anticipates not only a critical review (and thus more questions) of the problematics of parts one and two, but also a virtual, edited interview with curator Catherine David on her concept for *documenta 10*. There too, the love-hate relationship between cinema and the visual arts will be a central theme. Does the interaction between these two fields mean that after one hundred years the cinema is indeed ready for the museum? Does this inevitable withdrawal from the movie theaters indicate a fatal regression or rather a logical step towards a possible reanimation of the cinema?

Where is film?

The absurd question as to whether the cinema was born too early or too late perhaps best formulates the desperate impasse in which (the reflection over) the cinema is in. After all, what is the sense of questioning the concrete world of facts with such a wishful dream?[1] Last year the medium of film became one hundred years old, and in retrospect there is nothing more of that historical period we can change. It's not accidental however that the formulation of the problem sounds 'non-sensical,' because it originates from a need for re-orientation. For want of a perspective, one either symbolically and theoretically turns back in time,[2] or spatially, physically seeks new horizons.[3] The voice that introduced *Still/A Novel* for its television broadcast spoke explicitly of 'a travelogue in two parts, from the Netherlands to Hollywood and back.' Dercon opens his suitcase of cherished souvenirs and invites us on a geographical exploration spread out in time. The same question that director Werner Herzog asked himself on the top of the Tokyo Tower, which drove him to such places as the top of the Cerro Torre in Patagonia,[4] led Dercon to London, Los Angeles, Rotterdam, New York, Lille, Paris, Tourcoing, Zurich, Villeneuve d'Ascq, Tilburg, Eindhoven and Minneapolis. Where can we still find images that are adequate for our stage of civilization?
Since the loss of the *cinéma d'auteur*, after the New German Cinema's relatively brief period of glory, André Bazin's classic question, 'Qu'est-ce que

le cinéma?’[5] (What is film?) has been increasingly reformulated as ‘Où est-ce que le cinéma?’ (Where is film?) From Latin America to Kazakstan, the country of promise, according to the festivals and magazines, shifts almost every season. The most recent resurgence of the cherished cinema ideals from the post-war period is happening in the Far East. A film such as *Cyclo* (1995), by Tran Ahn Hung from Vietnam, pointedly recaptures the narrative pattern and semi-documentary approach of Vittorio De Sica’s *Ladri di biciclette* (1948), one of neorealism’s exemplary films. As it happens, the social context of these two films is also comparable. The logical, nearly schematic outcome of a bicycle being stolen is that an insignifi-

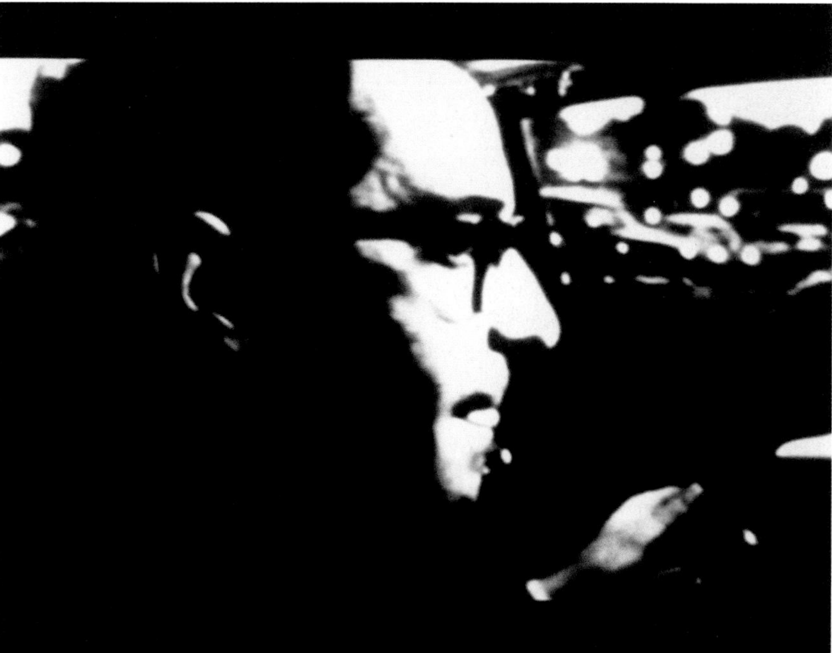

André Labarthe
Cinéastes de notre temps, 1965

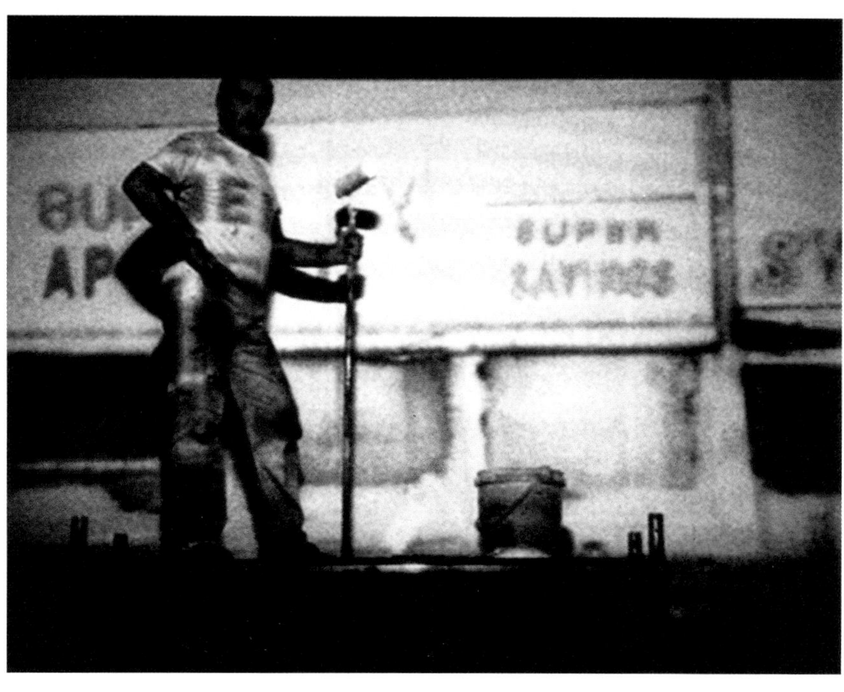

Jonas Mekas
New American Cinema, 1920/95
in Kunsthaus Zürich

cant individual goes under in a society that has just capitulated to the free-market economy. In the first issue of his magazine Trafic (not coincidentally a transportation term, which in French also connotes 'smuggling'), Serge Daney introduced the Iranian filmmaker Abbas Kiarostami as one of his latest discoveries. Even after his impotent exploration of the television universe,[6] Daney, the 'zappeur/passeur,' continued to look further for a suitable biotope for The Cinema. Indeed, it demands a rather specific constellation of political, economic and ideological factors in order to create something that can enter the nouvelle vague's consecrated tradition, from Vertov, Rossellini, Welles to Godard: a cinéma d'auteur with

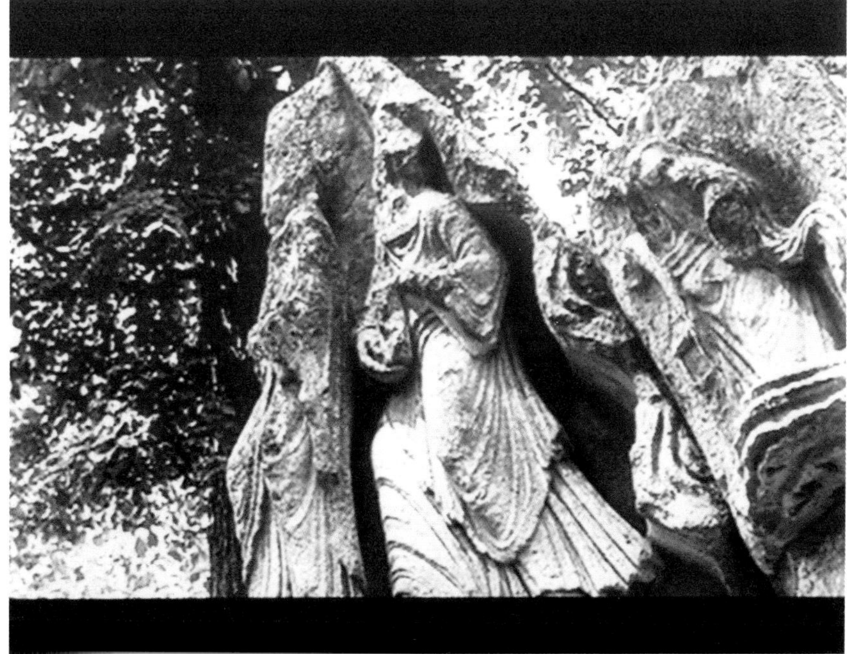

Chris Marker & Alain Resnais
Les statues meurent aussi, 1953

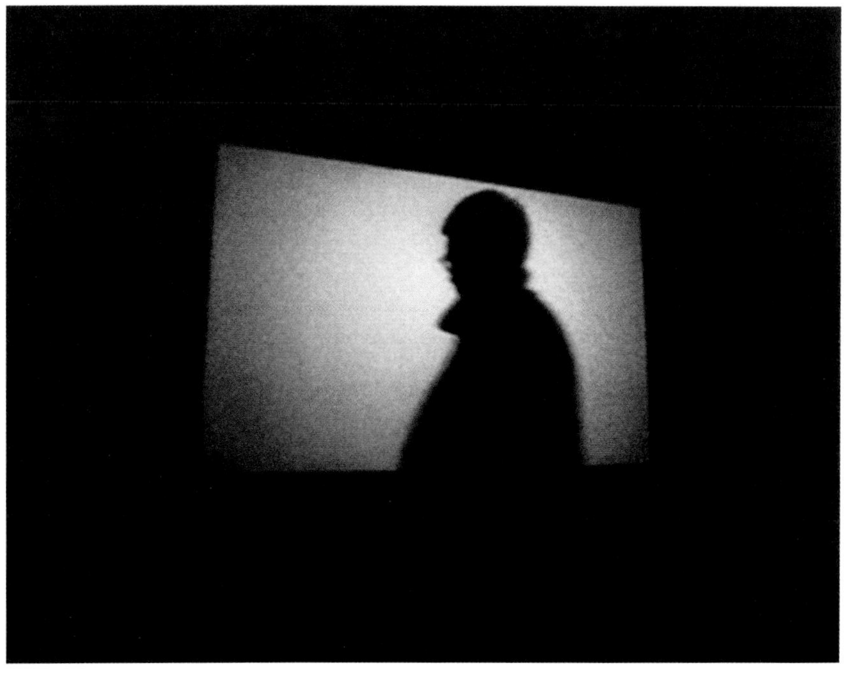

Chris Dercon with
Derek Jarman's Blue, 1993

a highly stylized, personal world view, an artistic vision that remains socially and even internationally relevant at the same time. Godard: 'With a man, a woman, and a car you had a trip through Italy. Replace the Jaguar with a cup of tea, and Ozu takes the place of Rossellini.... There was something: an image with hardly any movement, no modern TV images of merely comings and goings, instead of what happened in-between.'[7] With their misplaced national classifications and superficial redefinitions of always the same, by now unattainable, ideals of the cinema, the film festivals promise the public a world tour, but at the same time ask that one stay put within a hopelessly dated frame of reference. Godard fairly quickly grasped that his post-war cult of cinéphilism was a dead end. The favorable conditions that make a typical director's filmmaker such as Kiarostami (whose international career began with a Rossellini prize) possible are not only tied to location, they are also extremely temporary. Economically, everything evolves with increasing tempo; and the world's cinema talent, just like the world's fuel supply, is being ever more quickly exhausted.[8] Opposed to this escapist utopia, the blind belief that modern cinema can repeatedly bloom in a different spot, is the postmodern, self-critical inquiry within the typical, highly pronounced Western context. For Godard, the question is no longer whether a cinema can (temporarily) still be made that fulfills the social-utopian norms of modernism, but whether this is still meaningful, considering the profusion of images and mirror images, constructions and reproductions within our audio-visual culture. The cinema has been, is now history, and as such can only be, estranged from its original context, catalogued and commemorated in such things as empty churches.[9] While the philosophers are beginning to mourn increasingly louder, the movie theaters' public, with growing impatience, is on the lookout for something else, something new that can project it into a virtual (and even more multimedia-oriented) future. The desire for images has apparently remained intact, but its definition is temporarily missing. Jeff Wall: 'Fiction is the making visible of something that doesn't pre-exist the moment of photography.'[10] Perhaps by way of provocation, Chris Dercon gave his compact essay on the cinema the paradoxical title Still/A Novel, following the example of Carl Andre's typographical poem. It is as if a return to the origins of cinema is being offered, a rediscovery of the still image of photography and the narrative structure of the novel, the descriptive text, the literary tradition. Or does he merely wish to suggest that there are no more films, but just an album with a couple of collective souvenirs, the leftover stills of a much richer history? Perhaps indeed we are ending up once more at the art of novel writing, fiction without antecinematic reality. Can film after all still write history now that the world, due to the rise of digital-image manipulation, no longer needs to be analogically, and thus credibly, described? Besides, hasn't the cinema already long told all the stories there are to tell? It's not by coincidence that Godard begins his Histoire(s) du cinéma with the demarcation, 'Toutes les histoires qu'il y aurait. Qu'il y aura ou qu'il y aurait? Qu'il y a eu, qu'il y a eu.'[11]

Dercon begins his essay with the following quotation: 'Quand les hommes sont morts, ils entrent dans l'histoire. Quand les statues sont mortes, elles entrent dans l'art. Cette botanique de la mort, c'est ce que nous appelons la culture.'[12] The title and the approach of Still/A Novel can be interpreted as follows: everything is still and ready to be put on record. Godard wanders through his own document (it's much more than a documentary) as if in a mausoleum full of dying images. Dercon pointedly begins his story with a shot from La ville Louvre by Nicolas Philibert. For the last time, images are adulated as the artifacts of a culture that is being simultaneously preserved and destroyed. The canonization of those few images indeed throws an enormous shadow upon everything that can not be shown and that as such is becoming irrevocably blurred in the (collective) memory. Despite a comparable ambition and even construction, Still/A Novel is nevertheless much more a documentary than a document. Its emphasis in any case is on the stories to come. 'Qu'il y aura.' As an anthology, Still/A Novel is no less subjective than Histoire(s) du cinéma, but the choice for real (as opposed to imaginary) interlocutors ensures that the viewer doesn't think himself in a funeral parlor but rather in a reanimation room with numerous specialists combating the 'rigor mortis' of cinema.

What rhetorical question?

In order to find an answer to the numerous questions Dercon brings up, we must first consider the rhetoric of how his questions are formulated. Different from the ever conscious and deliberately irksome Godard, Dercon doesn't play his own 'candidly manipulative' physical presence quite so forcefully. He appears on screen only in silhouette or as a shadow. But the selection of the material, the delineation of the territory, and in this case also the mapping out of the route is nevertheless articulated by the vision of a supervising, controlling creator. The bridges that he erects between the places and the speakers are a second operative element in his story. To a certain degree, Still/A Novel demands the same mental athletics as watching Histoire(s) du cinéma does: Dercon also expects the viewer to be able to make the same mental leaps as he.
As opposed to the violent convulsions of a dying cinephile's consciousness, he presents us with a relentless, restless survey by a born optimist. For Dercon, the rousing of curiosity, the unremitting desire for the next opinion, the next point of view, is more important than finding definitive answers to dramatically posed questions. Still/A Novel does not offer us twenty-four truths per second, but it does present an extremely complex, apparently chaotic picture taken at the interface between the visual arts and the cinema. Works by Bruce Nauman, Stan Douglas, Tony Oursler, Matthew Barney flash by on the screen, hardly long enough to incite the memories of those already familiar with their oeuvres. Like Godard, Dercon addresses himself to a limited group of intimates familiar with the same names as he. Their ideal viewer possesses an enormous cultural reperatory

archive and can instantly recognize within the rapid edit all the artworks and references. He must also take part; he must project himself into it. A typical edit from the opening sequence of Still/A Novel is the fragment from La ville Louvre, when the camera passes by the famous Nike of Samothrace. The dancer Annabelle Whitford Moore, from Edison's early Kinetoscope film, instantly appears next to the statue, her fluttering arm movements equal in height to its wings. The association quickly blurs, but just as the security team in Philibert's film urges a fainted museum visitor to regain conciousness, we again get an insert. Film history's official first images, of the workers ('les ouvriers') leaving the Lumière factory,

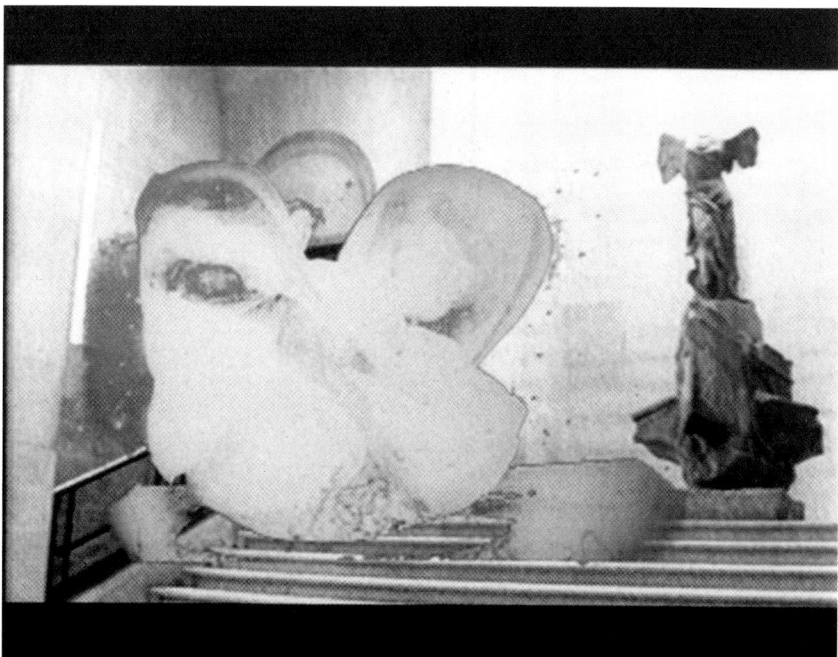

Nike of Samothrace and Annabelle Whitford Moore, 1894

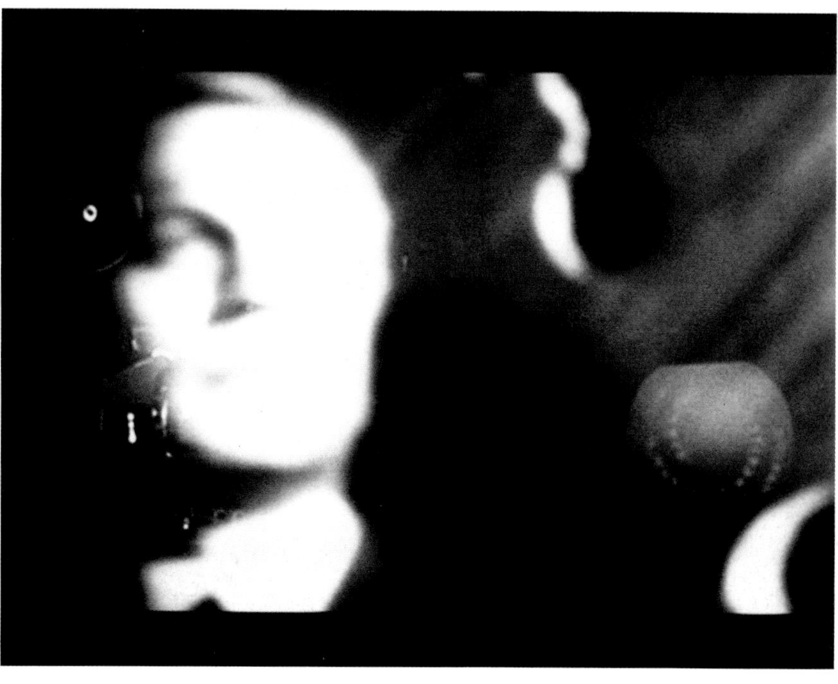

Orson Welles, Citizen Kane, 1941 and Marcel Duchamp, Anémic Cinéma, 1925

appear at exactly the same moment that the security team is asking the unconscious visitor to open his eyes ('ouvre les yeux!'). A couple of minutes later on a close-up shot from Jonas Mekas' New American Cinema, film theoretician Raymond Bellour starts to speak about the image's increased impact since the advent of projection. As he dwells on the seventeenth-century lanterna magica, we are suddenly shown a shot of a projection of Citizen Kane (1941). The fragment seems oddly framed, with the projector expressly in the picture and strangely enough also the reflection of one of Duchamp's Anémic Cinéma disks. Meanwhile Bellour discusses mirror images and the phenomenon of reproduction, and

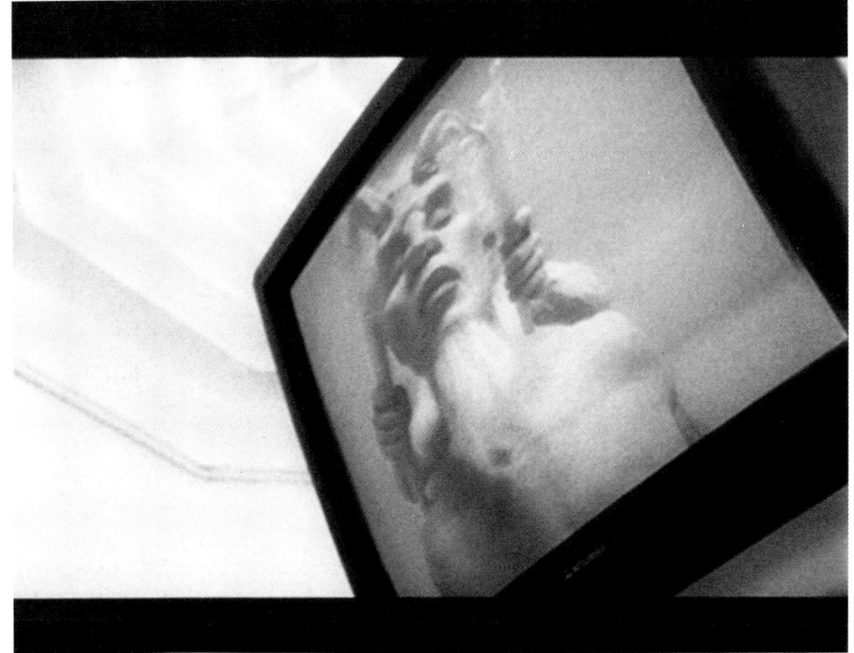

Matthew Barney, Drawing Restraint 7, 1993
in Museum Boijmans Van Beuningen, Rotterdam

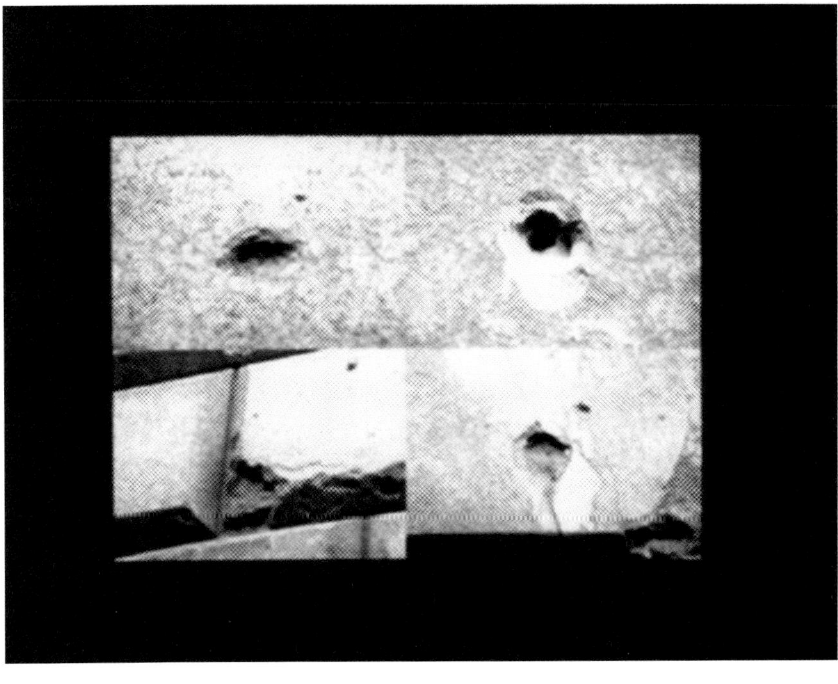

George Legrady
An Anecdoted Archive from the Cold War, 1994

the social context and utopian state so essential to Godard's projection theory. Replete with connotations, the images pursue one another at high speed, some being clarified by a voice, others by a subtitle. Sometimes the images complement what is being said and the name titles are withheld, sometimes the titles that appear in the upper corner lead (deliberately?) to confusion. Just like Godard (and long before him Bruce Conner), Dercon handles his material as if it is a collection of historico-cultural concepts that he in his own context can freely combine and contrast. In this way, we are first given artist Craigie Horsfield's name when we are shown, also for the first time, Hiroshi Sugimoto's photographs of drive-in theaters. Dercon counts on the viewer being familiar with this work and what the images stand for or at least that he is trying to follow the documentary with enormous concentration and an alert memory. Once introduced to us, we are expected to be able to recognize the speakers by their voices. Which is perhaps why in the beginning of part two of Still/A Novel Dercon lets Douglas Gordon sing along to the work of The Velvet Underground without the original being audible. Only later when this fragment is resumed, does he give the work's title. By way of this demanding rebus of loose statements and quotations, Still/A Novel assesses the existence of a collective memory for the cinema and the visual arts. A collective memory which since five to ten years is being increasingly exchanged for an individual mythology, a personal frame of reference.[13]

'Once something appears on TV, it too becomes television.'[14] Shown on the most conditioning of all the screening contexts, Still/A Novel automatically becomes a fleeting, ethereal product, too. As a documentary it is foremost an impression, a videographic account of a thematic expedition to a series of film-inspired exhibitions in 1995. Smuggled into a film festival like Rotterdam's, where both parts of Still/A Novel were projected together, Dercon's individualistic rhetoric was clearly difficult to appreciate. In Holland, the wintered film critics' reactions were in general negative, often even aggressive. They were, after all, robbed of something: the absolute certainty of a shared conviction, the myth of the 'art film.' Equally determining for an interpretation of Dercon's pictorial essay is therefore, next to the work's internal intertextual dialogue, the interference between the work and the milieu in which it is shown. Godard would prefer that his Histoire(s) du cinéma be seen in a museum rather than in a movie theater. Is this because such an institution offers a more appropriate, more lavishly furnished 'hors champs' (off-screen)? Curator Kerry Brougher was quite aware of the fact that his exhibition Hall of Mirrors – Art and Film since 1945 was taking place in the immediate vicinity of Hollywood. The enemy's camp is the best place, he feels, to make the public remember how much avant-garde filmmakers have influenced commercial film, and now even more than ever.[15] The curators of Spellbound: Art – Film in London deftly took advantage of the resurgent chauvinism to be found in Britpop, Britfilm and Britart. By way of a few precarious and carefully selected works, they essentially created a media-event, which claimed an exclusive tradition in passing.[16]

The most interesting aspect of Spellbound was its South Bank location: in The Hayward Gallery, in between the Museum of the Moving Image and The Royal Festival Hall. In addition to the confrontation of his tape in the Rotterdam Film Festival, Dercon created his own context for Still/A Novel. Combining a documentary with an exhibition automatically generated an in-between space, a field of meanings in which the project's position could be fully expressed. In the pure and strikingly empty spaces of Witte de With, Still/A Novel, as an exhibition, looked markedly static, perfectly complementing the busy, fleeting images of the documentary. In contrast to practically every other initiative that investigated the relationship between the visual arts and the cinema within the framework of its hundredth birthday,[17] Dercon didn't conjure his spaces into darkened projection rooms. He presented rather a surprising, concise and clear exhibition, a nearly pure conceptual confrontation between Eadweard Muybridge's motion studies and Jan Dibbet's contact sheets.

What lies in-between?

The impression of a severe, nearly ascetic academic exhibition was further strengthened and simultaneously ruptured by a triad of humorous drawings by Marcel Broodthaers, Carl Andre's typographic poem, and a series of publications in vitrines.[18] Strengthened, because the articles by Mel Bochner, Dan Graham and others evoked the presence of a complete discourse 'hors champs.' Ruptured, because the one-of-a-kind drawn or old-fashioned typed works pleasantly upset the schematic, serial structuring of the photographs. These small interjections are essential precisely because they help to animate Still/A Novel as a total project.[19] Just as Muybridge's motion studies only really came to life after he learned to project them with a zoopraxinoscope, Still/A Novel's meaning surfaces only when the different elements, the exhibition and the documentary, are brought together. The novice to the animation industry usually first learns 'inbetweening,' how to make the in-between drawings that fill in the crucial positions of an animated figure already established by the chief animator. Chris Dercon asks his audience to perform a similarly humble, obediant task. He broadly outlined the concepts of Still/A Novel, leaving it to the viewer to make a meaningful connection between them. In contrast to the film-and-art exhibitions in Zurich, Los Angeles and London, in Rotterdam Still/A Novel did not follow a neatly formulated, unequivocal concept. Instead of an obvious delineation and thus curtailment of the immense subject, instead of a simplifying historical analysis or a thematic deconstruction, Dercon opted for Sergei Eisenstein's strategy (and poetic freedom), with its dialectic of thesis, antithesis, and synthesis.[20] Like a spark, Still/A Novel's meaning must illuminate through the contrast between scarcity and abundance, order and chaos, essentialism and iconoclasm, cerebral serialism and suggestive polyphony.[21] The animated thought surfaces in a split second, in the black space between two photograms.

How the exhibition and the documentary work independent of each other is decidedly frustrating. Indeed, both were intended to provoke pertinent questions, rather than to exhaustively illustrate the curator's selective theories, as in Hall of Mirrors, 100 Jahre Kinobiscum, and Spellbound. In contrast to the one-time ideal of film as a 'Gesamtkunstwerk,' which time and again falls apart in exhibitions as a series of 'gesammelte Kunstwerke' (collected artworks), Dercon shows us rather a stock of 'gesampelte Kunstwerke' (selected artworks), fragments from conversations and visual quotations, suggestions for different strategies, demonstrations of old as well as new image techniques. That he rarely makes the connection between all of this material explicitly clear is perhaps a conscious decision. It's up to the viewer to complete the distance and take part in the travelogue. Still/A Novel reads a little like a CD-Rom, as an apparently inexhaustible source of information stemming from an open configuration of many image and text extracts. In an interview fragment, Rem Koolhaas talks of his cinematically inspired urge for decentralization.[22] As an architect, he also abandons the concentric principle in favor of a greater spread of the parts with many calm zones in between, dashes that must accentuate the breaks as well as they bridge them. He illustrates that these interzones do not necessarily need to be meaningless with films by Godard.

After Muybridge's horse and the Lumières' train, the future lies with the immobile motorist, the individual user on the information superhighway.[23] The nearly binary construction of Still/A Novel continually stimulates mental exercise: from (the memory of) the documentary's first part to its second, from the tightly framed and edited domain of theory to the smoother travel shots for the practice-oriented illustrations. The exhibition similarly required a switch over from the historical work by Muybridge to the contemporary work by Dibbets, each on its own floor at Witte de With. Dercon manifestly chose against an emphatic, demonstrative confrontation, in favor of an open comparison that called for considerable memory on the part of its viewer. Muybridge and Dibbets are moreover complementary photographers in that the first always let his subjects move while he stood still, whereas the second always moves with his camera in relation to his subject. While Muybridge applied himself solely to the analysis of physical movement, in his sequences Dibbets rather suggests the passage of time. This strictly divided combination caused the viewer to experience the effect of a space and time warp. In the documentary Still/A Novel, part two opens in a comparable manner with Overture, a work by Stan Douglas that as an installation tries to suggest the same effect: a meditative inversion of interior and exterior, of time and space.[24] As illustration to Marcel Proust's Remembrance of Things Past, we are shown footage dating back to Edison in which we follow a train's crossing through a mountain landscape, tunnel in, tunnel out. In this way Still/A Novel as a joint project offers a steady, panoramic overview at the same time as the impression of a conceptual vortex. While the viewer could systematically contemplate

the pictures at a distance in the exhibition, during the documentary it's more as if he's inside a zootrope, spinning round and round.[25]
'The picture, certainly, is in my eye. But I, I am in the picture.'[26] By filming his speakers or locations through reflecting glass, Dercon evokes several times in the documentary a similar feeling of a paradox-laden view.
As such, many images contain information on different levels, becoming in a way surrealistic collages. Framed as well behind glass (in a shot where the camera appears to be placed outside on the grass), Raymond Bellour relates the concept of the inversed space.[27] The implosion of our world view due to the acceleration of audio-visual culture means that the cinema could only be able to survive in the museum. Physical and mental inversion is the rhetorical exercise that makes Still/A Novel a fitting essay on the status of the moving image in the transition between the cinema and the new media. For example, Susan Meiselas, in a collaborative CD-Rom project with Ground Zero, tries to create a virtual homeland for the Kurds. New systems of communication generate new travelogues. The movie theater as mutual forum was exchanged for the television, which will soon be exchanged for the intercourse of the Internet. In this manner the last physical meeting places for cinephiles are indeed attaining the status of a museum, where the tradition is still nourished but no longer passed down.

The answer lies with the observer

In retrospect, Still/A Novel seems less Chris Dercon's valediction to Witte de With and more his declaration of intent as new director of the Museum Boijmans Van Beuningen. The very first thing that he presented at the museum was the installation of a 'Black Box,' a space for showing films. The name, in addition to being a loose translation of the concept of the

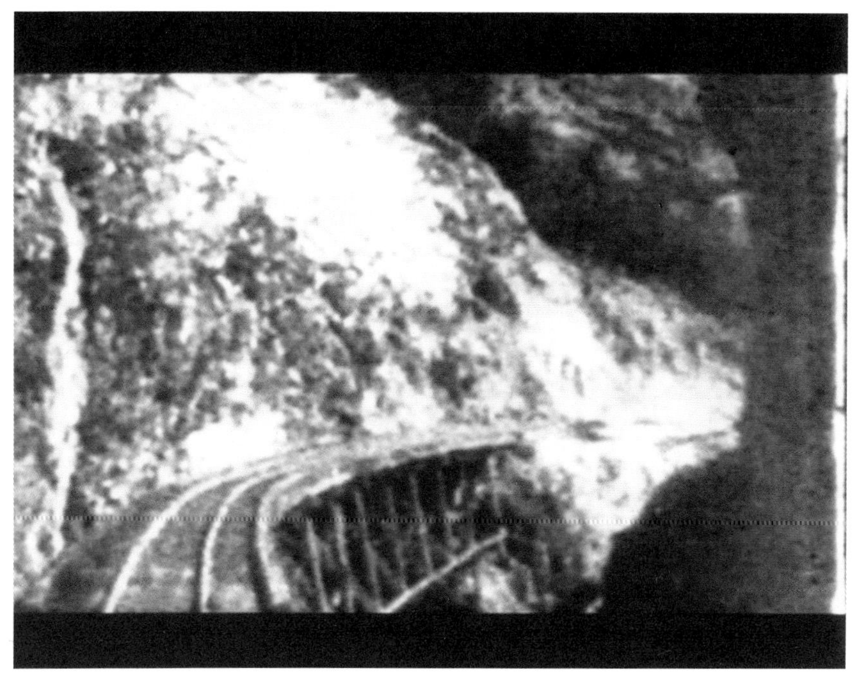

Stan Douglas, Overture, 1986

camera obscura, is also a symbolic reference to the 'Black Maria,' Edison's first film studio. There is as well the connotation of the black box as a technical witness to airplane crashes, a mysterious data bank of broken ambitions. A museum shows films not to preserve a culture but to inform the public of a culture that once was. However, just as in the beginning of the cinema when experience of the outside world was increasingly exchanged for simulacra, in recent years director filmmakers such as Godard, Straub/Huillet, Rivette and Pialat have all ended up with painting rather than natural referents as the subject of their films. Perhaps this is the start of a new culture, just as the museum itself is a more social continuation of the pri-

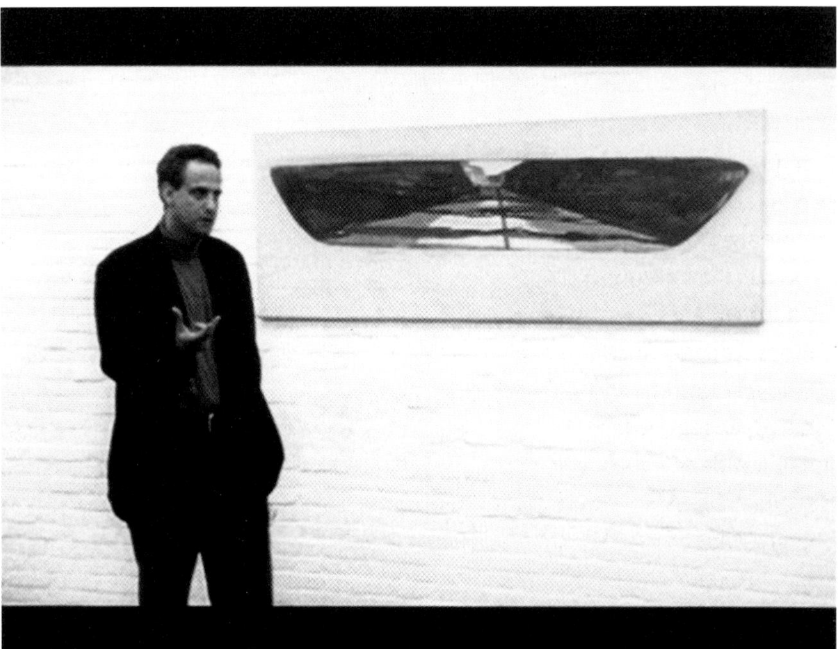

Luc Tuymans with Rear Mirror, 1986
in Stichting De Pont, Tilburg

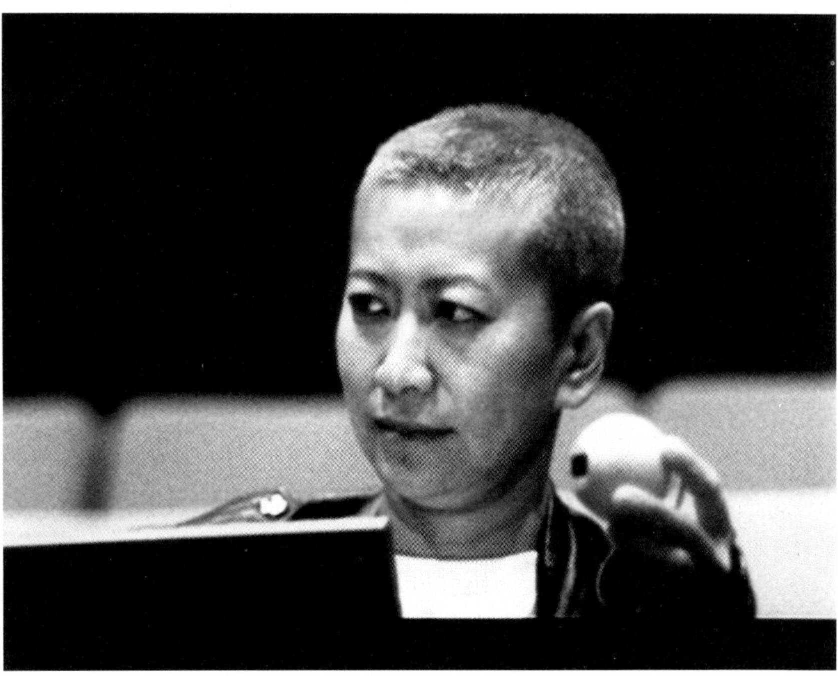

Shu Lea Cheang with Quickcam, 1995
in the Walker Art Center, Minneapolis

vate library, the archive, the statue gallery, the Wunderkammer.[28] According to the classic books on the precinema, the earliest predecessors to the moving image, the first sequential analyses of motion, the octopodan wild boar of Lascaux and the long rows of hieroglyphics in the pyramids, were always created and kept in dark caves. 'In order to survive it will vanish,' Dercon concludes upon his return home. In answer to the question of whether the cinema was born too early or too late, film festival director Marco Müller threw Dercon an equally rhetorical thought. Perhaps the cinema's importance as a metaphor was in fact 'to be a machine for observing the other arts.' The question, he feels, could also be formulated as: 'did the cinema die too early or too late?'

If we continue to reformulate the opening question (just as the placard TROP TÔT/TROP TARD and a couple of other fragments cyclically return in Still/A Novel), then we must, rather than seeking the best sanctuary for film, first ask ourselves whether it still makes sense to preserve it. Ensconsed in the museum, can film still reflect upon the world and still maintain the meaning of The Cinema? What is the most important thing that remains: the images or a way of looking? Has the time not come to, like Godard with his Histoire(s) du cinéma, philosophically finally deal with the enormous stock of film, to burn the old reels so that their fire can cast new shadows? Entrenched in the museum, can the camera obscura indeed still receive messages directly from the outside world? The cinema is absolutely not dead; it's only losing its relevance as a social phenomenon because it is falling out of the public eye.[29]

The first film-based artwork that Dercon showed in his black box was at least as exemplary as the initiation of the camera obscura itself. Bruce Nauman's Four Rotating Walls (1970), just like the entire project of Still/A Novel, is a study in inversion. Nauman makes an unstable space out of a darkened room by projecting on each of the four white walls an even whiter projection. There is nothing more to see than a tilting glass plate in black-and-white, which even then only becomes visible when its edge passes into the picture before the lens. The four rotating horizontal lines in the square space force the viewer to continually reorient himself. In Still/A Novel, we see Bruce Nauman speaking with his parallel image in a rectangular mirror. He talks, like Godard but in other words, about the difference in spatial and visual experience between the electronic image and the cinematic one, about 'projection' and 'rejection.' 'The television only gives us information in which you can't really participate. I'm interested in the contrast between real, spatial information and visual, intellectual information.'[30] Within the filmed images of Rotating Walls as well, the viewer can never move forward, as if into an illusion. He can never project himself into the image because the horizon, the only orientation point, disappears again and again. Thrown back upon his own experience, it's now up to the viewer himself to move, to choose a direction or at least to become conscious of his own viewing activity. The ubiquitousness of dark rooms, projected images and film installations also invites the contemporary specta-

tor to explore the multimedia field in a very simple manner. A visit to a gallery or museum immediately becomes an exercise in the logic of CD-Rom and the Internet as well. For film, when presented as an installation, looses its integrity in terms of playing time and narrative structure, because the moment in which the viewer enters is most often no more certain than the track that he will follow. One's view is manipulated differently than in the cinema, the deconstruction of the viewing process usually replaces an illusion of coherence. In order to force the viewer to be more active and to literally and figuratively move about, Dercon opted for the irritation of the still image, for the immobility of a collection of museum pieces.[31]
The bundle of questions that forms Still/A Novel's starting point can thus be summarized as follows: where and how can we still view the cinema? Are we still capable of observing the cinema's codes? During the last film festival in Rotterdam in 1996, Jonathan Crary was to have given a lecture at Witte de With, as the umpteenth insert to the project Still/A Novel. The idea unfortunately never came to fruition, but the intention behind it is clear. In his book Techniques of the Observer – On Vision and Modernity in the Nineteenth Century[32] Crary paradoxically argues that if we want to understand the principles of the moving image of the future, we must look back two centuries. After an enlightening overview of the aesthetic as well as the purely empirical and philosophical implications of the camera obscura, Crary guides us with great enthusiasm through the period in which the precinema most evolved, the first half of the nineteenth century (not the second half, in spite of Muybridge, Marey and Reynaud). In his Colour Theory of 1810 Goethe was the first to speak of the aftereffects of the image on the retina. He enriched Newton's theory on spectral colors with the effect of the afterimage. To this end, he asked the viewer to continue to observe, even after closing his eyes. In principle this small exertion meant the end of the concept of the camera obscura, a cultural revolution which is only just becoming fully visible. After all, every 'spectator' is also always to some degree an 'observer,' someone who by looking unconsciously observes all sorts of social codes and conventions. Crary relativizes the cult of the analogous image, photography, by pointing to the rapid acceptance of visual abstraction, which was already well established before photography with such optical toys as the thaumatrope, the phenakistiscope and the stereoscope. What Dercon with Still/A Novel suggests is that we too had better actively concentrate on the afterimages of the cinema rather than helplessly watch the medium's disappearance from our field of vision. In the future we can continue to cherish the remnants of the cinema as a series of objets trouvés, but we also can use them again as the foundations (as prima materia) or as a trusted construction strategy (the projection principle). It is no coincidence that the first exhibition catalog that was published by the Museum Boijmans Van Beuningen under Dercon was devoted to Cindy Sherman. In an exemplary manner, she began her œuvre by developing latent images from our collective memory of film. An everlasting image is first of all an unforgettable image.

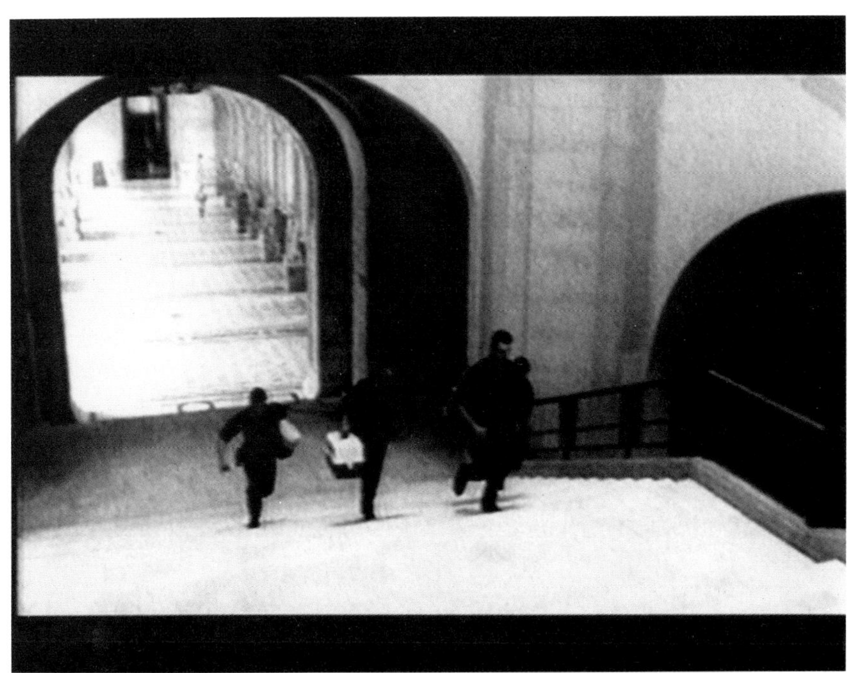

Nicolas Philibert La ville Louvre, 1989

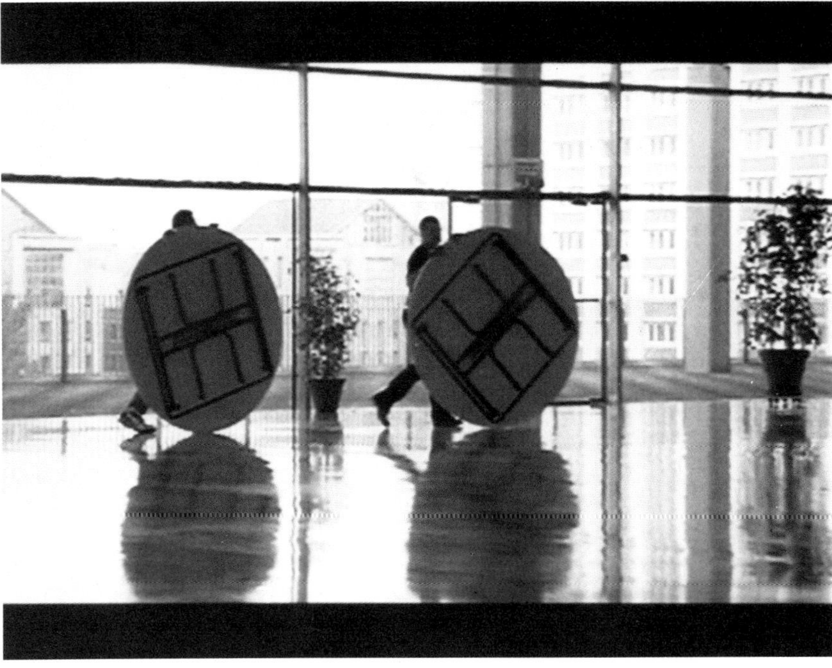

Euralille, Lille designed by Rem Koolhaas

1
Inspired by Jean-Marie Straub and Danièle Huillet, TROP TÔT TROP TARD (1980-81, 100 min. 16 mm). This film (based on texts by Friedrich Engels and Mahmoud Hussein) was also included in the exhibition Le monde après la photographie, curated by Régis Durand for the Musée d'Art Moderne (Villeneuve d'Ascq, 1995).

2
'We had never seen that before. A world that had no history and yet spent its time telling stories, and especially, apart from reading. Because writing, since Rimbaud and Mallarmé, was the terror. The blank page was the enemy. After Joyce and Duino's elegies, why write anymore? Whereas for us, facing the blank screen when the lights began to fade, what happened was the exact opposite of what drove Nicolas de Staël to suicide. A second light took shape in the darkness. The screen was no longer an obstacle but a friend, the cloth of Veronica and the Samaritan.' Jean-Luc Godard, 'A propos de cinema et d'histoire,' his acceptance speech for the Adorno prize, 17 September 1995 (Still/A Novel part 1).

3
'Let's go back to 1968, as I see it today, which is with too much clarity no doubt. After the months of May and June I had, more and more on my own, several experiences of dispossession. The first was traveling. The first trip to India, that is to say, the Third World. Illness followed. The first tuberculoses. The cinema had disappeared because I was experiencing my cinema with my own body like something which doesn't control itself. In fact, the cinema hadn't disappeared, it was I who had entered - somewhere - into film, playing for several years the role of incognito star in scenes where there was no one to watch me. My own super productions, announced by postcard, were modest: I was an absolute natural in "I'm going back to my hotel in Taroudant."' Interview with Serge Toubiana and Serge Daney in Persévérance (Paris: P.O.L. Éditeur, 1994), p. 102.

4
'There are just few images that remain. Just look outside, everything is built over. There are scarcely any possible images. Like an archeologist, you have to take a shovel and dig and just see if you can still uncover anything from this abused landscape. There is usually some risk to this. I'll never be able to escape that, and I see so few people who really dare to do something about our shortage - who know what to do with the lack of adequate images. We absolutely need images that harmonize with our cultural situation and what lies deep within us. Even if this means you have to go through war, or whatever else it takes.' Werner Herzog in Wim Wenders, Tokyo-Ga (1985, 80 min. 35 mm) (Still/A Novel part 1).

5
'Perspective was the original sin of Western painting. It was redeemed from sin by Niepce and Lumière. ... This production by automatic means has radically affected our psychology of the image. The objective nature of photography confers on it a quality of credibility absent from all other picturemaking. In spite of any objections our critical spirit may offer, we are forced to accept as real the existence of the object reproduced, actually re-presented, set before us, that is to say, in time and space. Photography enjoys a certain advantage in virtue of this transference of reality from the thing to its reproduction.' André Bazin, What is Cinema?, trans. Hugh Gray (Los Angeles: University of California Press, 1967), pp. 12-14.

6
'If television is a vehicle of culture, then cinema is a transmitter of real experiences. If television must have its professional code of ethics, the cinema's travel shots could be called its "matters of ethics." If television reveals its talent through programming, nothing will ever rid the cinema of its desire to produce. If, in short, television is our prose (and since we will never speak it well enough), the cinema's only chance is poetry.' Serge Daney's concluding sentence to Le salaire du zappeur (Paris: P.O.L. Éditeur, 1993), p. 189.

7
'We discovered the right to do our homework without as much as going to school. There was thus an absolute feeling of freedom. With a man, a woman, and a car you had a trip through Italy. Replace the Jaguar with a cup of tea and Ozu takes the place of Rossellini ... There was something: an image with hardly any movement, no modern TV images of merely comings and goings, and nothing of what happened in-between. Even if we didn't know how to make films, we knew that we could do it.' Jean-Luc Godard, 'A propos de cinema et d'histoire,' his acceptance speech for the Adorno prize, 17 September 1995 (Still/A Novel part 1).

8
'When the father of my father's father had a difficult task to accomplish he went to a certain spot in the forest, lit a fire and began a silent prayer; and what he needed to accomplish was realized. Later, when my father's father found himself confronted with the same task, he went to this very same spot in the forest and said: "we no longer know how to light a fire, but we do still know how to pray," and what he need to accomplish was realized. Even later (made inaudible) we go to the forest, we no longer know how to light a fire, we no longer know the mysteries of prayer, but we do still know the very spot in the forest where this happened and that this must suffice. And this was sufficient.' Opening line from Jean-Luc Godard, Hélas pour moi, (1992, 84 min, 35 mm).

9
'... the I like it or not rather than this is good or bad/the assistant's dilapidated car/exact

synchronization killed by the code/ the documentary divorced of fiction ...' quoted from Godard's poem 'La paroisse morte,' printed three times in Trafic no. 1 (Winter 1991).

10
'[Andy Warhol] made it clear that he was in a state of imitation of another production, another type of production - in his case, a kind of commodity production. And I think Warhol was interesting for that reason: that he recognized that art often had to come into those imitative relationships. ... But cinematography was based upon that and/or making things visible that didn't exist until they were assembled somehow artificially by the cinematographer and the film production in general as a whole and made visible. So fiction - what we call fiction - is the making visible of something that doesn't preexist the moment of photography. To me that's cinematography, or part of cinematography. And I like the fact that in that sense cinematography broadened out the notion of what photography could do.' Jeff Wall (Still/A Novel part 2).

11
(All the stories that would be. That will be or that would be? That have been, that have been) Histoire(s) du cinéma is Jean-Luc Godard's work in progress, which in total will consist of five chapters, the first three of which have already been realized. Chapter 1a: Toutes les histoires; chapter 1b: Une histoire seule; chapter 2a: Seul le cinéma; chapter 2b: Fatale beauté; chapter 3a: la monnaie de l'absolu; chapter 3b: la réponse des ténèbres; chapter 4a: Une vague nouvelle; chapter 4b: Montage mon beau souci; chapter 5a: le controle de l'univers; chapter 5b: les signes parmi nous. (1a: all the stories/histories; 1b: a single story/history; 2a: only the cinema; 2b: fatal beauty; 3a: the currency of the absolute; 3b: the reply of darkness; 4a: a new wave; 4b: editing, my old worry; 5a: the control of the universe; 5b: the signs among us). For stills see Jean-Luc Godard, Son + Image, ed. Raymond Bellour (New York: The Museum of Modern Art, 1992), p. 123ff.

12
(When men are dead they enter history. When statues are dead they enter art. This botany of death is what we call culture.) Chris Marker/Alain Resnais, Les statues meurent aussi (1953, 30 min., 35 mm).

13
An example of how Dercon takes off from his own mythology of art, a multiple of assumed, known points of reference, in order to put his subjective/associative discourse together: In Still/A Novel part 2, James Lingwood is presented as a blurred reflection on Stan Douglas's Der Sandmann, a project made in Berlin in 1995. The title and an overall picture of the work (with a large camera clearly in the center) is only shown to the viewer a half minute later. At the same time, Lingwood discusses the cyclic desire in art to no longer limit the telling of stories to one medium. For him, film is the Gesamtkunstwerk of the century. Dercon immediately adds on to this the voice of Harald Szeemann during his speech for the opening of 100 jahre Kinobiscum: Die 7. Kunst auf der Suche nach den 6 Andern, who elaborates on the Gesamtkunst and pubescent love. This is followed by images of the public and film posters of among others E.T. and Fassbinder. This is followed by Matthew Barney as a satyr with a Degas sculpture of a young ballerina in the background shot during the opening performance for the Matthew Barney exhibition at the Museum Boijmans Van Beuningen, 1996) and once again the voice of Lingwood, discussing naturalism in the late-nineteenth and late-twentieth century art.

14
'I am from the television generation. So even great works of cinema, I have seen on the television. Once something appears on TV, it too becomes television. So for me, the television itself or electronics are the great art form of the twentieth century. Film was finished when the still photograph was invented. For me, even looking at anything that would be considered avant-garde cinema feels nostalgic. And when I work in cinema, which we do occasionally in 16 mm or 35 mm, I think of it as a found object from the past that I am reinventing via the television.' Elizabeth LeCompte (of the Wooster Group) (Still/A Novel part 2).

15
Several themes emerge as common threads: the use and reconfiguration of Hollywood models of stardom; the return to the origins of film in an attempt to locate its fundamental relationship to the visual arts and to underscore the cinema's curious position between optics and illusion, science and secular mysticism, high art and popular culture; psychoanalytic and voyeuristic issues that shed light on gender, visual pleasure, surveillance, and spectacle; the meeting of film, painting, and photography within the concept of the tableau vivant; and the fragmentation of classic theater-based cinema within a culture dominated by the cinematic.' Kerry Brougher in his introduction to the catalogue for the exhibition Hall of Mirrors - Art and Film since 1945 for the Museum of Contemporary Art (Los Angeles, 1996) (New York: Monacelli Press, 1996).

16
'Indeed, the underlying argument of the show is that by grasping the relationship of art and film in Britain, we are forced not only to revise the orthodox histories of British art and film but also to recognize (and admire) British culture's wider ambitions.' Philip Dodd, 'Modern Stories,' in the catalogue for Spellbound: Art and Film in The Hayward Gallery (London: The Hayward Gallery and The British Film Institute, 1996).

17
Cfr. 100 jahre Kinobiscum: Die 7. Kunst auf der Suche nach den 6 Andern, curated by Harald Szeemann for the Kunsthaus (Zurich, 1995-96).

18
Dan Graham, 'Muybridge Moments, From Here to There?' Arts Magazine, vol. 41, no. 4 (February 1967), pp. 23-24. Mel Bochner, 'Serial Art,' Arts Magazine, vol. 41, no. 8 (Summer 1967), pp. 39-43. Mel Bochner, 'The Serial Attitude,' Artforum, vol. 6, no. 4, (December 1967), pp. 28-33. Hollis Frampton, 'Eadweard Muybridge: Fragments of a Tesseract,' Artforum, vol. 11, no. 7 (March 1973), pp. 43-52. Dan Graham, 'Photographs in Motion,' in cat. Articles (Eindhoven: Stedelijk Van Abbemuseum, 1978), pp. 11-13.

19
Norman McClaren's dictum (on a little card mounted above his animation camera: 'The philosophy behind this machine: * animation is not the art of DRAWINGS-that-move but the art of MOVEMENTS that are drawn. * What happens between each frame is much more important than what exists on each frame. * Animation is therefore the art of manipulating the invisible interstices that lie between the frames.' Originally published in Gretchen Weinberg, 'MC et Moi,' Film Culture 25 (Summer 1962), p. 47. McClaren's emphasis is taken from The Velvet Light Trap, no. 24, (Fall 1989), p. 68

20
'So, montage is conflict. Conflict lies at the basis of every art. (A unique "figurative" transformation of the dialectic.) The shot is then a montage cell. Consequently we must also examine it from the point of view of conflict. Conflict within the shot is: potential montage, that in its growing intensity, breaks through its four-sided cage and pushes its conflict out into montage impulses between the montage fragments. ... If we are to compare montage with anything, then we should compare a phalanx of montage fragments - "shots" - with the series of explosions of the internal combustion engine, as these fragments multiply into a montage dynamic through "impulses" like those that drive a car or a tractor.' Sergei Eisenstein, 'Beyond the Shot,' (1929) Selected Works, vol. 1 Writings 1922-34, ed. and trans. Richard Taylor (London: British Film Institute, 1988), pp. 144-145.

21
'Intelligence is understanding before confirming; it's looking further into an idea, to look for a limit, to look for its opposite. As a result, it is understanding the others differences between oneself and the others, between the for and against, to find one's way little by little. Oh, I know that the whole world dislikes this intellectual moral. People like bright colors, and just looking for the differences between black-and-white seems a bit grey. I think they are fanatics, boring dogmatics. In the first place: we always know in advance what they are going to say. But to the contrary, I'm not saying that it's the skeptics who are amusing, but the people who love paradoxes. And one paradox is, when faced with an obvious idea, to look for the other idea.' Jean-Luc Godard and Anne Marie Miéville in Deux Fois Cinquante Ans de Cinéma Français (video, 51 min, 1995) (Still/A Novel part 2).

22
'I think indeed that a sort of saturation point has been reached for the congestion of images. And what I find interesting, and this holds true for urban development as well, is that the whole idea of centrality and of the middle and of the most important and of the triumph of the municipal is at the moment being in one way or the other exchanged for a sort of calm. Where everything doesn't happen simultaneously but where great distances come between events. Where events are presented with a sort of nonchalance, so that, if you want to ignore them, you can ignore them. With regard to this, Godard, I believe, was one of the first to use that sort of stillness or breathing space ... it's not that his films aren't full, but that they are void of a sort of visual force and just full of ideas. And it took me a long time. I discovered this in urban development before film. I was once a scriptwriter, and I still consider what I do script writing, but by other means. And I still think that what actually drives our work is editing.' Rem Koolhaas (Still/A Novel part 1).

23
'After the long, long development of "dynamic" moving vehicles, we are now entering the era of the static vehicle: an audiovisual vehicle, vector of apparent motion, of that sense of inertia induced by traveling vast distances -- which is a substitute for physical displacement that has become more or less redundant with the immediacy of telecommunications technologies. Hence the spontaneous generation of videodisks, and of interactive screens simulating visits to all sorts of places - cities, stately homes, museums.' Paul Virillio, 'Cataract Surgery: Cinema in the Year 2000,' Alien Zone - Cultural Theory and Contemporary Science Fiction Cinema, ed. Annette Kuhn, (London: Verso, 1990), p. 170.

24
'Overture associates cinema (four silent documentary films from 1899/1901) with a text modified by the artist (Marcel Proust's Remembrance of Things Past) effecting a collage of images without a known author and texts in which a famous writer marks the end of an epoch. The texts, however, have been transformed by Douglas to become anonymous literature, outside all specifics, reflecting a will to blur the notion of "an author" or at least to reduce his presence in the works.' Introduction by Christine van Assche to cat. Stan Douglas, (Paris: Editions du Centre Pompidou, 1993), p. 18. Overture was also presented in Witte de With in the exhibition Stan Douglas/ Diana Thater (1994).

25
'This both at once, this being caught inside the illusion and this looking on

nonetheless form without, would, he understood, suit his purposes perfectly. It would manifest that peculiar feeling you have when you dream and even while captured by the emotions of its drama you can speak of yourself as someone else: "You're only dreaming you know." So in his collage he will use the zootrope is such a way that, simultaneously inside the illusion and outside it, the little girl will dream of taking the veil. And, inevitably, her dream will be pulsatile. The surge of the wings beating up and down from within the illusion will visually rhyme with the flickering staccato of the zootrope's motion, a rhythm that will simultaneously construct the gestalt and threaten it with dissolution, with a breakup into its separate, impotent fragments.' Rosalind E. Krauss on the collage 'Dans mon colombodrome' from A Little Girl Taking the Veil by Max Ernst (1930), in which Ernst glued the figure of a little girl inside a zootrope with doves by Marey. Quoted from The Optical Unconscious (Cambridge: The MIT Press, 1993), p. 207.

26
Hal Foster, 'The Real Thing,' in cat. Cindy Sherman (Rotterdam: Museum Boijmans Van Beuningen, 1996), p. 77.

27
'The room became a sort of reversible place. With that arose an archeology of the camera obscura and the lanterna magica which in the late eighteenth century and into the early nineteenth century brutally cut across the concept of the room in its most simplified sense, the bedroom. When photography constructed the idea of the darkroom, the bourgeoisie simultaneously at the end of the century invented for itself a very special room, different from all the others, the movie theater. For me, it was basically a sort of installation that succeeded, that had a particular destiny. It's the destiny to which Godard has become so attached with his ever mythic and nearly animal-like, ferocious defense of projection. Raymond Bellour (Still/A Novel part 1).

28
In the Kunst- und Ausstellunghalle der Bundesrepublik Deutschland in Bonn, three successive, large exhibitions were organized that thematically formed an ideal introduction for film's centenary anniversary: The Desire to See, The Panorama as a Medium of Mass Entertainment in the 19th Century (1993); Bunuel – Auge des Jahrhunderts (1994); and Wunderkammer des Abendlandes – Museum und Sammlung in Spiegel der Zeit (1995).

29
In response to Chris Dercon's question as to whether a new genre is being created by all the recent films devoted to the phenomenon of cinema, Chantal Akerman negatively replies: 'Godard says something about himself in his work. Something which I find personally alarming. Godard is getting locked into a sort of autism. Which is sad for people like me because it is because of him that we make films. The path he's following is leading to a sort of autism; and I find that alarming.' (Still/A Novel part 1). In addition to this 'autistic' inclination towards recluseness, Godard, the director's filmmaker par excellance, is now of course being gagged because for every film he makes on the cinema he is only concerned with copyrights. See as well the fragment with the flickering placard 'NO COPYRIGHT' in Deux Fois Cinquante Ans de Cinéma Français, which was also used in Still/A Novel part 2.

30
'On TV there is no projection. There is a rejection – you are rejected in your armchair or on your bed. In pictures you are projected, but you still have to decide what to be. In TV there is just transmission of something. (People like to say, "What do you mean exactly?" I would answer, "I mean, but not exactly.")' Jean-Luc Godard interviewed by Gavin Smith in Film Comment, vol. 32, no. 2 (1996), p. 39.

31
Cf to the interview 'Ja er zijn nog sterke beelden,' (Yes, there still are powerful images.) with Jan Braet in Knack, vol. 25, no. 51 (21 December, 1995).

32
'Most of the historically important functions of the human eye are being supplanted by practices in which visual images no longer have any reference to the position of an observer in a "real," optically perceived world. ... To comprehend this relentless abstraction of the visual and to avoid mystifying it by recourse to technological explanations, many questions would have to be posed and answered. Some of the most crucial of these questions are historical. If there is in fact an ongoing mutation in the nature of visuality, what forms or modes are being left behind? ... How is the body, including the observing body, becoming a component of new machines, economies, apparatuses, whether social, libidinal, or technological? In what ways is subjectivity becoming a precarious condition of interface between rationalized systems of change and networks of information?' chapter 1, 'Modernity and the Problem of the Observer,' Techniques of the Observer – On Vision and Modernity in the Nineteenth Century, (Cambridge: The MIT Press, 1990), p. 2.

Marcel Broodthaers
Cheval au galop, Avant Muybridge,
Après Muybridge, 1973-74
ink on canvas
27 x 25 cm each
collection Reiner Speck, Cologne

Cheval au galop.

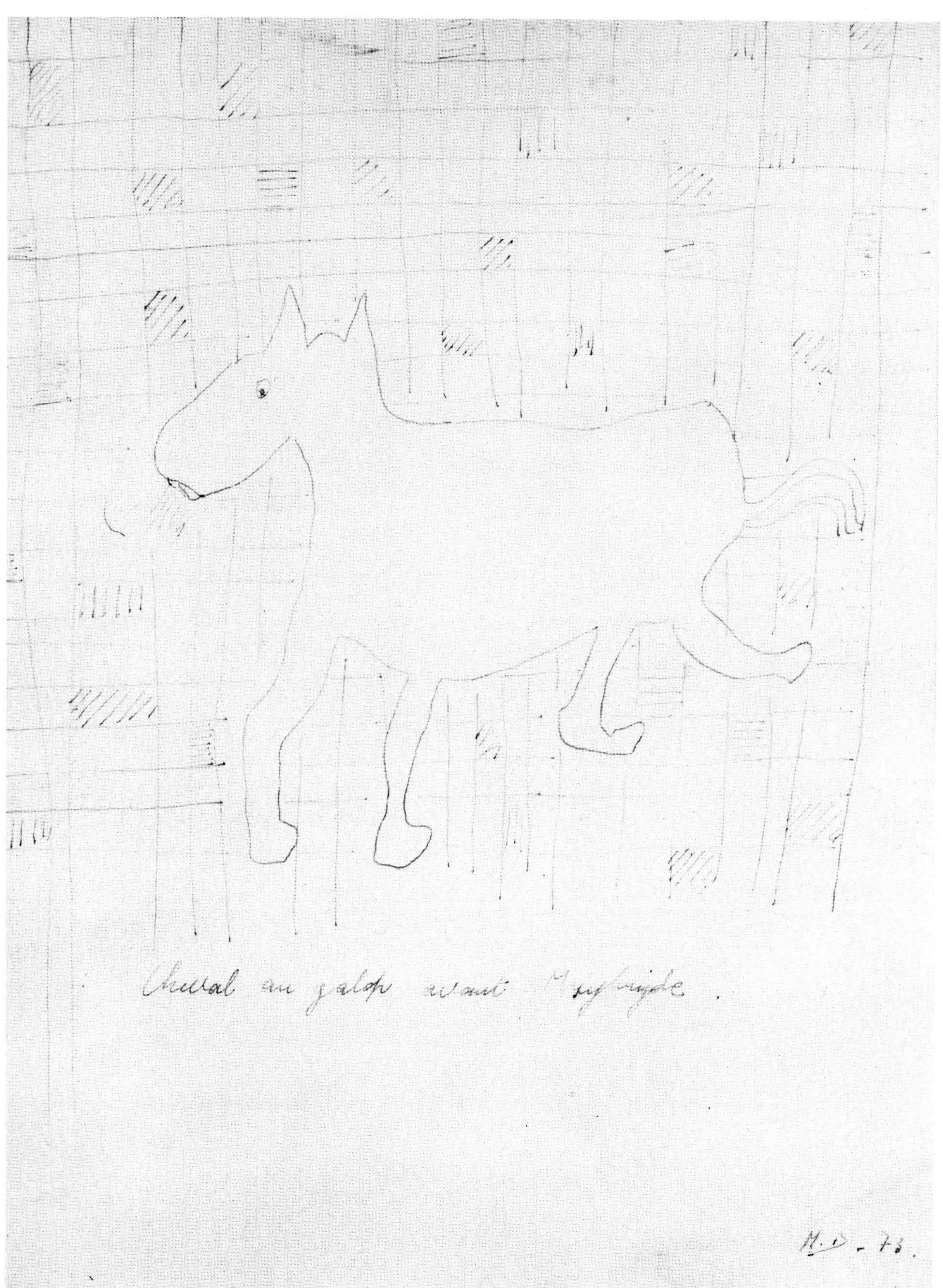

Cheval au galop avant Muybridge.
M.D - 73.

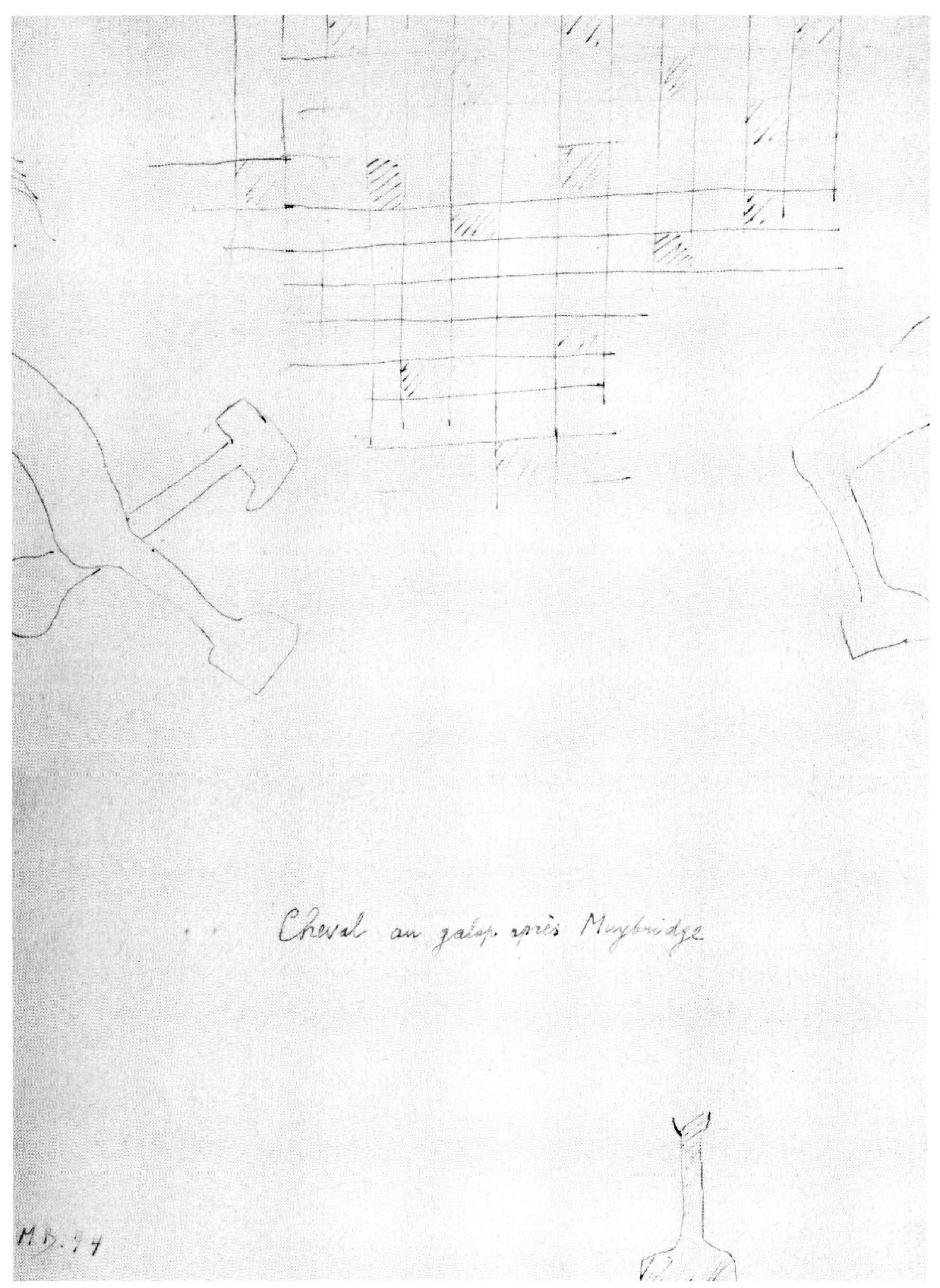
Cheval au galop après Muybridge
M.B. 74

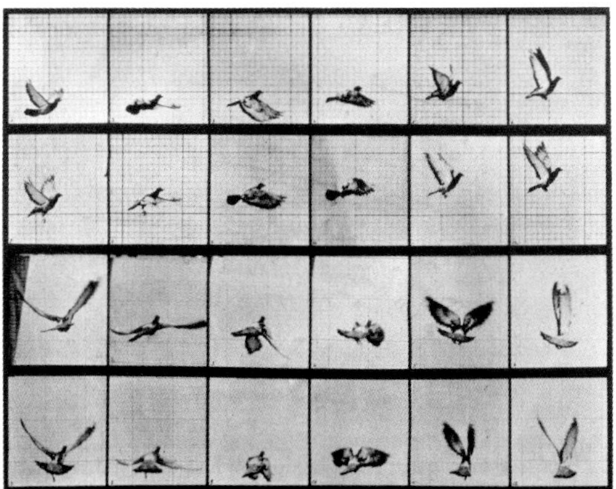

Eadweard Muybridge, Animal Locomotion
Plate 757. Pigeon Flying
collotype, print: 24.4 x 31.4 cm
private collection
courtesy Bonnefantenmuseum, Maastricht

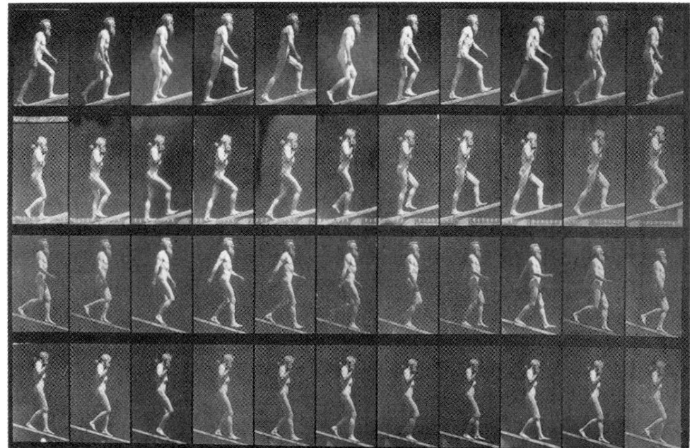

Eadweard Muybridge, Animal Locomotion
Plate 489. A: Ascending incline.
B: Ascending incline with a 50-lb. dumbbell.
C: Descening incline. D: Descending incline with a 50-lb. dumbbell.
collotype, print: 21.8 x 34.3 cm
collection Ydessa Hendeles, Toronto
courtesy Ydessa Hendeles Art Foundation, Toronto

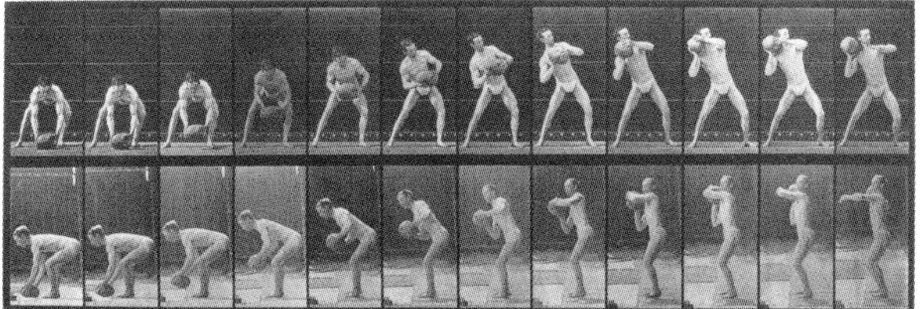

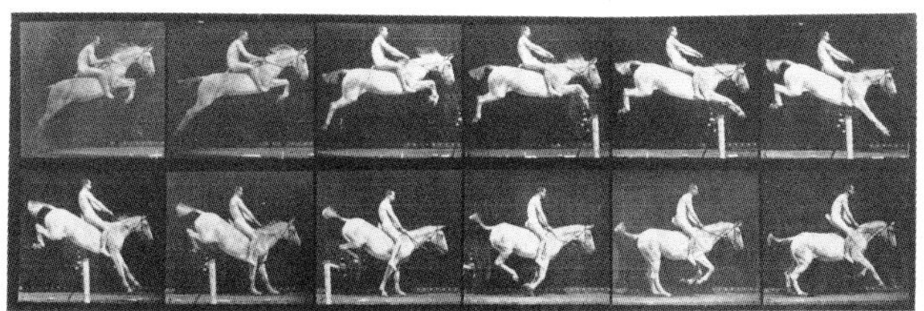

Eadweard Muybridge, Animal Locomotion
Plate 318. Lifting a 75-lb. rock
collotype, print: 15 x 45 cm
private collection
courtesy Bonnefantenmuseum, Maastricht

Eadweard Muybridge, Animal Locomotion
Plate 643. 'Pandora' jumping a hurdle, bareback, clearing and landing; male nude
collotype, print: 14.5 x 46 cm
private collection
courtesy Bonnefantenmuseum, Maastricht

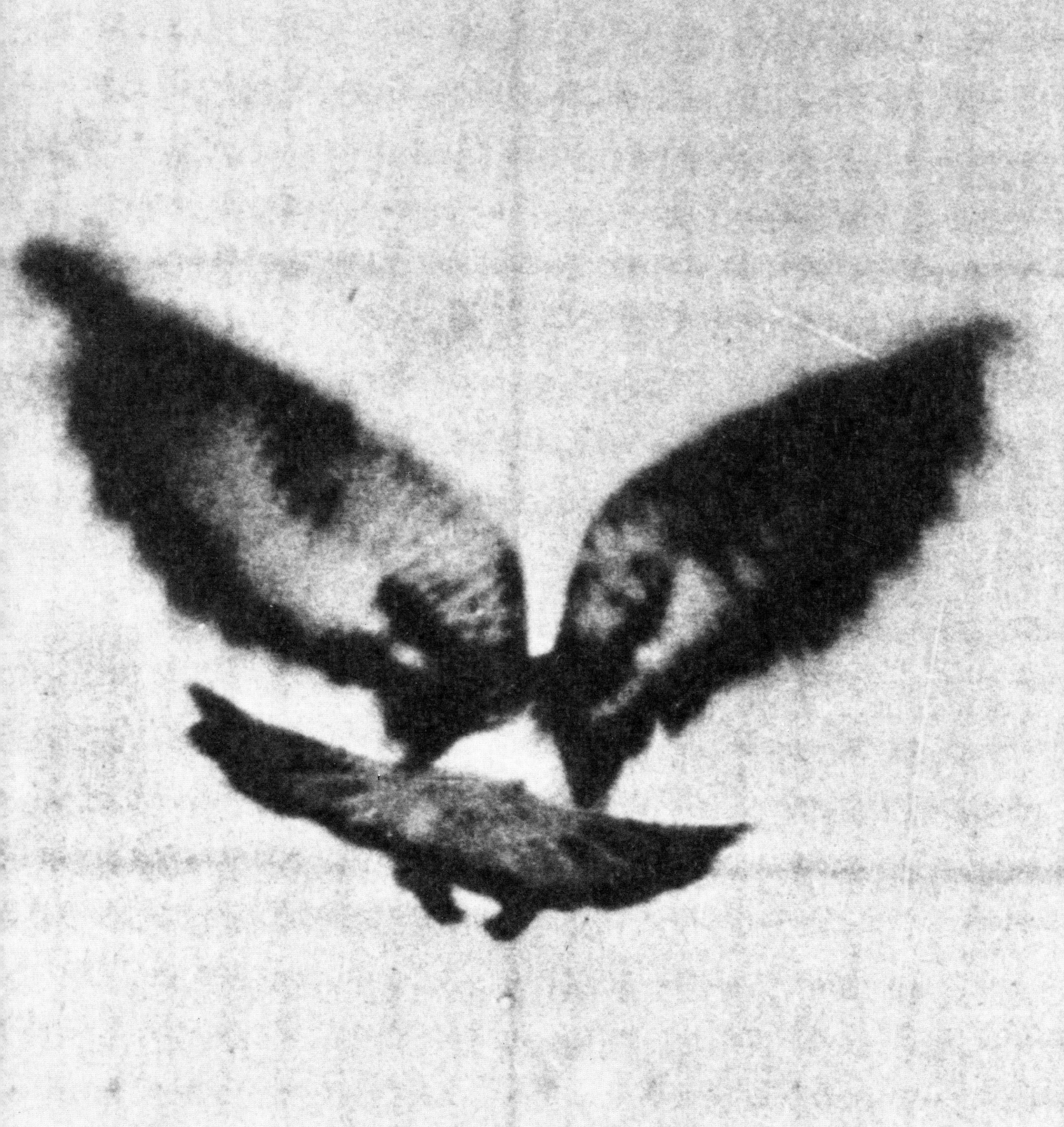

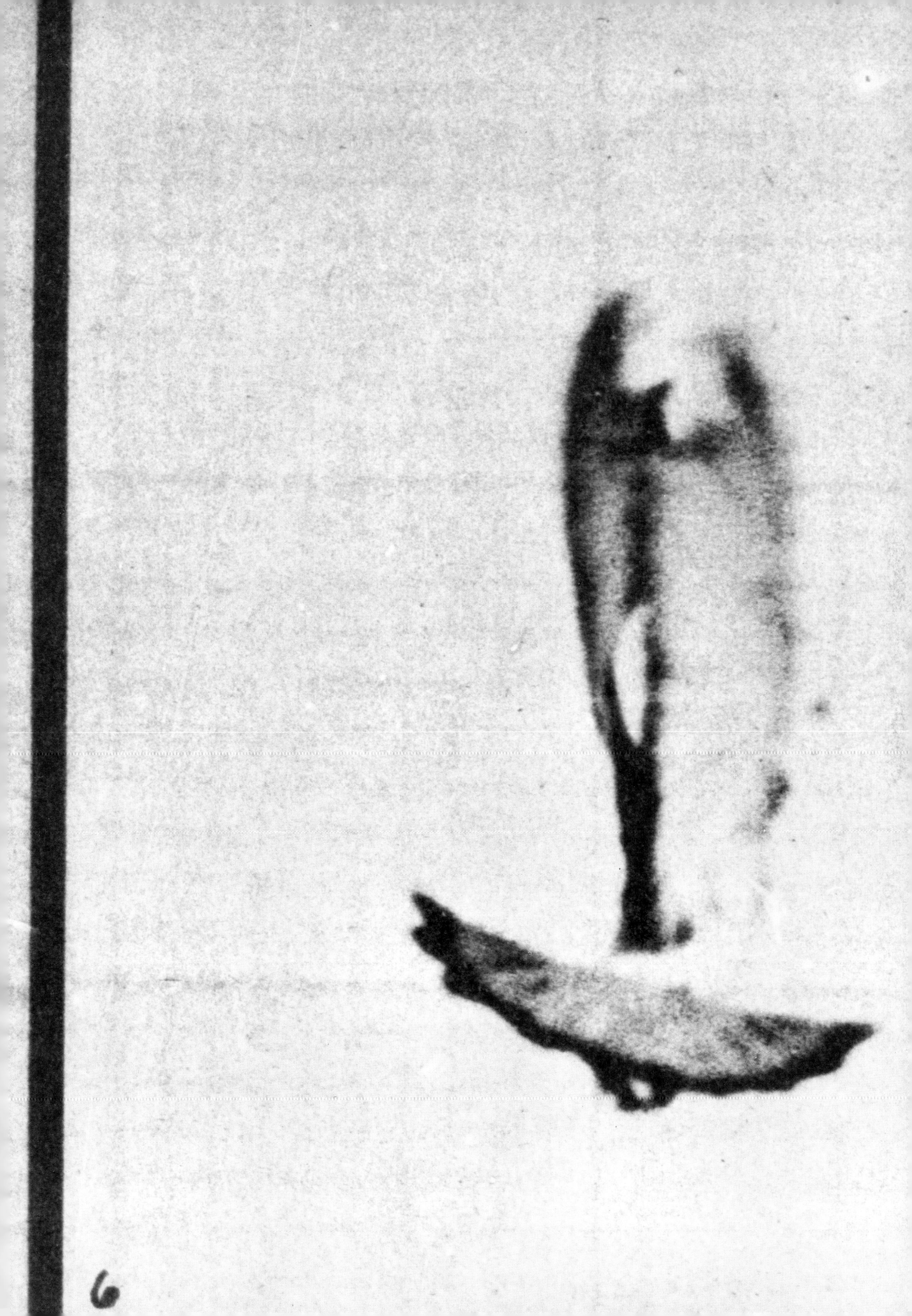

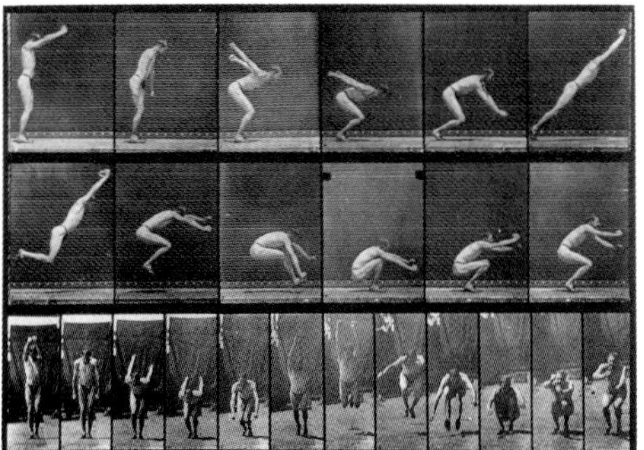

Eadweard Muybridge, Animal Locomotion
Plate 163. Jumping, standing broad jump
collotype, print: 22.5 x 32.5 cm
private collection
courtesy Bonnefantenmuseum, Maastricht

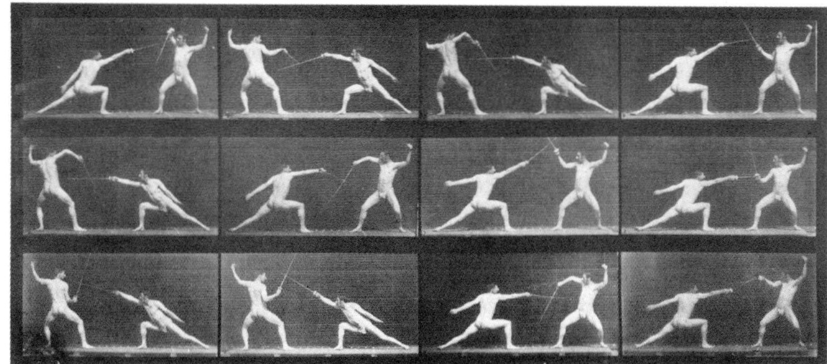

Eadweard Muybridge, Animal Locomotion
Plate 349. Fencing
collotype, print: 18 x 42.4 cm
collection Ydessa Hendeles, Toronto
courtesy Ydessa Hendeles Art Foundation, Toronto

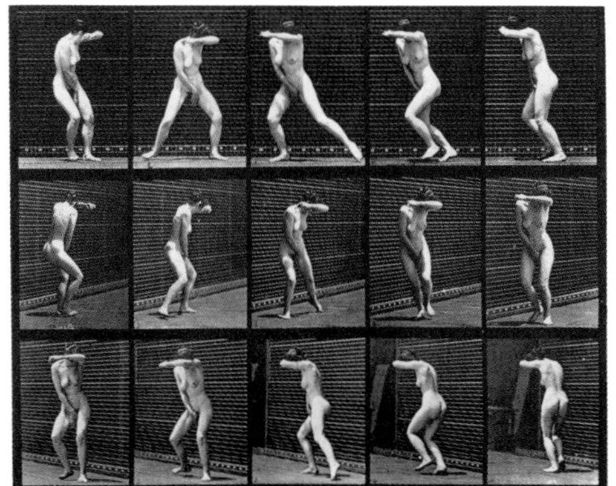

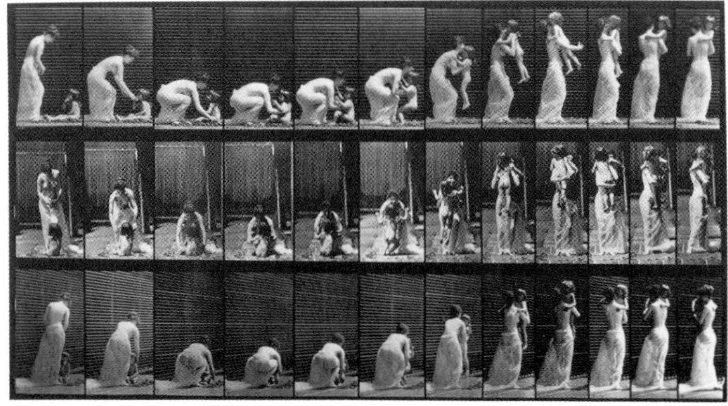

Eadweard Muybridge, Animal Locomotion
Plate 73. Turning around in surprise
and running away
collotype, print: 24.5 x 31 cm
collection Ydessa Hendeles, Toronto
courtesy Ydessa Hendeles Art Foundation, Toronto

Eadweard Muybridge, Animal Locomotion
Plate 214. Lifting a child from the ground and turning around
collotype, print: 19.5 x 36.1 cm
collection Ydessa Hendeles, Toronto
courtesy Ydessa Hendeles Art Foundation, Toronto

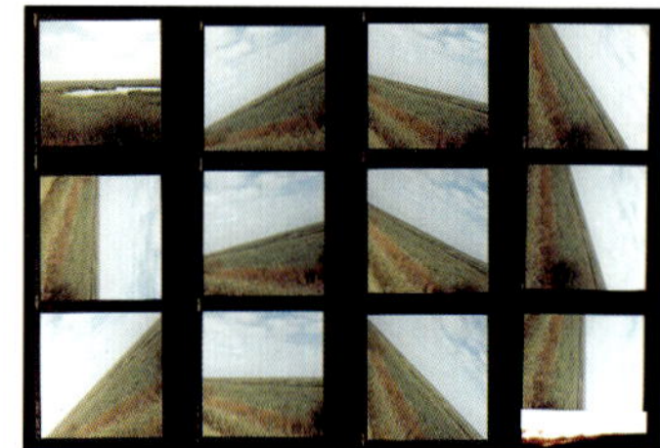

Jan Dibbets
0° — 135°, 1972
contactsheet
collection of the artist

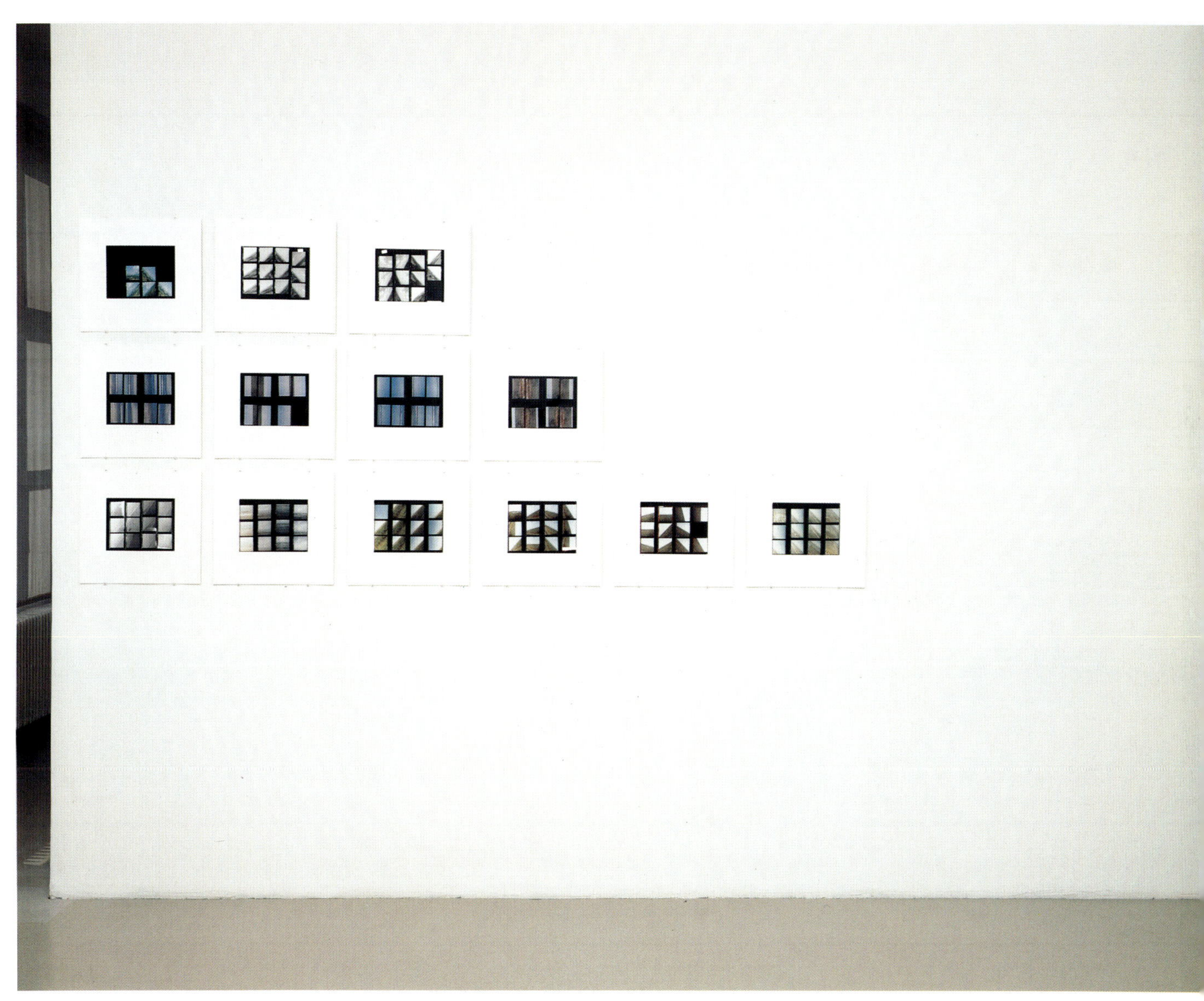

Jan Dibbets
0° — 135°, 1972
installation view at Witte de With

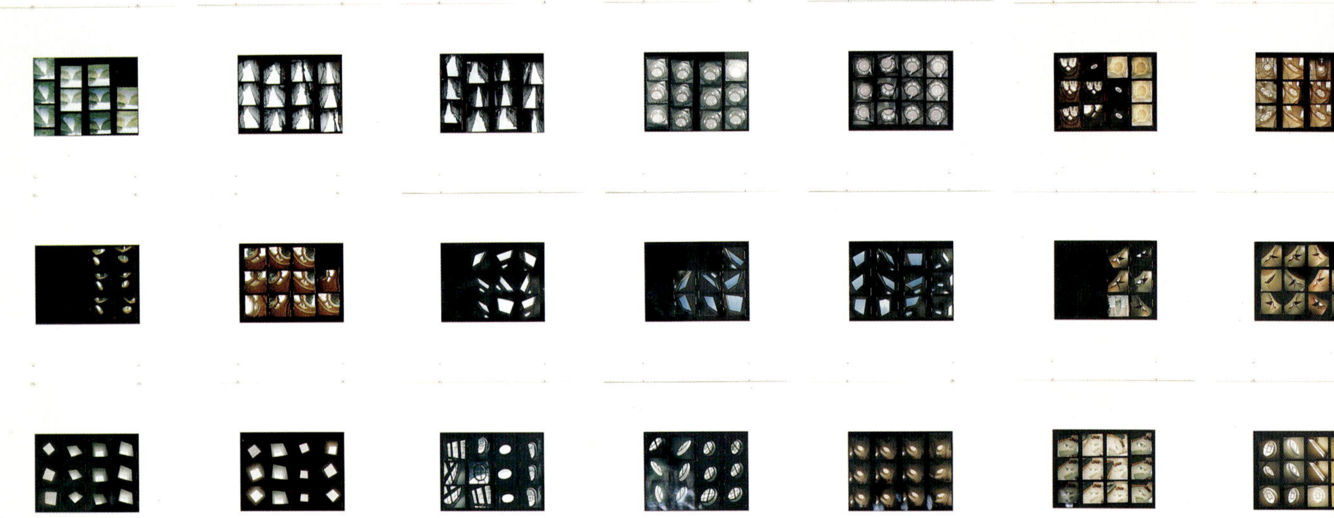

Jan Dibbets
Windows, 1987-95
contactsheets
collection of the artist
installation view at Witte de With

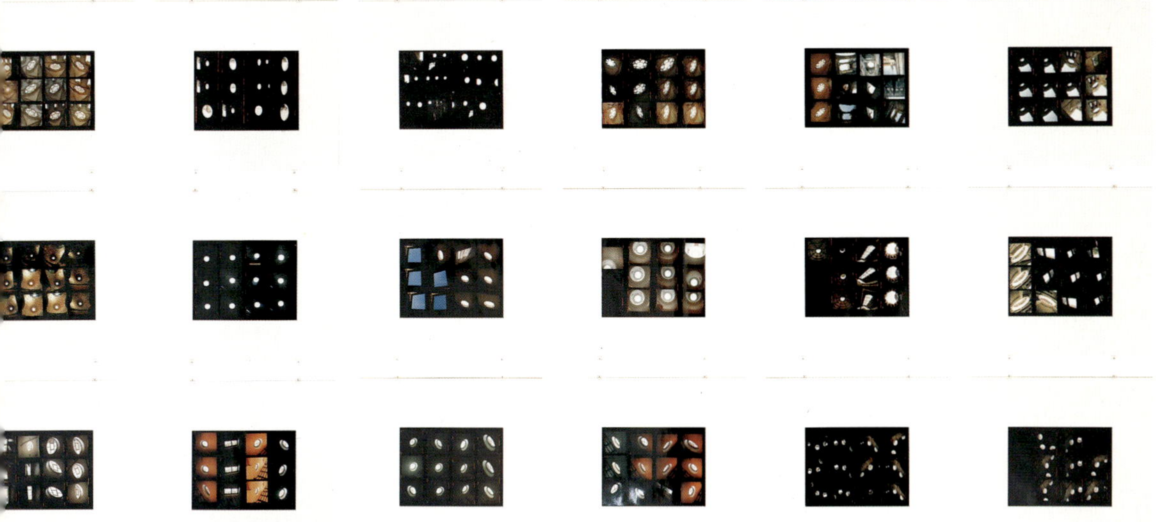

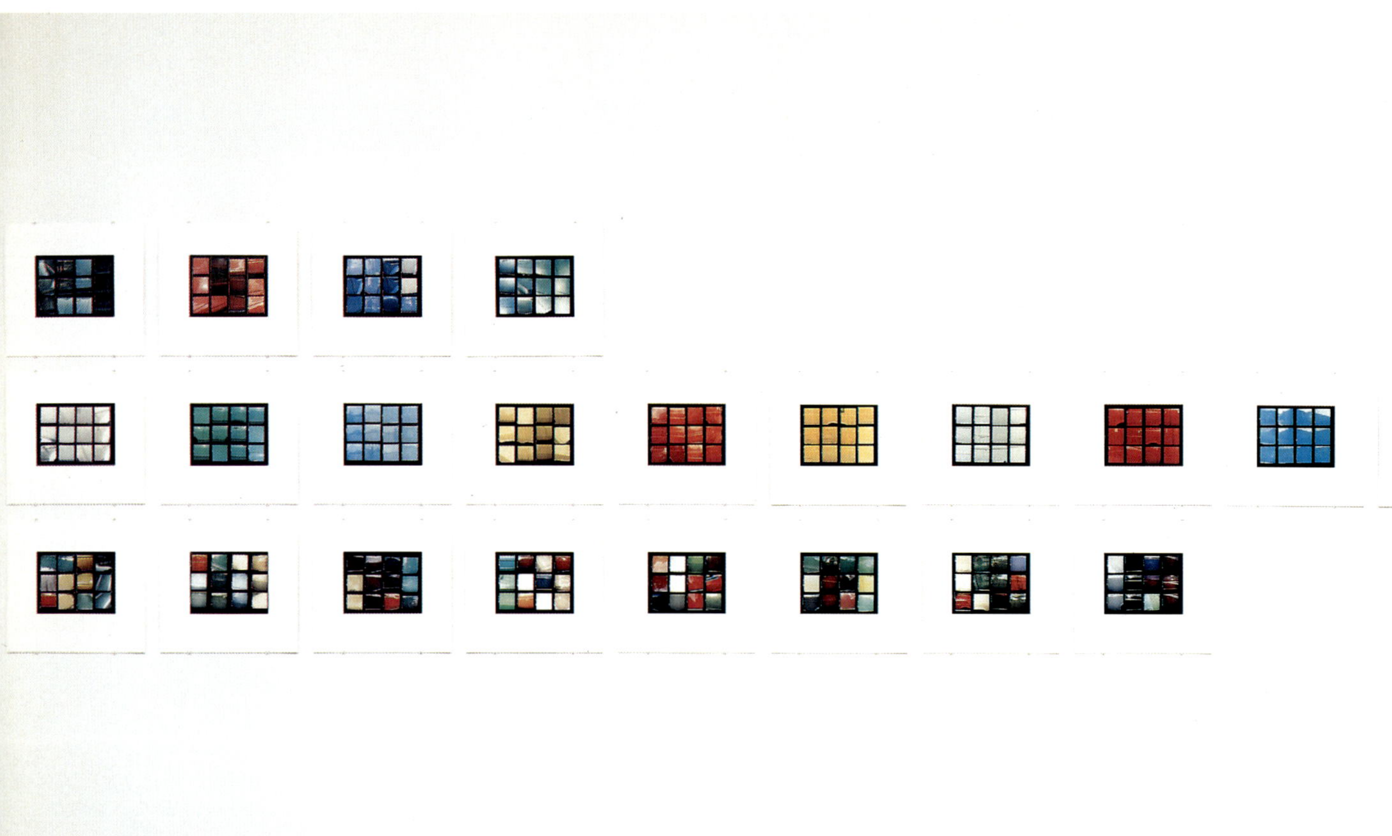

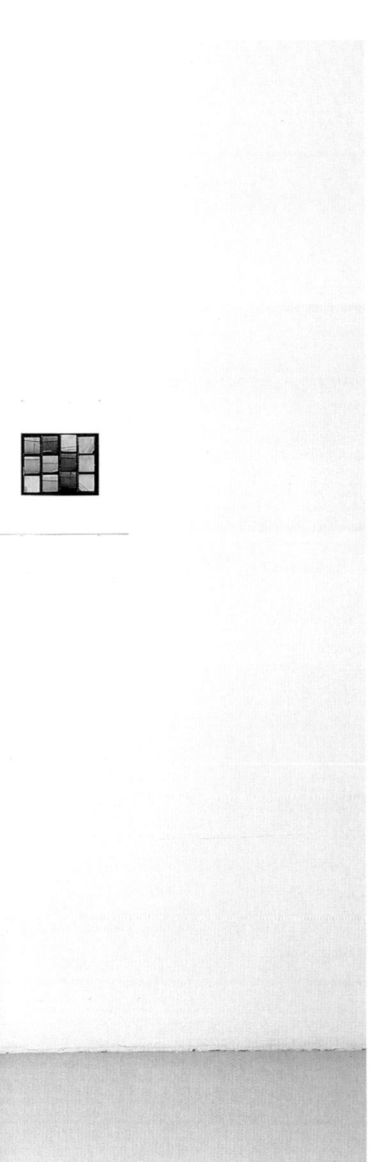

Jan Dibbets
Colour Studies, 1975
contactsheets
collection of the artist
installation view at Witte de With

Carl Andre
<u>STILL/A NOVEL</u>, 1972
(pages 55-62 out of 98)
typoscript on paper
27.8 x 21.7 cm each
collection of the artist
courtesy of the Stedelijk Museum,
Amsterdam

MAJORLARKYNSATTHEDOORCALLINGINTOTHEDARKNES.
N TA IR S
A HL NO W
C ER TO H
I DO OD O
U OJ TE A
O OA HH R
Y RM ET E
E CU DT Y
R AO AA O
A LY RS U
O LE KN I
H IE NY C
W NS EK A
S GT SR N
SENKRADEHTOTNINACIUOYERAOHWSALROJAMUOYEEST
SWHOAREYOUICANTSEEYOUMAJORLARKYNSATTHEDOOR
E TE RU C
H SR KO A
T EA YY L
O EO NE L
T YH SE I
N OW AS N
I US TT G
G MS TN I
N AE HA N
I JN EC T
L OK DI O
L RR OU T
A LA OO H
C AD RY E
ROODEHTTASNYKREHTOTNIGNILLACERAOHWSSENKRAD
CALLINGINTOTHEDARKNESSWHOAREYOUICANTSEEYOU
T DG YS M
A AN OE A
S RI UN J
N KL IK O
Y NL CR R
K EA AA L
R SC ND A
A SR TE R
L WO SH K
R HO ET Y
O OD EO N
J AE YT S
A RH ON A
M ET UI T
UOYEESTNACIUOYTASNYKRALROJAMGNILLACROODEHT

EADWEARDM
UYBRIDGED
ISCHARGIN
GHISPISTO
LINTOTHEC
HESTOFMAJ
ORLARKYNS

mmmmmmuuuuuuyyyyyybbbbbbrrrrrriiiiiiddddddggggggeeeeee
mmmmmmuuuuuuyyyyyybbbbbbrrrrrriiiiiiddddddggggggeeeeee
mmmmmmuuuuuuyyyyyybbbbbbrrrrrriiiiiiddddddggggggeeeeee
mmmmmmuuuuuuyyyyyybbbbbbrrrrrriiiiiiddddddggggggeeeeee
mmmmmmuuuuuuyyyyyybbbbbbrrrrrriiiiiiddddddggggggeeeeee
rrrrrreeeeeeppppppllllllyyyyyyiiiiiinnnnnnggggggaaaaaa
rrrrrreeeeeeppppppllllllyyyyyyiiiiiinnnnnnggggggaaaaaa
rrrrrreeeeeeppppppllllllyyyyyyiiiiiinnnnnnggggggaaaaaa
rrrrrreeeeeeppppppllllllyyyyyyiiiiiinnnnnnggggggaaaaaa
rrrrrreeeeeeppppppllllllyyyyyyiiiiiinnnnnnggggggaaaaaa
rrrrrreeeeeeppppppllllllyyyyyyiiiiiinnnnnnggggggaaaaaa
ttttttoooooonnnnnncccccceeeeeeggggggoooooooooooodddddd
ttttttoooooonnnnnncccccceeeeeeggggggoooooooooooodddddd
ttttttoooooonnnnnncccccceeeeeeggggggoooooooooooodddddd
ttttttoooooonnnnnncccccceeeeeeggggggoooooooooooodddddd
ttttttoooooonnnnnncccccceeeeeeggggggoooooooooooodddddd
ttttttoooooonnnnnncccccceeeeeeggggggoooooooooooodddddd
eeeeeevvvvvveeeeeennnnnniiiiiinnnnnnggggggmmmmmmaaaaaa
eeeeeevvvvvveeeeeennnnnniiiiiinnnnnnggggggmmmmmmaaaaaa
eeeeeevvvvvveeeeeennnnnniiiiiinnnnnnggggggmmmmmmaaaaaa
eeeeeevvvvvveeeeeennnnnniiiiiinnnnnnggggggmmmmmmaaaaaa
eeeeeevvvvvveeeeeennnnnniiiiiinnnnnnggggggmmmmmmaaaaaa
eeeeeevvvvvveeeeeennnnnniiiiiinnnnnnggggggmmmmmmaaaaaa
jjjjjjoooooorrrrrrllllllaaaaaarrrrrrkkkkkkyyyyyynnnnnn
jjjjjjoooooorrrrrrllllllaaaaaarrrrrrkkkkkkyyyyyynnnnnn
jjjjjjoooooorrrrrrllllllaaaaaarrrrrrkkkkkkyyyyyynnnnnn
jjjjjjoooooorrrrrrllllllaaaaaarrrrrrkkkkkkyyyyyynnnnnn
jjjjjjoooooorrrrrrllllllaaaaaarrrrrrkkkkkkyyyyyynnnnnn
jjjjjjoooooorrrrrrllllllaaaaaarrrrrrkkkkkkyyyyyynnnnnn
ssssssmmmmmmyyyyyynnnnnnaaaaaammmmmmeeeeeeiiiiiissssss
ssssssmmmmmmyyyyyynnnnnnaaaaaammmmmmeeeeeeiiiiiissssss
ssssssmmmmmmyyyyyynnnnnnaaaaaammmmmmeeeeeeiiiiiissssss
ssssssmmmmmmyyyyyynnnnnnaaaaaammmmmmeeeeeeiiiiiissssss
ssssssmmmmmmyyyyyynnnnnnaaaaaammmmmmeeeeeeiiiiiissssss
ssssssmmmmmmyyyyyynnnnnnaaaaaammmmmmeeeeeeiiiiiissssss
mmmmmmuuuuuuyyyyyybbbbbbrrrrrriiiiiiddddddggggggeeeeee
mmmmmmuuuuuuyyyyyybbbbbbrrrrrriiiiiiddddddggggggeeeeee
mmmmmmuuuuuuyyyyyybbbbbbrrrrrriiiiiiddddddggggggeeeeee
mmmmmmuuuuuuyyyyyybbbbbbrrrrrriiiiiiddddddggggggeeeeee
mmmmmmuuuuuuyyyyyybbbbbbrrrrrriiiiiiddddddggggggeeeeee
mmmmmmuuuuuuyyyyyybbbbbbrrrrrriiiiiiddddddggggggeeeeee

LARKYNSST
AGGERINGB
ACKWARDUN
DERTHEIMP
ACTOFTHES
HOTSMUYBR
IDGEFIRES

MMMMMMUUUUUUYYYYYYBBBBBBRRRRRRIIIIIIDDDDDDGGGGGGEEEEEE
MMMMMMUUUUUUYYYYYYBBBBBBRRRRRRIIIIIIDDDDDDGGGGGGEEEEEE
MMMMMMUUUUUUYYYYYYBBBBBBRRRRRRIIIIIIDDDDDDGGGGGGEEEEEE
MMMMMMUUUUUUYYYYYYBBBBBBRRRRRRIIIIIIDDDDDDGGGGGGEEEEEE
MMMMMMUUUUUUYYYYYYBBBBBBRRRRRRIIIIIIDDDDDDGGGGGGEEEEEE
MMMMMMUUUUUUYYYYYYBBBBBBRRRRRRIIIIIIDDDDDDGGGGGGEEEEEE
MMMMMMUUUUUUYYYYYYBBBBBBRRRRRRIIIIIIDDDDDDGGGGGGEEEEEE
DDDDDDRRRRRRAAAAAAWWWWWWIIIIIINNNNNNGGGGGGAAAAAAGGGGGG
DDDDDDRRRRRRAAAAAAWWWWWWIIIIIINNNNNNGGGGGGAAAAAAGGGGGG
DDDDDDRRRRRRAAAAAAWWWWWWIIIIIINNNNNNGGGGGGAAAAAAGGGGGG
DDDDDDRRRRRRAAAAAAWWWWWWIIIIIINNNNNNGGGGGGAAAAAAGGGGGG
DDDDDDRRRRRRAAAAAAWWWWWWIIIIIINNNNNNGGGGGGAAAAAAGGGGGG
DDDDDDRRRRRRAAAAAAWWWWWWIIIIIINNNNNNGGGGGGAAAAAAGGGGGG
DDDDDDRRRRRRAAAAAAWWWWWWIIIIIINNNNNNGGGGGGAAAAAAGGGGGG
UUUUUUNNNNNNSSSSSSAAAAAAYYYYYYIIIIIINNNNNNGGGGGGHHHHHH
UUUUUUNNNNNNSSSSSSAAAAAAYYYYYYIIIIIINNNNNNGGGGGGHHHHHH
UUUUUUNNNNNNSSSSSSAAAAAAYYYYYYIIIIIINNNNNNGGGGGGHHHHHH
UUUUUUNNNNNNSSSSSSAAAAAAYYYYYYIIIIIINNNNNNGGGGGGHHHHHH
UUUUUUNNNNNNSSSSSSAAAAAAYYYYYYIIIIIINNNNNNGGGGGGHHHHHH
UUUUUUNNNNNNSSSSSSAAAAAAYYYYYYIIIIIINNNNNNGGGGGGHHHHHH
UUUUUUNNNNNNSSSSSSAAAAAAYYYYYYIIIIIINNNNNNGGGGGGHHHHHH
EEEEEERRRRRREEEEEESSSSSSMMMMMMYYYYYYAAAAAANNNNNNSSSSSS
EEEEEERRRRRREEEEEESSSSSSMMMMMMYYYYYYAAAAAANNNNNNSSSSSS
EEEEEERRRRRREEEEEESSSSSSMMMMMMYYYYYYAAAAAANNNNNNSSSSSS
EEEEEERRRRRREEEEEESSSSSSMMMMMMYYYYYYAAAAAANNNNNNSSSSSS
EEEEEERRRRRREEEEEESSSSSSMMMMMMYYYYYYAAAAAANNNNNNSSSSSS
EEEEEERRRRRREEEEEESSSSSSMMMMMMYYYYYYAAAAAANNNNNNSSSSSS
EEEEEERRRRRREEEEEESSSSSSMMMMMMYYYYYYAAAAAANNNNNNSSSSSS
WWWWWWEEEEEERRRRRRTTTTTTOOOOOOTTTTTTHHHHHHEEEEEELLLLLL
WWWWWWEEEEEERRRRRRTTTTTTOOOOOOTTTTTTHHHHHHEEEEEELLLLLL
WWWWWWEEEEEERRRRRRTTTTTTOOOOOOTTTTTTHHHHHHEEEEEELLLLLL
WWWWWWEEEEEERRRRRRTTTTTTOOOOOOTTTTTTHHHHHHEEEEEELLLLLL
WWWWWWEEEEEERRRRRRTTTTTTOOOOOOTTTTTTHHHHHHEEEEEELLLLLL
WWWWWWEEEEEERRRRRRTTTTTTOOOOOOTTTTTTHHHHHHEEEEEELLLLLL
WWWWWWEEEEEERRRRRRTTTTTTOOOOOOTTTTTTHHHHHHEEEEEELLLLLL
EEEEEETTTTTTTTTTTTEEEEEERRRRRRYYYYYYOOOOOOUUUUUUSSSSSS
EEEEEETTTTTTTTTTTTEEEEEERRRRRRYYYYYYOOOOOOUUUUUUSSSSSS
EEEEEETTTTTTTTTTTTEEEEEERRRRRRYYYYYYOOOOOOUUUUUUSSSSSS
EEEEEETTTTTTTTTTTTEEEEEERRRRRRYYYYYYOOOOOOUUUUUUSSSSSS
EEEEEETTTTTTTTTTTTEEEEEERRRRRRYYYYYYOOOOOOUUUUUUSSSSSS
EEEEEETTTTTTTTTTTTEEEEEERRRRRRYYYYYYOOOOOOUUUUUUSSSSSS
EEEEEETTTTTTTTTTTTEEEEEERRRRRRYYYYYYOOOOOOUUUUUUSSSSSS
EEEEEENNNNNNTTTTTTMMMMMMYYYYYYWWWWWWIIIIIIFFFFFFEEEEEE
EEEEEENNNNNNTTTTTTMMMMMMYYYYYYWWWWWWIIIIIIFFFFFFEEEEEE
EEEEEENNNNNNTTTTTTMMMMMMYYYYYYWWWWWWIIIIIIFFFFFFEEEEEE
EEEEEENNNNNNTTTTTTMMMMMMYYYYYYWWWWWWIIIIIIFFFFFFEEEEEE
EEEEEENNNNNNTTTTTTMMMMMMYYYYYYWWWWWWIIIIIIFFFFFFEEEEEE
EEEEEENNNNNNTTTTTTMMMMMMYYYYYYWWWWWWIIIIIIFFFFFFEEEEEE
EEEEEENNNNNNTTTTTTMMMMMMYYYYYYWWWWWWIIIIIIFFFFFFEEEEEE

LARKYNSRU
NNINGTHRO
UGHTHEKIT
CHENANDSI
TTINGROOM
ATTEMPTIN
GTOESCAPE

eeeeeeeAAAAAAAdddddddWWWWWWWeeeeeeeAAAAAAArrrrrrrDDDDDDDmmmmmmm
eeeeeeeAAAAAAAdddddddWWWWWWWeeeeeeeAAAAAAArrrrrrrDDDDDDDmmmmmmm
eeeeeeeAAAAAAAdddddddWWWWWWWeeeeeeeAAAAAAArrrrrrrDDDDDDDmmmmmmm
eeeeeeeAAAAAAAdddddddWWWWWWWeeeeeeeAAAAAAArrrrrrrDDDDDDDmmmmmmm
eeeeeeeAAAAAAAdddddddWWWWWWWeeeeeeeAAAAAAArrrrrrrDDDDDDDmmmmmmm
eeeeeeeAAAAAAAdddddddWWWWWWWeeeeeeeAAAAAAArrrrrrrDDDDDDDmmmmmmm
eeeeeeeAAAAAAAdddddddWWWWWWWeeeeeeeAAAAAAArrrrrrrDDDDDDDmmmmmmm
UUUUUUUyyyyyyyBBBBBBBrrrrrrrIIIIIIIdddddddGGGGGGGeeeeeeeDDDDDDD
UUUUUUUyyyyyyyBBBBBBBrrrrrrrIIIIIIIdddddddGGGGGGGeeeeeeeDDDDDDD
UUUUUUUyyyyyyyBBBBBBBrrrrrrrIIIIIIIdddddddGGGGGGGeeeeeeeDDDDDDD
UUUUUUUyyyyyyyBBBBBBBrrrrrrrIIIIIIIdddddddGGGGGGGeeeeeeeDDDDDDD
UUUUUUUyyyyyyyBBBBBBBrrrrrrrIIIIIIIdddddddGGGGGGGeeeeeeeDDDDDDD
UUUUUUUyyyyyyyBBBBBBBrrrrrrrIIIIIIIdddddddGGGGGGGeeeeeeeDDDDDDD
UUUUUUUyyyyyyyBBBBBBBrrrrrrrIIIIIIIdddddddGGGGGGGeeeeeeeDDDDDDD
iiiiiiiSSSSSSScccccccHHHHHHHaaaaaaaRRRRRRRgggggggIIIIIIInnnnnnn
iiiiiiiSSSSSSScccccccHHHHHHHaaaaaaaRRRRRRRgggggggIIIIIIInnnnnnn
iiiiiiiSSSSSSScccccccHHHHHHHaaaaaaaRRRRRRRgggggggIIIIIIInnnnnnn
iiiiiiiSSSSSSScccccccHHHHHHHaaaaaaaRRRRRRRgggggggIIIIIIInnnnnnn
iiiiiiiSSSSSSScccccccHHHHHHHaaaaaaaRRRRRRRgggggggIIIIIIInnnnnnn
iiiiiiiSSSSSSScccccccHHHHHHHaaaaaaaRRRRRRRgggggggIIIIIIInnnnnnn
iiiiiiiSSSSSSScccccccHHHHHHHaaaaaaaRRRRRRRgggggggIIIIIIInnnnnnn
GGGGGGGhhhhhhhIIIIIIIsssssssPPPPPPPiiiiiiiSSSSSSStttttttOOOOOOO
GGGGGGGhhhhhhhIIIIIIIsssssssPPPPPPPiiiiiiiSSSSSSStttttttOOOOOOO
GGGGGGGhhhhhhhIIIIIIIsssssssPPPPPPPiiiiiiiSSSSSSStttttttOOOOOOO
GGGGGGGhhhhhhhIIIIIIIsssssssPPPPPPPiiiiiiiSSSSSSStttttttOOOOOOO
GGGGGGGhhhhhhhIIIIIIIsssssssPPPPPPPiiiiiiiSSSSSSStttttttOOOOOOO
GGGGGGGhhhhhhhIIIIIIIsssssssPPPPPPPiiiiiiiSSSSSSStttttttOOOOOOO
GGGGGGGhhhhhhhIIIIIIIsssssssPPPPPPPiiiiiiiSSSSSSStttttttOOOOOOO
lllllllIIIIIIInnnnnnnTTTTTTTooooooo TTTTTTThhhhhhhEEEEEEEccccccc
lllllllIIIIIIInnnnnnnTTTTTTToooooooTTTTTTThhhhhhhEEEEEEEccccccc
lllllllIIIIIIInnnnnnnTTTTTTToooooooTTTTTTThhhhhhhEEEEEEEccccccc
lllllllIIIIIIInnnnnnnTTTTTTToooooooTTTTTTThhhhhhhEEEEEEEccccccc
lllllllIIIIIIInnnnnnnTTTTTTToooooooTTTTTTThhhhhhhEEEEEEEccccccc
lllllllIIIIIIInnnnnnnTTTTTTToooooooTTTTTTThhhhhhhEEEEEEEccccccc
lllllllIIIIIIInnnnnnnTTTTTTToooooooTTTTTTThhhhhhhEEEEEEEccccccc
HHHHHHHeeeeeeeSSSSSSStttttttOOOOOOOfffffffMMMMMMMaaaaaaaJJJJJJJ
HHHHHHHeeeeeeeSSSSSSStttttttOOOOOOOfffffffMMMMMMMaaaaaaaJJJJJJJ
HHHHHHHeeeeeeeSSSSSSStttttttOOOOOOOfffffffMMMMMMMaaaaaaaJJJJJJJ
HHHHHHHeeeeeeeSSSSSSStttttttOOOOOOOfffffffMMMMMMMaaaaaaaJJJJJJJ
HHHHHHHeeeeeeeSSSSSSStttttttOOOOOOOfffffffMMMMMMMaaaaaaaJJJJJJJ
HHHHHHHeeeeeeeSSSSSSStttttttOOOOOOOfffffffMMMMMMMaaaaaaaJJJJJJJ
HHHHHHHeeeeeeeSSSSSSStttttttOOOOOOOfffffffMMMMMMMaaaaaaaJJJJJJJ
oooooooRRRRRRRlllllllAAAAAAArrrrrrrKKKKKKKyyyyyyyNNNNNNNsssssss
oooooooRRRRRRRlllllllAAAAAAArrrrrrrKKKKKKKyyyyyyyNNNNNNNsssssss
oooooooRRRRRRRlllllllAAAAAAArrrrrrrKKKKKKKyyyyyyyNNNNNNNsssssss
oooooooRRRRRRRlllllllAAAAAAArrrrrrrKKKKKKKyyyyyyyNNNNNNNsssssss
oooooooRRRRRRRlllllllAAAAAAArrrrrrrKKKKKKKyyyyyyyNNNNNNNsssssss
oooooooRRRRRRRlllllllAAAAAAArrrrrrrKKKKKKKyyyyyyyNNNNNNNsssssss
oooooooRRRRRRRlllllllAAAAAAArrrrrrrKKKKKKKyyyyyyyNNNNNNNsssssss

MUYBRIDGE
AFTERFIRI
NGFOLLOWI
NGMAJORLA
RKYNSCLOS
ELYTHROUG
HTHEHOUSE

Still/A Novel

Connections with the Eye of the Camera

Erik Eelbode

'Do I really see something different each time,
or do I only interpret what I see in a different way?'

At first sight it seemed a little like a footnote, the starting point of the exhibition Still/A Novel. Footnote 39, for example, in a recent Mel Bochner catalogue: 'Around 1967 Bochner had purchased two well-known "serial" photographs, both of which would be of major significance for his own work: a plate from Eadweard Muybridge's Animal Locomotion and Walker Evans's famous window, Penny Picture Display, Savannah of 1936.'[1] One note in passing is that in those days photography of such quality must have still been affordable. A more relevant point for Still/A Novel was that in the late sixties, apart from Mel Bochner, a considerable number of artists, including Carl Andre, Sol LeWitt, Dan Graham, Robert Smithson, Hollis Frampton, Marcel Broodthaers and Jan Dibbets, were going back to Muybridge's œuvre, which was then receiving little attention. Some of their works were inspired by his motion studies; and they published texts setting out Muybridge's influence on their own methods. The process-like character and the serial structure, which they identified in Muybridge's series of photographs, proved to be the crucial aspects.

In a similar broad movement, Witte de With wanted to draw attention to the origins of the cinema and focus on the relationship between photography, cinema and art through these 'motion pictures' by Muybridge, by confronting some one hundred of his collotypes with poems by Carl Andre, three drawings by Marcel Broodthaers and, above all, four hundred contact prints by Jan Dibbets. Add to this the television essay Still/A Novel by Chris Dercon, and the footnote becomes a stream. A flood of connections and associations to which perhaps only a similarly constructed, possibly multimedia, text could do justice. At the same time I recall earlier studies undertaken at Witte de With into the connections between contemporary art and photography. In De Afstand (Distance) (1990), Michelangelo Pistoletto e la Fotografia (1993) and Walker Evans & Dan Graham (1992) clear and far from obvious statements about this were made, which cast a new light on such concepts as 'medium,' 'œuvre,' 'history' and 'the ambiguous position currently occupied by photography between art and the media.'[2]

With some modifications, it proved possible to return to several of these themes in Still/A Novel and to comment on, for example, current 'sitings' of photography, its 'history' (including the blind spots) and on possible, changing locations and interpretations of two 'related' œuvres, those of Muybridge and Dibbets.

Initially, footnotes formed the model for this fragmentary text accompanying Still/A Novel – as an exhibition about photography.

More than the eye can see/An instrument that enlarges vision

> 'Mr. Muybridge's photographs are, perhaps, rather of indirect importance to the artist, as showing him what actually takes place, than as a direct means of assisting him to represent what the eye sees. The eye certainly does not see an instantaneous phase, such as is shown by one of Mr. Muybridge's photographs, but it sees a resultant of many motions, and it is this resultant which the artist generally aims at reproducing.... Scientifically the inquiry is most interesting, but though Mr. Muybridge's labor has been watched with much attention ... we doubt whether the contribution to art will be of much importance. Art for the purpose of representation does not require to give to the eye more than the eye can see; and when Mr. Sturgess gives us a picture of a close finish for the Gold Cup, we do not want Mr. Muybridge to tell us that no horses ever strode in the fashion shown in the picture. It may indeed be fairly contended that the incorrect position (according to science) is the correct position (according to art). Nor is this a paradox; for only extremists contend that art must discard every other consideration in an endeavor to represent merely the True.'[3]

This view was expressed in an unsigned text in The Photographic News of 1889, when Muybridge's main studies were gradually reaching cruising speed. The rumors and quasi-didactic anecdotes surrounding his work regularly and persistently take precedence over the possible interpretations and repercussions of his research. Yet from the outset they were significant: 'The meaning of the term "truth to nature" lost its force ... the photograph demonstrated that for many artists truth had really been another word for convention.'[4] Because of or despite this, scientists like Mach, Marey and Edison and artists like Meissonier, Bouguereau, Alma Tadema, Millais, Whistler, Puvis de Chavannes and Rodin eagerly subscribed in 1887 to the first edition of Muybridge's Animal Locomotion: an Electro-Photographic Investigation of Consecutive Phases of Animal Movement, 1872-1885. Two shorter, more popular editions, Animals in Motion and The Human Figure in Motion, followed in 1899 and 1901 respectively, and for generations of artists they formed a valuable store of movement sequences.

There is a further important point to be noted in the text by the anonymous contributor to The Photographic News. He writes, 'to represent what the eye sees ... and does not see' and thus moves, no doubt unwittingly, into previously unexplored but fundamental territory. Eduardo Cadava sums up this essential feature of photography, which had never before been demonstrated so clearly as through Muybridge's work (and through that of Étienne-Jules Marey, of which more later) as follows: 'Photography reveals what sight cannot see, what, before sight, makes sight impossible. The photograph tells us that when we see we are unconscious of what our seeing cannot see.'[5] This is a reference to Walter Benjamin, who is also accorded a prominent place by Rosalind Krauss:

> 'It was in 1931, in his "Small History of Photography" that Walter Benjamin first used the term "optical unconscious." With the photographs of Muybridge or Marey undoubtedly in mind, he speaks of how the naked eye cannot penetrate movements of even the most ordinary kind. "We have no idea at all," he says, "what happens during the fraction of a second when a person steps out." But photography, he exults, "with its devices of slow motion and enlargement, reveals the secret. It is through photography that we first discover the existence of this optical unconscious, just as we discover the instinctual unconscious through psychoanalysis."'[6]

For Benjamin, in this sense the camera is an 'instrument that enlarges vision.'

Muybridge may be regarded as an undoubted 'enlarger' of photographic vision and one of the keenest researchers in this field, but the whole undertaking to which his name continues to be linked is considerably more complex than the following standard statement suggests: 'In 1872 Eadweard Muybridge became the first person to record motion and duration photographically.' A first requirement, for example, was a major technological development. The earliest photographs could not 'capture' movement, simply because of the extremely long exposure times required to produce a visible image. This aspect of making visible what up to then could not be seen has a 'history' of its own (which we shall not go into here).
And even the familiar 'Muybridge's horse' anecdote turns out, on closer inspection, not to be without precedent. In the eighteenth and nineteenth centuries artists were already studying the true action of horses' legs in movement. Géricault and Meissonier, for example, rejected the prevailing flying gallop position, but could not offer a more 'correct' alternative. Around the middle of the nineteenth century there was a stream of treatises from veterinarians, cavalrymen and physiologists, 'and usually the intention was as much to provide the artist with visual material as it was to establish new and more accurate information for science.'[7] Lieutenant-Colonel Émile Duhousset almost got it right, without the aid of photography, in 1874 in his book Le Cheval. In addition to solid analyses of works of art – from the Greeks to Meissonier – he probably also made use of mechanical chronographic recordings by the physiologist Étienne-Jules Marey (1830-1904). 'Despite the fact that his illustrations are almost exactly correct, Duhousset still believed that ultimately the camera would supply the correct and irrefutable answers.'[8] He was not to know that Muy-

bridge, inspired by Marey's earlier research, had already done so two years before. Influenced in turn by these photographs, Marey decided that he would from then on record his experiments by photography alone.

Étienne-Jules Marey and Eadweard James Muybridge: the two EJMs of serial photography, as Siegfried Zielinski calls them. In an article with this title he disregards the uninteresting 'Who was first?' issue and concentrates on an often relevant comparison of their working methods. Not so much the differences in technical approach, but their photographs themselves seem to cover widely divergent matters. Muybridge's people and animals in movement look more realistic: 'They correspond more closely to what they refer to in the reality beyond the image.'[9] They are meant to give an impression of the physicality of a moving object in a (perspectivist) space. They are strictly mimetic – Muybridge tries to show nature 'as it really is' – and at the same time they remain hyperconstructed 'illusions.' Muybridge's commissioned photographs are 'sensations of volumes (in time), in the two-dimensional plane.' They report in detail on an external reality. Marey's chronophotos, on the other hand, are more compact and concise; in them a multiplicity of movements is compressed into a single image according to constructivist principles. They do not imitate, but show 'models' of bodies in motion. The prime concern here was not simply to depict external reality, but scientific experiment to 'make visible' an internal reality. According to Zielinski, Muybridge takes us directly to the pioneering phase of the audiovisual industry, but no further. His subject is spectacle, entertainment. Muybridge's photographs are 'earth bound' and subject to the laws of gravity. Marey, in contrast, reaches further, seizing many of the movements of his figures (literally) out of the air: the flight of birds, a pole-vaulter, the fall of a cat. Bodies are reduced to the structure of their locomotion. They become 'measurable,' stylized, stripped of their physical complexity, and comprehensible as 'constructions.' Marey was a revolutionary visionary, Muybridge a showman and a conjurer. For the dream factory of film, Muybridge's method (isolating separate moments of motion, frame by frame) proved to be the most useful and effective, but when one looks at these photographs as individual stills, they very quickly lose (for Zielinski) their 'aesthetic stimulus': 'At rest, they have no attraction. It is only in rapid succession that they articulate time, not in stationary juxtaposition. Media history has made them look shabby, worn out from being used a billion times.'[10] Whereas Marey's simultaneous images continue to fascinate and inspire. In his undisguised, almost emotional 'preference' for Marey, Zielinski is certainly not alone. This is evident not only from a number of relatively recent exhibitions and publications;[11] even the painter and photographer Thomas Eakins, who was a friend of Muybridge and a member of the committee at the University of Pennsylvania that supervised his animal locomotion experiments, in his own photographic work in 1885 preferred Marey's synthesis to Muybridge's analysis.

Marion Faller and Hollis Frampton
14. Gourds vanishing (var. 'Mixed Ornamental') from Sixteen Studies from Vegetable Locomotion, 1975
black-and-white photograph
27.9 x 35.6 cm
collection Albright-Knox Art Gallery, Buffalo, New York
Evelyn Rumsey Cary Fund, 1983

Another curiously relevant figure, though he rarely comes into the picture in this context, is the Frenchman Albert Londe, who in 1882 was taken on by Professor Charcot as a photographer at the proto-psychiatric clinic la Salpêtrière in Paris. Londe set to work with a kind of compressed version of the 'array' used by Muybridge: nine – later twelve – lenses attached to a mechanically powered, rotating plate, a system which recalls Marey's chronophotographic gun. With this apparatus Londe succeeded in recording (hallucinatory) series of 'pathological movements,' epileptic or hysterical attacks. But 'Londe is in no way concerned with any kind of recomposition of the movements he records,' writes Michel Frizot significantly. 'His camera, which allows him to study every form of movement in a scientific way, ... is perfectly adapted to the aim he sets himself: to obtain telling series of successive exposures which can be used for visual analysis on the basis of parameters or simply stored as documentary material.'[12] Alongside his medical work, Londe and Paul Richer, a lecturer in anatomy at the École des beaux-arts in Paris, carried out a number of motion studies related to Muybridge's research. One of Richer's diagrams, based on Londe's plates, is Un homme nu descendant un escalier (Nude Descending a Staircase). Londe's last two publications of 1903, Atlas sur les allures du cheval (Atlas on the Allures of the Horse) (yet again) and Album de chronophotographies documentaires à l'usage des artistes (Album of Documentary Chronophotography Used by Artists) completely transcend any possible medical application. The second

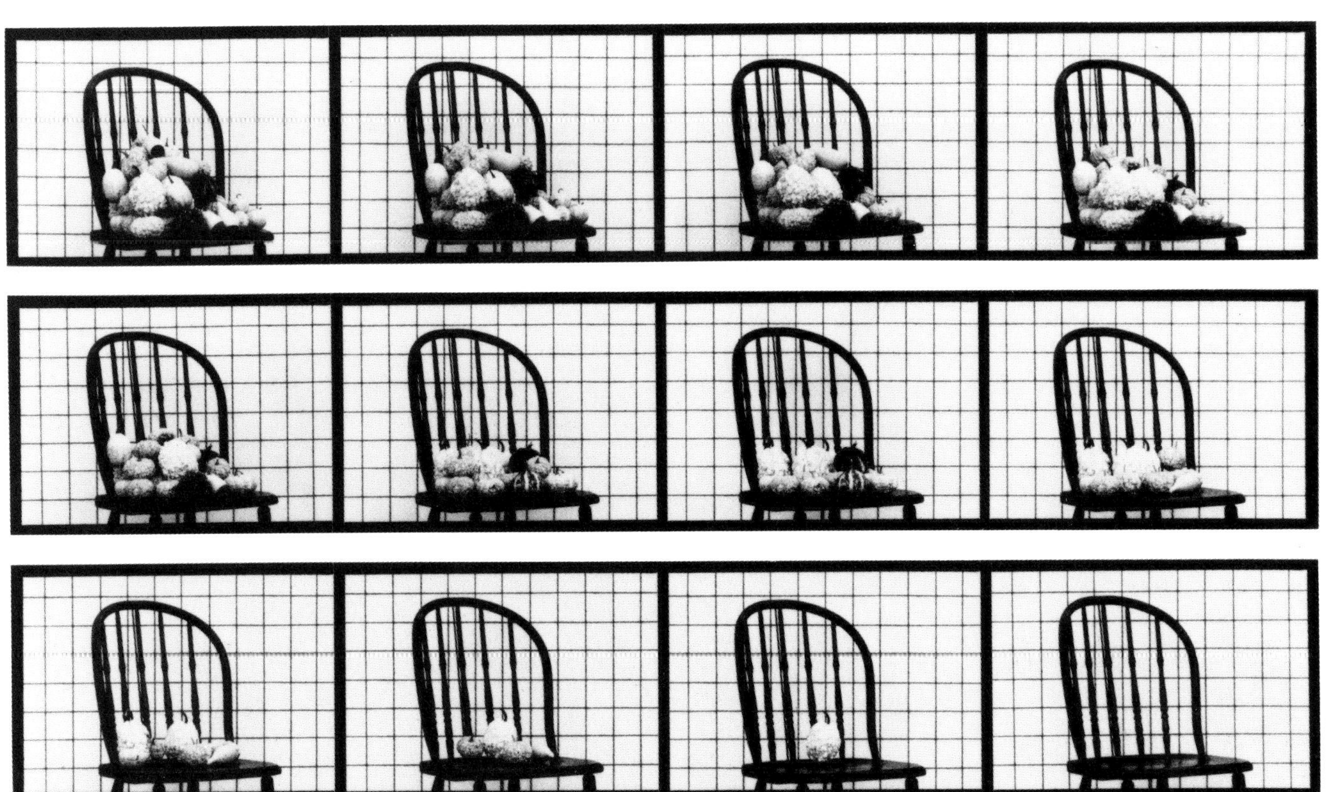

book even includes several studies of the motion of waves in the sea which 'in their aesthetic representation come very close to the conceptual work of the seventies, and in particular that of Jan Dibbets.'[13]

A series is no longer a 'picture'

One aspect which has so far been largely ignored or reduced to just a footnote in many photohistorical outlines and in analyses of media history dealing with the possible 'Muybridge-Marey legacy' is the measured and carefully considered use of photography by conceptual artists in the late sixties and early seventies.

There were various reasons why they initially turned to Muybridge – Londe was probably unknown to them – and only to a lesser extent to Marey. In the light of the comparison outlined above (the two EJMs), it could indeed be said that Marey's images were 'newer' and 'more interesting' and that 'the decomposition carried out by Muybridge' produced 'few specific images from the photographic point of view.'[14] However, the last thing that conceptual artists seemed to be looking for were 'aesthetic stimuli' (such as Zielinski finds in abundance in Marey) or photographically interesting images. The 'non-specific image' was exactly what concerned them.

A second and perhaps more important reason for their choice was the fact that Muybridge 'successively decomposed the fluid movements of living bodies in sequentially related frames. Here was the one-image-at-a-time analytic syndrome, gathering coherence through the linear aggregation of the frames (twenty-four in two horizontal tiers of twelve),'[15] as Max Kozloff says, with a barely concealed hostile undertone which betrays his preference as well for Marey. Muybridge's serial method of working and presenting was annexed as one of the constituent techniques of conceptual art, although not to a fanatical degree.

Of course Muybridge did not have a monopoly on working and thinking in series and sequences. The idea of producing successive photographic images went back to the 1850s and arose from Joseph Plateau's discoveries concerning the so-called after-image (the theoretical basis of cinema).[16] But Rilke too, discussing Rodin's 'stepping' sculptures, had already talked about 'simultaneity always containing an implicit experience of sequence.'[17] And in his writings Ludwig Wittgenstein – who was widely read by artists in the late sixties – talks about photography remarkably often. For him photography became a 'starting point for philosophical ideas and at the same time a practical proof of the various aspects of the objects such as the "fixed, existing" from which the world – a linking of facts – is put together.' For Wittgenstein this photographic conversion requires the use of serial or frequently repeated images, as can be seen in his travel photographs or in his own photo album.[18]

Nor was an awareness of the value and possible impact of photographic series restricted to the conceptualists, as the example of László Moholy-

Marion Faller and Hollis Frampton
782. Apple advancing (var. 'Northern Spy') from Sixteen Studies from Vegetable Locomotion, 1975
black-and-white photograph
27.9 x 35.6 cm
collection Albright-Knox Art Gallery, Buffalo, New York
Evelyn Rumsey Cary Fund, 1983

Nagy shows. He ends one of his important texts for the modernist Neue Fotografie, written between 1923 and 1926, with a separate and extraordinarily relevant section on Series (Photographic Image Sequences of the Same Object):

> 'There is no more surprising, yet, in its naturalness and organic sequence, simpler form than the photographic series. This is the logical culmination of photography. The series is no longer a "picture," and none of the canons of pictorial aesthetics can be applied to it. Here the separate picture loses its identity as such and becomes a detail of assembly, an essential structural element of the whole which is the thing itself.'[19]

Misunderstandings/Illusions/False Impressions

One of the original period documents on display at Still/A Novel was 'The Serial Attitude,' a text by Mel Bochner which appeared in Artforum in 1967. It also points in the first instance to the universality of 'working in series.'[20] 'Serial order is a method, not a style,' Bochner immediately asserts.

> 'The results of this method are surprising and diverse. Eadweard Muybridge's photographs, Thomas Eakins's perspective studies, Jasper John's numerals, Alfred Jensen's polyptychs, Larry Poons's circles, dots and ellipsoids, Donald Judd's painted wall pieces, Sol LeWitt's orthogonal multi-part floor structures, all are works employing serial logics.'

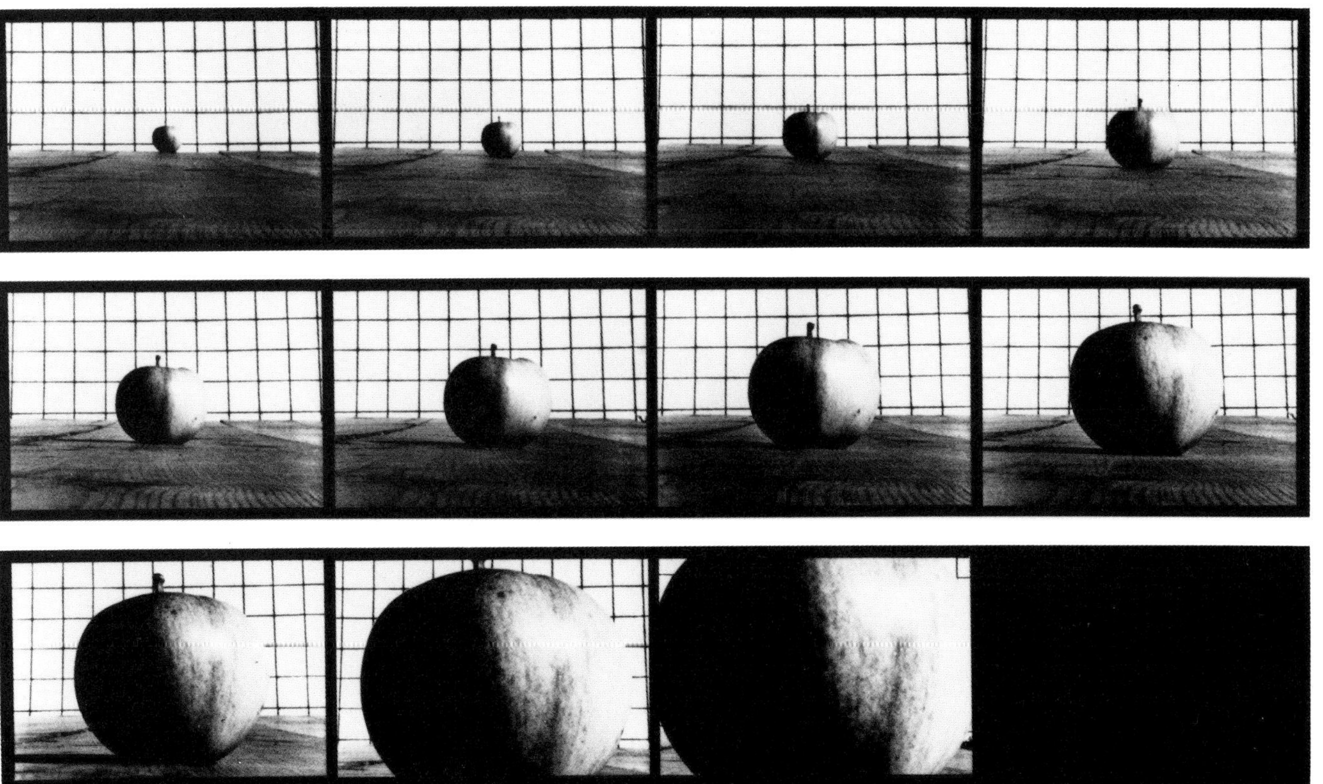

Seriality has no predetermined form or reserved places, although Muybridge is of course an outstandingly inspiring example.

'Muybridge's photographs are an instance of the serialization of time through the systematic substraction of duration from event. Muybridge simultaneously photographed the same activity from 180°, 90°, and 45° and printed the three sets of photographs parallel horizontally. By setting up alternative reading logics within a visually discontinuous sequence he completely fragmented perception into what Stockhausen called, in another context, a "directionless time-field."'

The concept of simultaneity (with Duchamp's Nude Descending a Staircase (1912) as an early example) is also discussed and hence the experiments of Marey, whom Bochner, like Dan Graham, evidently values greatly for the inventive way in which he could visualize the passage of time. At the end of 1966, Bochner had himself begun using photography, as the result of a project in which he wanted to capture the passing of time (Block Setups for First Photo Piece). He too, immediately came up against the ambiguity of the photographic image: 'the photographs were full of mysterious distortions, unpredictable foreshortenings, and even spherical aberrations.... Bochner's substitution of the photograph for the sculptured object was enormously prescient, for it was just after this moment that conceptual and earthwork artists began to realize that many of their works existed and were experienced principally as photographs.'[21] It was no coincidence that Mel Bochner gave his concise theory of photography (1967-70) the main title Misunderstandings. It consists of ten index cards, on each of which Bochner wrote a quotation about photography in block letters. They range from Mao Tse Tung to Merleau-Ponty and include three pirate quotes which are pronouncements of his own under a 'false' name – 'the intention of which was to undermine belief in the illusions of language (as his projects had undermined belief in the illusions of photography).'[22]

At that time there were remarkably few illusions about photography among conceptual (and other) artists. Robert Smithson had no trouble adding more quotes to Bochner's Misunderstandings:

'Artists who are bothered by unreality distrust the eye of the camera. "There are enough shadows in my life already," says Carl Andre in a discussion about photography. "I've looked at so many photos that I can't bear to see another one," says Michael Heizer. "I would like to make an abstract film," says Andy Warhol. As long as there are cameras around, no artist will be free from amazement.'[23]

But despite his strong reservations about photography (because it 'fossilizes and sterilizes'), Smithson still believed it to be essential within the changes that were taking place in art.

'In the crisis of modernism, in which Smithson, in the sixties, took a leading part, photography does indeed have a deciding role to play. In this it is similar to language, which flows between the different media and forms of art, playing one off against the other, making disturbing

Albert Londe
La vague, vue de face (The wave, seen from front), 1903
black-and-white photograph
collection Bibliothèque Nationale, Paris

comparisons and spectacular reversals of scale, from macrocosm to microcosm, from the whole to the infinitesimal fragment. Photography, like language, can relativize and contextualize a work, or stop it from existing solely in the splendid isolation of the medium's modernist autonomy. At the same time, it becomes, once again like language, a continuous babble that "covers" more than it "discovers."'[24]

If Muybridge were alive today, he'd turn over in his grave, claimed Hollis Frampton in 1979. As a filmmaker and theoretician, he approached photography with another, though not less critical, vision. False Impressions is the title of a series of color xerographs from the same year in which he aimed to unmask the codes of visual mass culture in advertising, film and photojournalism through a form of proto-appropriation of advertising images.[25] Seven years prior, Frampton began work on Magellan, a somewhat megalomaniac undertaking intended to reconstruct 'the history of cinema as it should have been' that was based on the five-year voyage of the Portuguese discoverer. The series of films lasted for 36 hours. While working on them, Hollis Frampton produced several series of photographs which build on the 'perceptual areas analogous to film.' Both Marey and Muybridge were quasi-literally brought in. A Visitation of Insomnia (1970-73), for example, includes a number of sequences in which Frampton tries

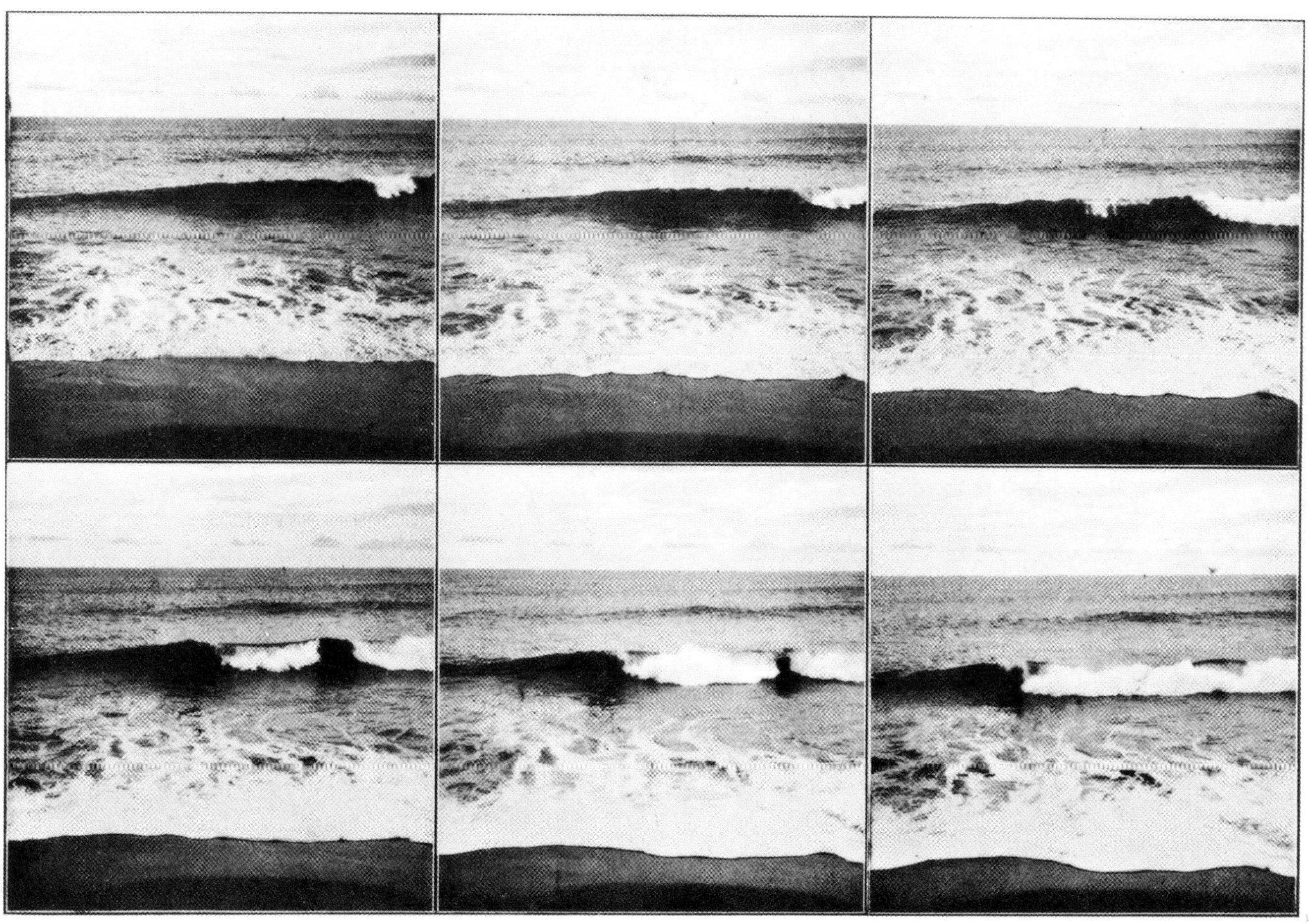

to repeat Marey's chronophotography: different exposures of a moving, nude woman are contained in one image. 'The photograph,' writes Frampton in the context of Marey, 'could no longer contain the contradictory pressures to affirm time and to deny it. It split sharply into an illusionistic cinema of incessant motion and a static photographic art that remained frozen solid for decades.'[26] The admiring undertone in this statement can also be detected in the curious 'earnestness' with which the images in Insomnia are charged. This seems slightly different in Sixteen Studies from Vegetable Locomotion which he did in 1975 with Marion Faller. No longer animals or people in motion, but (homegrown) vegetables. Even Muybridge's archetypal Cartesian grid is caricatured here. The laughter is real, but passes, and what remain are the images of a hopeless immobility. False Illusions.[27]

Photography produces its own reality/Variations and verifications

The encounter between Eadweard Muybridge and Jan Dibbets was the main component of Still/A Novel. One hundred collotypes from about 1887. Four hundred contact sheets dating from 1967 to 1995.

Two pioneers. A photographer pur sang – taken out of his historical nineteenth-century context and placed today into a conceptual setting – alongside an artist who works with photography but certainly does not regard himself as a photographer pur sang nor entirely as a conceptual artist, although in quite a few texts he is described as one of the photographic trailblazers of that movement. 'Of course theoretically it was an important moment,' said Dibbets already in 1980. 'But otherwise there is nothing more to say about conceptual art. It is the final completion of minimal art – it is nothing,'[28] as was painting for him at first. He gave it up in the sixties, though essentially he has always remained a 'painter.' Then Jan Dibbets discovers photography and at once in a way in which he can link up both abstract art and the possibility of working with recognizable forms. One of Dibbets's early, and indisputably conceptual projects, Roodborst territorium/Sculptuur 1969, in which he gives a photographic account of how he moved the territory of a robin in the Vondelpark in Amsterdam by way of posts, is for him less relevant in this context.

> 'I introduced photography in my work with the perspective corrections.... I'm trying to put photography within art on a new track. I think it will be a lifetime's task: to develop a new ABC for photography. ... Up to now photography meant making a picture: you tried to capture an interesting image. I believe you can also make uninteresting images special, by adding something, by doing something with them. That added value makes it art. Muybridge was the first to do something with photography in that sense.'[29]

Dibbets and Muybridge do have some points in common. The evolution of both œuvres is similarly compact, and both show a high degree of internal

cohesion. Both men work 'lightly,' lucidly and (often misleadingly) 'straightforwardly.' The two œuvres are 'elementary' and rest on isolated observation.[30] Both are distinct purists. Muybridge empties his images until only a universal frame of reference is left. Dibbets excludes all narrative, rejects figuration and otherwise leaves every photograph as it is.
In both Muybridge and Dibbets a single photograph taken out of context loses (almost) all meaning.

In Still/A Novel 'study material' by both was shown: in Muybridge's case for the instruction (and enjoyment) of artists and scientists, in Dibbets's case for himself, in a wide selection of contact sheets. By definition, contacts show everything – the whole of the developed film, complete with the edges of the negative and the number. For most photographers contact sheets are private territory; they are their store cupboard, their memory from which choices should be made – this will be a photograph, this will not. In this sense, contact sheets are an unknowable, awesome and unfathomable reservoir of denied images.
In his contact sheets, however, Jan Dibbets does not seek out errors or triumphs; no decisive moments, he shows everything. Based on an awareness that 'for the camera every moment is equally important or, if you like, equally unimportant.' That Dibbets accords his contacts a quasi-autonomous status that puts them on the same 'level' as his final artworks became fully clear in this exhibition. Certainly from the point of view of 'research,' it is in these contact prints, above all, that the most unmistakable parallels with Muybridge's collotypes can be seen.
Each sets down a development, a process, a state of affairs in a linear continuum. They connect distinct observations. Both work serially. However, Muybridge's motive is scientific 'clarity.' Dibbets aims to lift the photograph out of its limitations to the fragmentary and 'to open the way towards abstractions, without violating the characteristics of the medium. For him, the use of sequences is not an aim in itself;'[31] he is concerned with the ultimate image that a series of photographs produces.
For Muybridge the photograph is evidence; for Dibbets it is 'the work. His installations exist only for and through photography.'[32] Muybridge observes. Dibbets 'translates' those observations on the flat plane, with all the changes which that involves.[33] Dibbets intensifies the observation, pushing the (illusion of) 'clarity' to the limit.
Muybridge's collotypes suggest the difference between knowing and seeing. Dibbets's work is founded on it. Thought hurries to the aid of observation. In Dibbets's analytical perception of the essence of photography, a tense relationship is maintained between the visual and the conceptual. The visual aspect of each work remains primal, precisely in order to let the idea emerge more clearly. Jan Dibbets questions a way of looking, a vision Jonathan Crary summarizes and explains as the representation model of the camera obscura, a model with a single, central viewpoint located in a 'chamber' in which images of an outside world are projected. This comes

down to an act of 'idealized' looking in which the ideality is determined by the separation from, the break with, the physical body of the viewer.[34] Dibbets seems to be seeking among other things ways of going beyond the possibilities of the perspectivist box of the camera, or at least exposing its ambiguity. After all, photography, which is the triumph of Renaissance perspective, at the same time has within it – through the infinite variations in visions and the possibilities for putting viewpoints opposite each other or bringing them together – the potential to play down that central perspective until it finally disintegrates, dissolves. Jan Dibbets makes full use of this ambiguous nature of photography.[35] More than that, for him 'photography produces its own reality.'[36]
He does that fully in his perspective corrections of the late sixties and in *Louverdrape* and *Shutterspeed Pieces*, both of 1971, which are based on elementary starting points such as the gradual opening and closing of sun blinds or exploring all of a camera's shutter variations. This reflective use of the conditions of the camera 'as if the apparatus itself began registering its own parameters, was only possible on the basis of the *legacy* of conceptual art and thanks to a revaluation in ideas about the mechanical properties of photography. The camera only expresses what it is: a system suitable for describing the world from a certain, measured angle.'[37] It describes and verifies. In these preoccupations with the 'photographic machine' too – in these 'verifications' of the *objectivity* of the camera, which in this sense could equally well be called a *clarification process* – the *démarches* of Muybridge and Dibbets converge and diverge.

Dibbets's later sequences, writes Marcel Vos, 'curve around an "empty" center, expand from that center in all directions.... This outward movement, this movement toward infinity, however keeps turning back to the center in which it is anchored: the point where the human eye coincides with the eye of the camera.'[38] And connects with it.

> 'Do I really see something different each time,
> or do I only interpret what I see in a different way?
> I am inclined to say the former.'[39]

1
Richard S. Field, Mel Bochner: Thought Made Visible 1966-1973 (New Haven: Yale University Art Gallery, 1995), p. 68.

2
Jean-François Chevrier, 'Entre les beaux-arts et les médias,' Galeries Magazine, no. 37 (June/July 1990), quoted in Walker Evans & Dan Graham (Rotterdam: Witte de With, 1992), p. 6.

3
The Photographic News (21 March 1889). Reprinted in Photography in Print. Writings from 1816 to the Present, ed. Vicki Goldberg (New York: Touchstone Book, Simon and Schuster, 1981), p. 188.

4
Aaron Scharf, Art and Photography (London: Penguin Books, 1986), p. 211.

5
Eduardo Cadava, 'Words of Light. Theses on the Photography of History,' Fugitive Images. From Photography to Video, ed. Patrice Petro (Bloomington: Indiana University Press, 1995), p. 223.

6
Rosalind E. Krauss, The Optical Unconscious (Cambridge: The MIT Press, 1993), p. 178.

7
Op. cit., note 4.

8
Op. cit., note 4, p. 212.

9
Siegfried Zielinski, 'Die 2 EJMs der Reihenphotographie. Zu einigen ihrer Differenzen in der Annäherung an den Körper vermittels aufzeichnender Apparate,' Eikon, Internationale Zeitschrift für Photographie & Medienkunst, no. 7/8 (1993), p. 37.

10
Ibid., p. 42.

11
Op. cit. note 9, p. 43. For example, an exhibition on chronophotography at the Filmmuseum (Frankfurt, 1985), which did not cover Muybridge; an exhibition on the measurement of time at the Deutsches Museum (Munich, 1990) and an exhibition at the British Film Museum (London, 1992) also concentrated on Marey. One recent publication is François Dagognet, Étienne-Jules Marey. A Passion for the Trace (New York: Zone Books, 1992).

12
Michel Frizot, 'Vitesse de la Photographie. Le mouvement et la durée,' Nouvelle Histoire de la Photographie, ed. Michel Frizot (Paris: Adam Biro, 1994), p. 251.

13
Ibid., freely translated.

14
Op. cit., note 12, p. 246.

15
Max Kozloff, 'The Etherealized Figure and the Dream of Wisdom,' Vanishing Presence (Minneapolis: Walker Art Center, 1989), p. 50.

16
Michel Frizot, Dictionnaire de la Photo (Paris: Larousse, 1996), p. 135.

17
Herta Wolf: Skulpturen - Fragmente (Vienna: Wiener Secession, 1992), p. 130. This in the context significant quote from Rilke continues as follows: 'One of the striking aspects of modern sculpture is the way in which it manifests its maker's growing awareness that sculpture is a medium peculiarly located at the juncture between stillness and motion, time arrested and time passing. From this tension, which defines the very condition of sculpture, comes its enormous expressive power.'

18
Text at the exhibition Het spel van het (onzegbare) naamloze (The Play of the Unsayable) concept by Joseph Kosuth. (Vienna: Wiener Secession and Brussels: Palais des Beaux Arts, 1989-90) The complete, valuable text reads as follows: 'In addition to music, architecture and technology, photography is an example of the extension of Wittgenstein's philosophical method, in which the concept of play as an ordering principle in language is applied in order to grasp the limits of the thinkable and sayable and to put questions in new ways. Seeing, and thus photographic seeing too, is in this sense a way of describing objects in general. Wittgenstein's attempts center on the desire to throw light on the relationships between the objects or between them and himself.... "Philosophy is not a doctrine, but an activity." Photography is part of this process of clarification, particularly in the area of "that which cannot be expressed through utterances, but only shown." Essential to this is the supplementary, broadening function of photography for Wittgenstein's philosophy. He makes himself, his friends and relatives the objects of observation, whose visual premise changes. At first the moment of showing relates only to Wittgenstein; early on he depicts himself in a series of automatic exposures. It is not until the photographs of the late 1930s which he took himself or had taken according to his directions that a stabilization in physiognomy and posture is seen. The anti-aesthetic attitude in his photographs links the gesticulatory intention to a repeatedly expressed desire for the greatest possible clarity, which is reflected in the simplicity of the conditions in which the photographs were taken. The amateurish nature of Wittgenstein's photographs serves to clarify the elements of the medium related to the psychology of observation. The extent of time and space, and the memory value of the photographic image and its limits are examined here. In this way Ludwig Wittgenstein makes a contribution to photographic historiography which has so far received little attention.'

19
László Moholy-Nagy, 'From Pigment to Light,' Telehor, vol. 1, no. 2 (1936), pp. 30-36. Reprinted in Moholy-Nagy Documentary Monographs in Modern Art, ed. Richard Kostelanetz (London: Penguin Books, 1970), p. 56. Moholy-Nagy continues: 'In this concatenation of its separate but inseparable parts a photographic series inspired by a definite purpose can become at once

the most potent weapon and the tenderest lyric. The true significance of the film will only appear in a much later, less confused and groping age than ours. The prerequisite for this revelation is, of course, the realization that a knowledge of photography is just as important as that of the alphabet. The illiterate of the future will be ignorant of the use of camera and pen alike.'

20
Mel Bochner, 'The Serial Attitude,' Artforum, vol. 6, no. 4 (December 1967), p. 28. The opening quotation (Josiah Royce, Principles of Logic) immediately offers a usable definition of a series: 'What is a series? Any row, array, rank, order of precedence, numerical or quantitative set of values, any straight line, any geometrical figure employing straight lines, and yes, all space and all time.' In another important article of 1967, 'Serial Art, Systems, Solipsism,' Bochner offers this definition: 'Seriality is premissed on the idea that the succession of terms (divisions) within a single work is based on numerical or otherwise predetermined derivation (progression, permutation, rotation, reversal) from one or more of the preceding terms in that piece. Furthermore the idea is carried out to its logical conclusion, which, without adjustments based on taste or chance, is the work.'

21
Op. cit., note 1, p. 25-26. In connection with this observation, which also applied to a certain extent to the recent exhibition Paul Thek – The wonderful world that almost was at Witte de With (Rotterdam et al., 1995) for example, Field continues: 'In their turn, Bochner's installation pieces and constructions would share the same fate. Although they can be reinstalled during the artist's lifetime, it remains that most are known through photographic experience. One claims that the unique quality of the work lies in the tensions it sets up between theory and practice, thought and experience, diagram and material, drawing and installation. But the fact of the matter is that most historians, critics, and viewers have had to abstract their "experiential ideas" from reproductions (photographs) rather than from the actual installed piece.' On this point Philippe Dubois remarks that in Earth and Land Art photography is not just a means for the documentary reproduction of a work; the photographic vision is already integrated in the concept of the project in advance.

22
Op. cit., note 1, p. 33.

23
Robert Smithson, 'Art Through the Camera's Eye,' Kunst- en Museumjournaal, vol. 5, no. 6 (1994), pp. 15-23.

24
Régis Durand, Le Monde Après la Photographie (Villeneuve d'Ascq: Musée d'Art Moderne, 1995), pp. 31-32. Durand based his title on a phrase from Robert Smithson's text 'Fragment of a Conversation' from 1969, which at the same time approaches his complex and specific vision of photography: 'because photography does not make Nature an impossible concept. It somehow mitigates the whole concept of Nature in that the earth after photography becomes more of a museum.' Régis Durand: 'What is photographed becomes museum material, and thus a "ruin," like the various "monuments" that Robert Smithson himself photographed and commented on in "A Visit to the Monuments of the Passaic." Similar in this to the concept of non-site, photography is characterized by the passage from the whole to the fragment, from the formless and the limitless to the formed and the frame, from the continuous to the discontinuous. While seeming to work as a discovery and description – as a celebration even – it really partakes in the current entropic process. ... It is precisely this complex status that makes it so interesting, in my view. Some of Robert Smithson's contemporaries, for example, have taken a stand, with regard to a type of photography whose impact appears limited – indifference, purely instrumental or documentary use, etc. With Robert Smithson, we are confronted with a thought that marks a turning point in the history of representation and contemporary art.'

25
Bruce Jenkins, Susan Krane, Hollis Frampton. Recollections. Recreations, (Cambridge: The MIT Press, 1984), p. 25. If Muybridge were still alive today ... recycles an advertisement from The New York Times which shows a series of shoes photographed against a grid background. Frampton and Marion Faller combine this advertisement with several 'authentic' Muybridge photos, some of their own tributes to the master (Sixteen Studies from Vegetable Locomotion) and a joke on Muybridge from a humorous magazine in which a man stubs his toe and hops painfully through the following frames.

26
Op. cit., note 25, p. 70.

27
That Hollis Frampton indeed approached Muybridge with the same, critical, respect as Marey is evident from the impressive article 'Eadweard Muybridge: Fragments of a Tesseract,' Artforum, vol. 11, no. 7 (March 1973), pp. 42-52, from which the following quotation is taken: 'Having once consciously fastened upon time as his grand subject, Muybridge quickly emptied his images as nearly as he could of everything else. His animals, athletes, and subverted painters' models are nameless and mostly naked, performing their banalities, purged of drama if not of occasional horseplay, before a uniform grid of Cartesian coordinates, a kind of universal "frame of reference," ostensibly intended as an aid in reconcil-

ing the successive images with chronometry, that also destroys all sense of scale (the figures could be pagan constellations in the sky) and utterly obliterates the tactile particularity that is one of the photograph's paramount traits, thereby annihilating any possible feeling of *place*. About all that is left, in each case, is an archetypal fragment of living action, potentially subject to the incessant reiteration that is one of the most familiar and intolerable features of our dreams.'

28
Lien Heyting, 'Jan Dibbets. De liefde voor de natuur is de motor achter alle grote kunst,' *NRC Handelsblad* (15 February 1980), p. 7. Dibbet's complete statement reads as follows: 'Of course theoretically it was an important moment, when artists said: we're not going to execute our ideas, because the idea is enough in itself. But otherwise there is nothing more to say about conceptual art. It is the final completion of minimal art - it is nothing.'

29
Op. cit., note 28.

30
Rudi Fuchs, *On Jan Dibbets, La XXXVI Biennale di Venezia, Padiglione Olandese* cat. (1972). 'All this is relevant with regard to Dibbets because his art concerns the isolation of observation as an autonomous operatio.'

31
Alexander van Grevenstein, *Jan Dibbets. Bonnefanten/Saenredam* (Maastricht: Bonnefantenmuseum, 1978), n.p.

32
Michel Nuridsany, *Ils se disent peintres. Ils se disent photographes* (Paris: ARC/Musée d'Art Moderne de la Ville de Paris, 1981), n.p.

33
Ron Kaal, 'Schilderen met de camera' *Elsevier*, vol. 28, no. 48 (25 November 1972), p. 149.

34
Jonathan Crary, *Techniques of the Observer. On Vision and Modernity in the Nineteenth Century* (Cambridge: The MIT Press, 1992).

35
After: Régis Durand, 'L'exacte simplicité de Jan Dibbets,' *Art Press*, no. 91 (April 1985).

36
Fotografie als Kunst. Kunst als Fotografie, Das Medium Fotografie in der bildenden Kunst Europas ab 1968, ed. Floris M. Neusüss (Cologne: DuMont Buchverlag, 1979), p. 30, also contains an accurate description of the perspective corrections: 'Since the eye of the viewer of a picture is always compelled to assume the standpoint of the photographer, it is impossible for the viewer to penetrate behind the true relationships in the image, unless the photographer discloses them visually. The rectangular outlines which are seen in the photographs by Jan Dibbets are really outlines of trapezoids, which begin to spread out in the direction leading away from the viewer. These trapezoids have been laid out on the ground so that their widening is "corrected" to the form of rectangles by the foreshortening perspective of the camera. Photography produces Its own reality, which does not correspond to outwardly appearing circumstances.'

37
Michel Frizot, 'Photographie et langage,' freely translated, op. cit., note 12, p. 726. 'Verifications' (*Verifiche*) is a photographic series by Ugo Mulas from the 1970s.

38
M.M.M. Vos, 'On Photography and the Art of Jan Dibbets,' *Jan Dibbets* (Minneapolis and New York: Walker Art Center and Rizzoli, 1987), pp. 25-26.

39
Ludwig Wittgenstein, *Philosophical Investigations*, trans. G.E.M. Anscombe (Oxford: Basil Blackwell, 1974) p. 212.

You can tell if you're
in an attractive American spot: it's
littered with trash.

the frenCh call it
tRompette des morts. its
colors
blAck
To
grEy
woRk
to hidE it, but not
effectivLy (we overcome
aLl
sUch
natural deviceS).

deviCes, natural but
undergrOund, inexplicable,
some yeaRs keep it from
appeariNg: we look this year
for
instance
'till we were blUe
in the faCe
withOut success, another year
all you had to do was
Park
go In
any wOods:
there were mIllions of them
everywhere.
they Dry
wEll
for winter uSe.

Zeger Reyers
Onder-tussen (In-between), 1996
Installation view at Witte de With

John Cage, *M-writings '67-'72*
(London: Marion Boyars Publishers, 1973), p. 149.

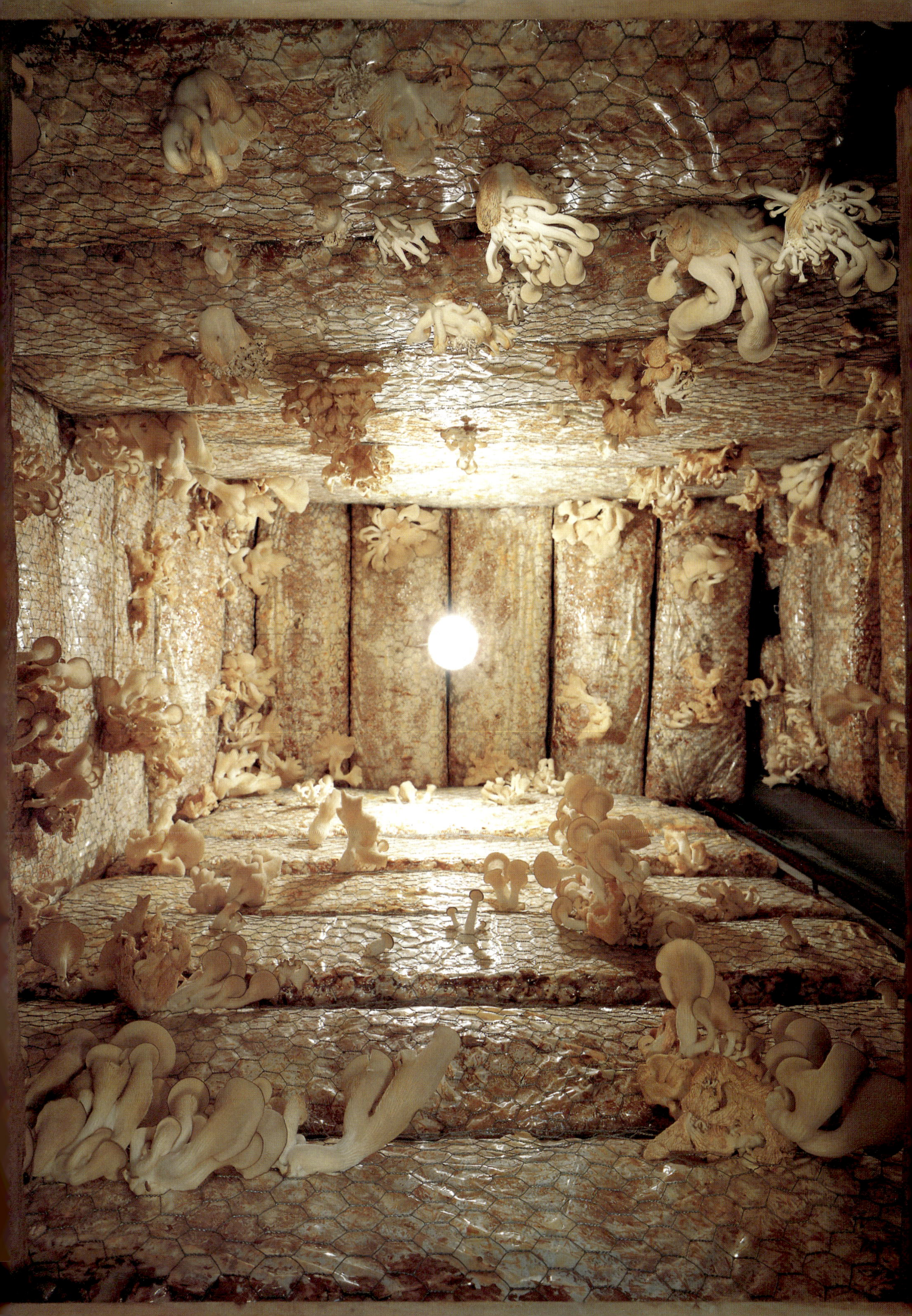

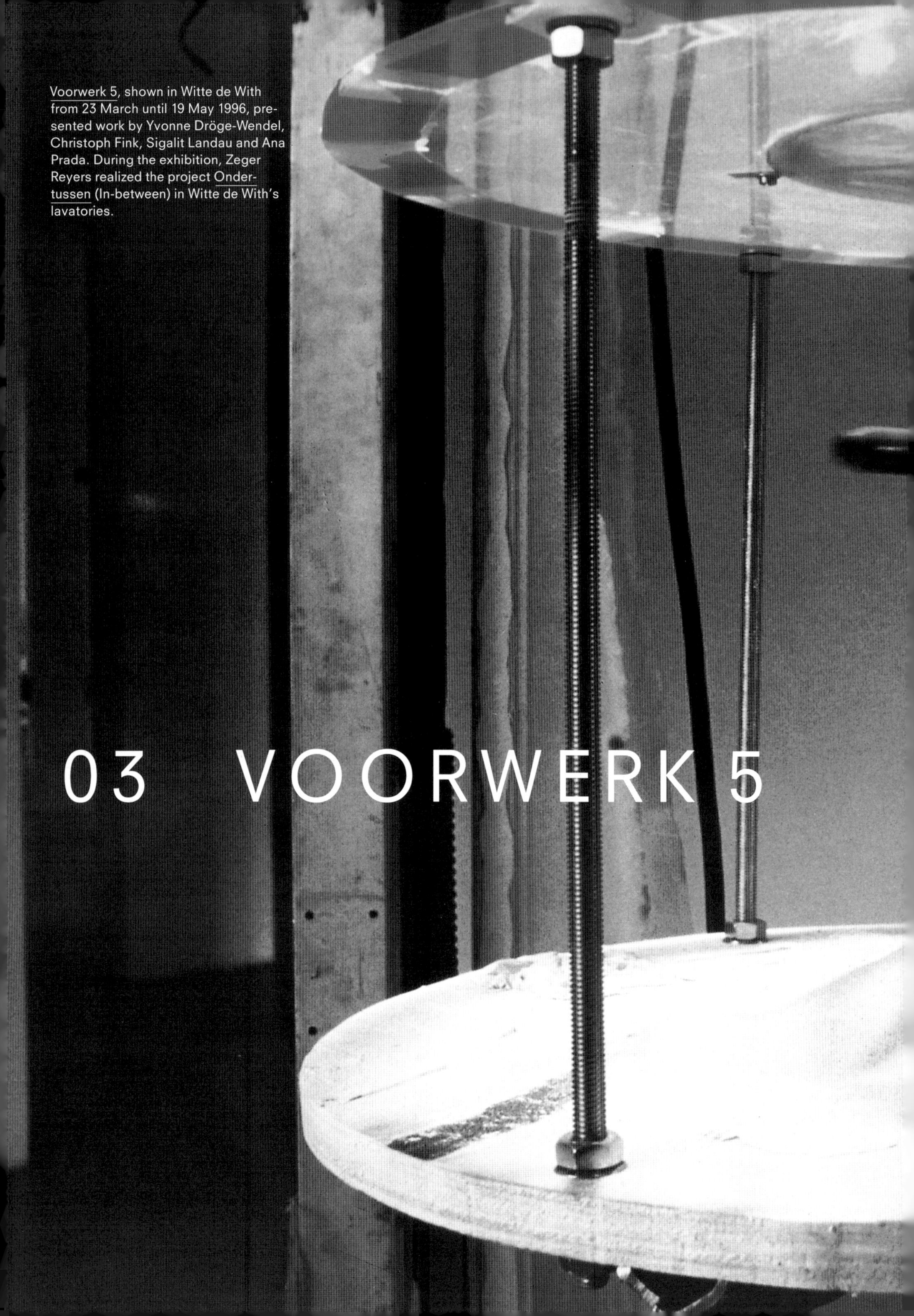

Voorwerk 5, shown in Witte de With from 23 March until 19 May 1996, presented work by Yvonne Dröge-Wendel, Christoph Fink, Sigalit Landau and Ana Prada. During the exhibition, Zeger Reyers realized the project Ondertussen (In-between) in Witte de With's lavatories.

03 VOORWERK 5

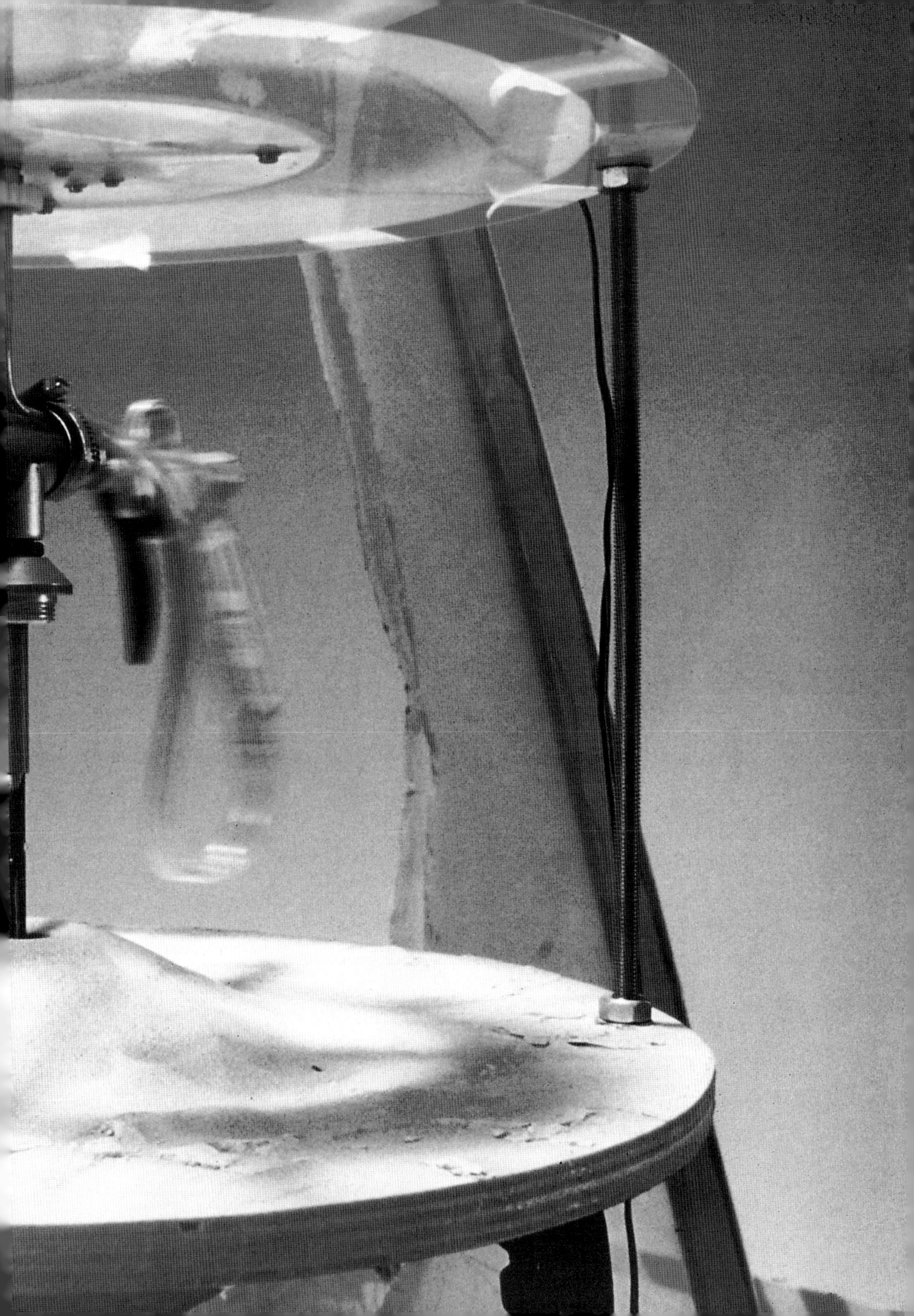

Nick de Ville

Ana Prada

The most seemingly self-evident and modest thing that one can ask of a contemporary work of art is that it should be of interest – that the work should have the capacity to engage the viewer's interest. For the artist to have such an ambition may seem only a modest starting point, but it is from the engagement of the viewer's interest that everything else follows, most particularly the intellectual endeavor which is required by the viewer to follow the complexity of the artist's thought. This text seeks to offer an understanding of some of the ways in which Ana Prada's sculptures so ably intrigue the viewer, and in so doing, it also hopes to reveal something of her working methods.

The sculptures Prada has made since the late eighties have a number of consistent attributes. They are remade in the gallery each time they are exhibited. They are generally fixed to the wall, and sometimes require a specific architectural detail, such as a corner, to play off. They always have as their chief motif and mainspring a domestic object, usually something fairly small and of a type likely to be discovered amongst any collection of household junk. Each chosen object shows that it has been worked upon in the studio – pulled apart, examined and cut to reveal its hidden visual possibilities. This process reaches its final resolution when – and if – the object surrenders up some way of allowing Prada to incorporate it in the configuration of a sculpture.

In her working process, Prada can be imagined as roaming a series of related domains. These domains have been defined for us through the problematized oppositions and 'differently structured possibilities'[1] of recent art theory. Domains and their boundaries (or our present supposed indifference to such matters) are equally the stuff of *categories* and *binary oppositions* and *disciplines*. These critical terms have been employed in the undoing of what William Tucker has characterized as 'an ideal condition of self-contained, self-generating apartness for the work of art, with its own rules, its own order, its own materials, independent of its maker, of its audience and of the world in general.'[2] The terms have been used in attacking the autonomous status of the art object and have made us familiar with the possibility of conflating the sculptural form and the everyday object. They also allow us to acknowledge the importance of the issue of context and relative meaning for recent art production. It therefore does not seem to be claiming anything striking for Prada's work to remark that it constantly

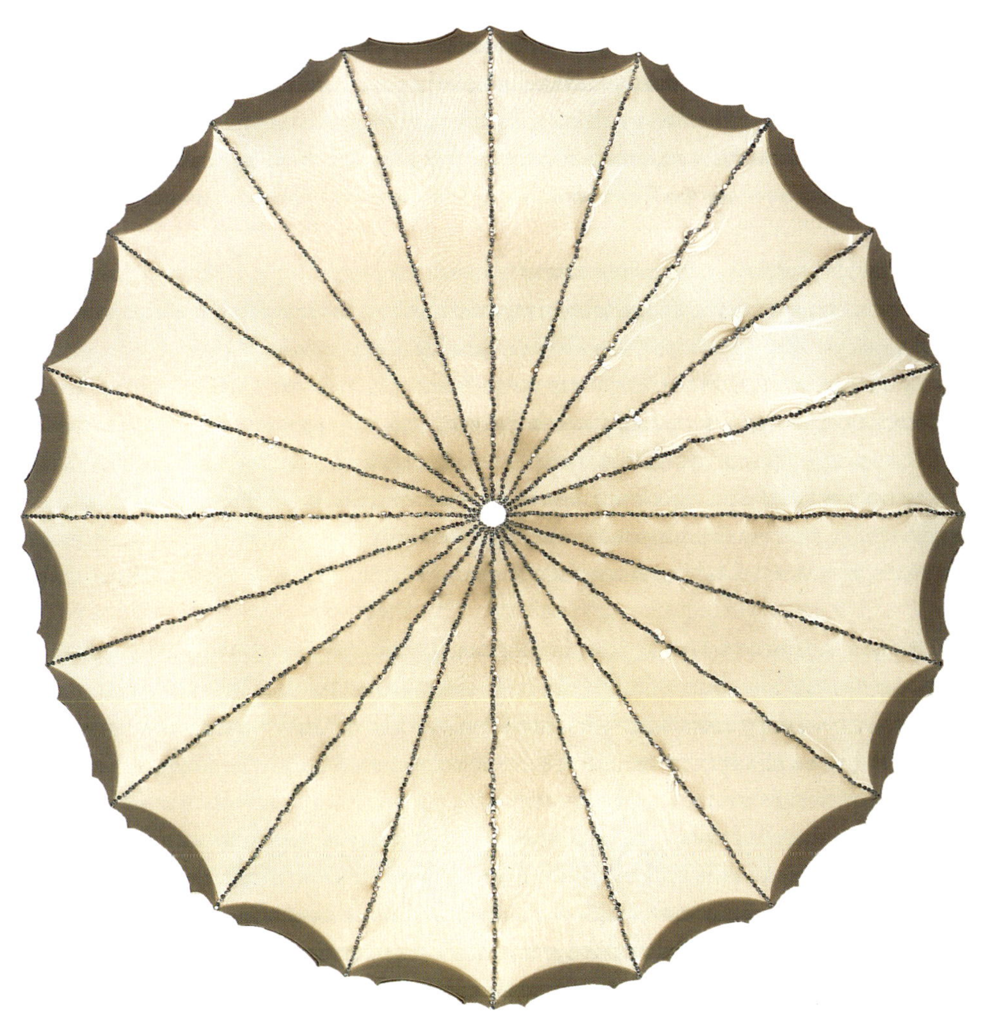

Ana Prada
20 Seams, 1994
pantyhose and nails
Ø 97 cm
collection of the artist

evokes boundary slippage between domains; that there is in her sculpture a ceaseless scattering of taxonomies. However, it is only by understanding how her sculptures *in their own particular way* test these domains that we will fully grasp why it is that her work engages our interest to the degree that it does. In particular, it is by examining the ways in which the domain of the object, the domains of sculpture and painting are disturbed and undone by her works that we can have access to how they act upon us so successfully.

The Object

The appearance of everyday objects insinuated into formal sculpture is not an unusual act in the art of the twentieth century. We are familiar with the experience of seeing everyday objects in all manner of guises – of looking at the detail in a David Smith sculpture and suddenly realizing we are looking at a spanner or some other blacksmith's tool. Everyday objects appear in endless proliferation in the genre of the assisted ready-made, that ubiquitous twentieth-century celebration of the poetic transubstantiations of ordinary things. (As an example of this it is useful to think of Joan Brossa's adaption of the assisted ready-made to his own poetic sensibility. The dissimilarities to be found in the work of Brossa and Prada are important to emphasis since both are Spanish and might, at first glance, be considered members of a national school.) In fact, Prada's use of everyday objects resists historical comparisons. Her sculptures do not relate easily to any of the preexisting discourses concerning the object in art, and an attempt to define them by such means unduly forecloses their richness of meaning.

More helpful than trying to define historical precedents for Prada's use of everyday objects is to consider – with a closer focus – the type of objects she chooses to use. As a starting point the claim made by Estrella de Diego that in Prada's choice of objects and their subsequent utilization there is a play on feminine/masculine stereotypes seems particularly useful. De Diego notes that 'A first look reveals the chosen objects as strongly connoted entities, firmly linked to the feminine universe. Condemned to it, one could say, by historical associations.'[3] This reading of Prada's choice of objects

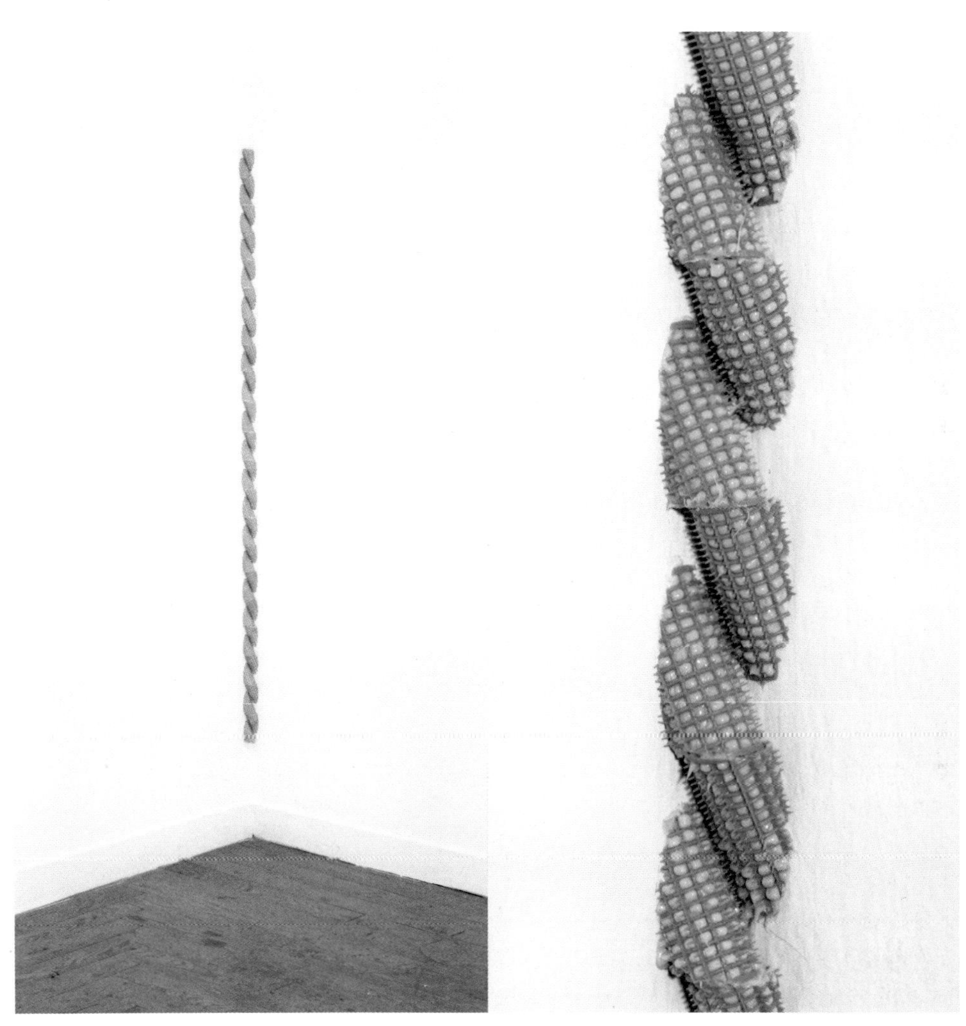

Ana Prada
Blue Plait, 1994
plastic hair rollers and silicone
200 x 4 x 4 cm
collection of the artist

hints at sexual politics. However, Prada does not present the issue with the aggressive edge we associate with eighties feminism. If this is sexual politics then her approach seems distinctly personal and muted. The reason may be, in part, that only some of the objects she chooses to use, such as the plastic hair rollers in *Blue Plait* (1994), are distinctly gendered by usage. The articulation of difference in Prada's work is more subtle and subversive and, in seeking to disturb the binary opposition that sexual politics depends upon, she embeds the issue of gender and sexual identity more deeply in her working processes. The most revealing way of understanding this aspect of Prada's work is not to focus on either the artistic precedents for her use of objects-as-sculpture, or on the narratives to be deduced from the genus of objects she selects, but rather to look at the way her work employs the *relationship* between these two topics. If we take this approach, what gradually becomes clear is that for Prada it is sculptural ideals far removed from the legacy of Duchamp that are of central significance. If we consider the procedures that she subjects her chosen objects to, we find ourselves reluctantly forced to conclude that they are most characteristic of that central strand of abstract formalism that we find running through much of the history of twentieth-century sculpture. Hers is a repertoire of classic formal concerns – interior form/exterior form, positive object/negative space. Yet the objects she chooses to implicate in this sculptural analysis – brown paper bag (*Secret Place*, 1991), Volvic water bottles (*Agua-Marina*, 1991), red balloons (*Striped Composition*, 1993), plastic picnic knives (*Untitled*, 1995), clothes pegs (*Gusano Geometrico* [Geometrical Caterpillar], 1995) – are of such modest pretensions that the entire performance perplexes us and the performance of high-minded sculptural rigor is peppered with darts of irony. We might anticipate that the modesty of Prada's chosen object would translate into a sculptural project with only modest implications but, in fact, the quixotic incongruity of this key relationship gives her work considerable abrasive power. The elusive key to her sculptures turns out to be an act of hybridization of such breathtaking absurdity that it is scarcely surprising that our expectations for the contemporary sculptural object are so unsettled. Even accepting this new perception, her work still induces a puzzlement for which there is no easy solution, although we may also suspect that we are in the presence of an unusual wry detachment; feminine, but never overtly feminist.

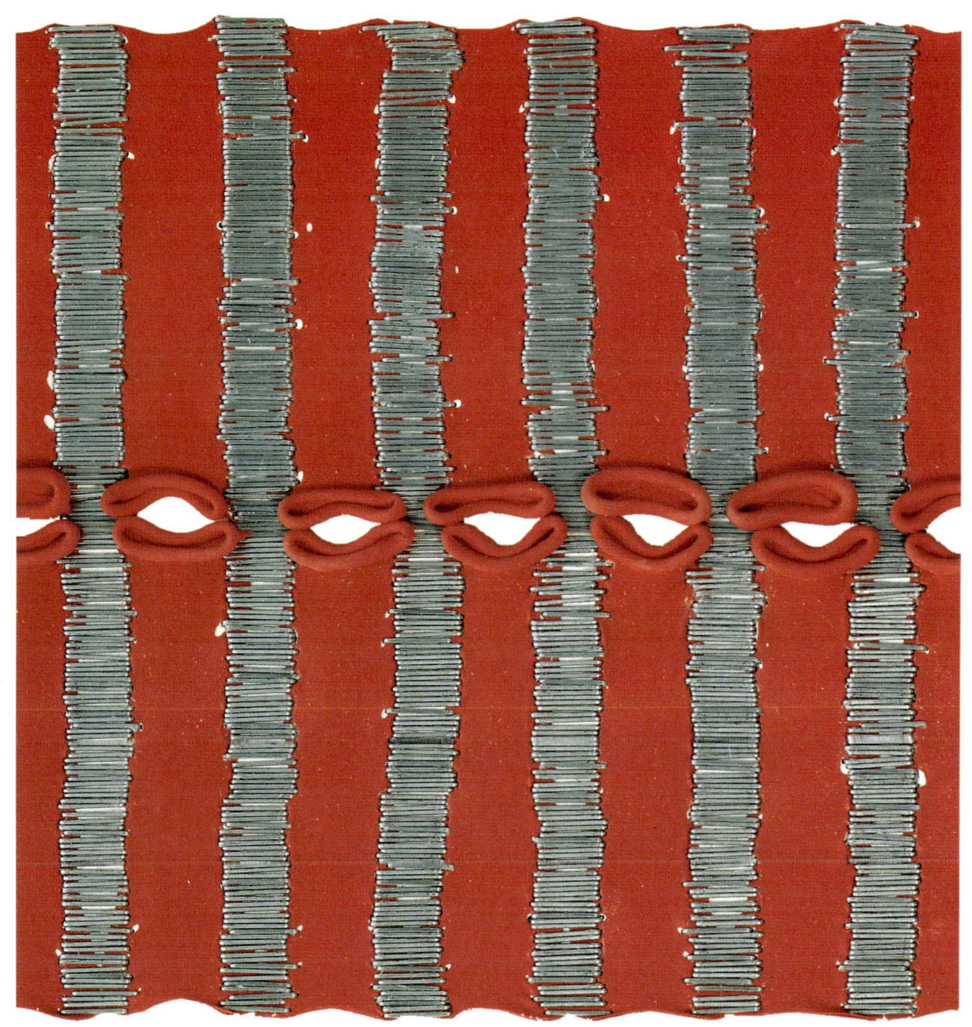

Ana Prada
Striped Composition, 1993 (detail)
balloons and staples
16 x 181 cm
collection of the artist

The Mechanics of Sculpture

At this point we can acknowledge, as we pass it, the boundary that marks the beginning of the second domain of Prada's work. It is here that Prada begins to deploy the mechanics of sculpture to find a particular attribute in her chosen object. Whereas the first phase of her search has been in some senses womanly, like window shopping, the second phase is (stereotypically) manly. In this domain the disciplines of carving and modeling are the cardinal exemplars. Her work here can be typified as the drive to discover clear and distinctive forms. She attends to the constructed entity of her chosen object as formal essence – to the transition of the egg cup's stem as it becomes the cup-like container for the egg – to the possibility of the wick of a candle becoming a hidden potential allowing the candle to be deployed as an element in the repetition of a decorative pattern – to the topography of the curve of a lip on a ladle protruding from the larger curved surface of the ladle itself – to the potential for the mouth and neck of a balloon to be made more nozzle-like, more like a puckered orifice, yet less like a balloon. The cut is Prada's principle method in the search for this potential. Subjecting objects to the cut is her way of opening out their characteristics and of revealing something unfamiliar and unexpected latent within them. Her objects do not necessarily reveal their invisible possibilities easily, so Prada cuts them time and time again in the attempt to discover new internal spaces, new contour lines, new forms, new figurative associations. In her hands the procedure of the cut is the weapon of discipline. It is a parody of rigor and of the scientific process out of which she extracts a flower, a fungus or a decorative frieze.

The Look of Painting

In many of Prada's sculptures, objects are deployed in some form of array or decorative repeat, or as an element in a larger figure or form. In these works it is most easily seen how she trespasses on the domain of painting. In some ways the signs are obvious – her sculptures cling to the wall, to flatness, like paintings. The silicone used in a number of them performs like glue and at the same time suggests the texture of paint. However, when we look more closely we see that the trespass is more comprehensive. In the middle distance of the gallery space sculptures such as *Untitled (Green Candles*, 1995) or

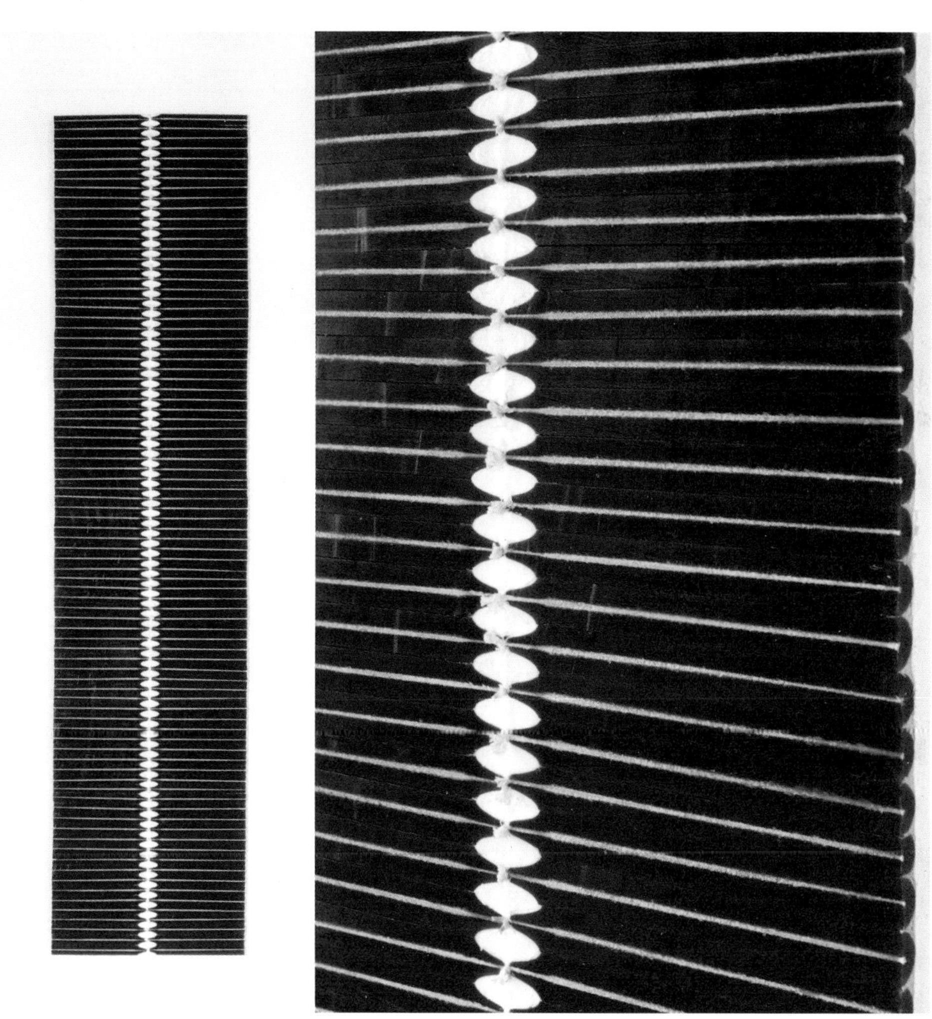

Ana Prada
Untitled, 1995
candles and silicone
168.5 x 40 x 1.5 cm
collection of the artist

20 Seams (1994) give a strong suggestion of the ornamental filigrees of Islamic architecture. From a distance the viewer sees *20 Seams* as a round symmetrical figure. It only resolves itself into its constituent elements of twenty stockings – with their seams of tacks – when the viewer examines the work up close. We experience a purposeful disruption of the image between one scale level and another. The detail is not unproblematically in the service of the image which the sculpture initially presents to its audience. The work anticipates – and even emphasizes – the mobility of the viewer. As one moves towards and away from the sculpture, the changing visual field provokes the need to constantly reformulate one's reading because detail and incident are handled in contradictory ways at the two different scales. If this description sounds oddly reminiscent of much which is innovative in contemporary painting it is because Prada's sculpture is, initially, preeminently pictorial. The paradox of a sculpture that behaves, in some ways, like a painting can be explained by Prada's wish to submit her chosen objects to one of the central ideals of the painterly sensibility. She requires the objects she uses in her sculptures to *depict* themselves, and her emphasis – usually by way of the cut – on certain characteristics of the objects is, in effect, an attempt to get them to picture themselves as objects the viewer has to examine repeatedly. They do not lose their original identity, but have superimposed upon them another *pictured* identity, the consequence of being made strange by the cut.

The boundary slippage evoked in these works has few clear antecedents, but the following observations by Fred Orton on the sculpture of Jasper Johns suggests the possibilities of the same conflation of domains: 'Johns distinguishes his sculptures from "ordinary things" by giving them another surface and another tactility but in a way that does not make them thoroughly unimpeachable as "separate things" that can be seen as sculptures. Their surface effect is like that of painting.... Having decided to make sculptures, Johns made "separate things" that problematized their separateness from the "ordinary things" they came in place of and, in some cases, their difference from paintings. In doing this, they also problematized the beholder's relation to them. Although each sculpture has its own "certain place," that place is also uncertain. Rather than the "certainty," "steadiness," "loftiness," and "harmonious adjustment to the environment" that Rilke required of sculpture, each sculpture effects a kind of instability and uncertainty.'[4]

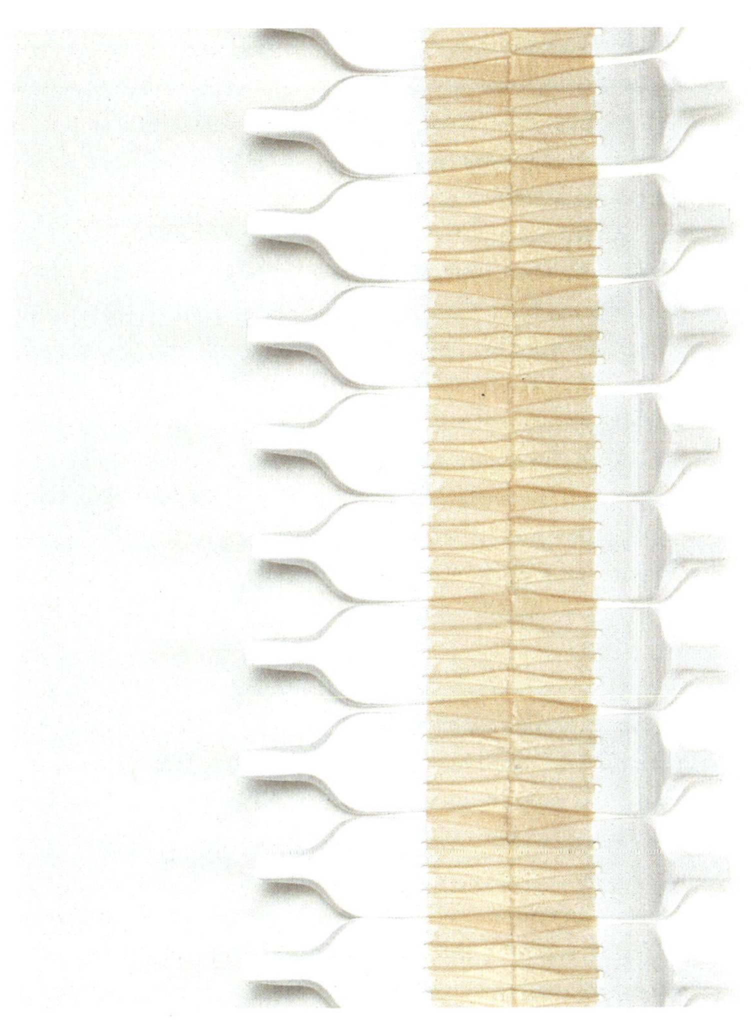

Ana Prada
Forked Piece, 1993 (detail)
plastic forks and adhesive tape
154 x 14 x 3 cm
collection of the artist

The Performance of Objecthood

There is one final boundary that has to be considered when reading Prada's work. This is the tension between sculpture as autonomous object and sculpture as the residue of a performance. More distinctly than in the work of most other sculptors, Prada rhetorizes the making of her work as a performance, explicitly displaying the obsessive repetitions of making and the bodily labor. There is in her work the partial but significant replacement of sculpture's objecthood by the process of its making. This performance is not seen by the viewer, but it can be readily imagined, as can the work's destruction at the end of the exhibition. The need for her to perform the making of her pieces each time they are shown, and the frailty of the materials from which they are made, undermines the temporal persistence of the sculptural object. In her attitude to making sculpture there is a deliberate avoidance of monumentality and permanence. In her wish for the work to be temporary and fragile there is a refusal of the obviously portentous, just as there is in her work a confounding of categories and professionalized domains. What may seem categorical and didactic in the hands of art theorists is shown by her work to be intensely convoluted and rich. The concerns her sculptures present resemble the system of balance and counter-balance necessary in the branches of an immense mobile. And if this image, itself, suggests the portentous then let it finally be noted that what interests the viewer most vivaciously in Prada's work is her lightness of touch and her distinctive ironic tone.

1 Rosalind Krauss, 'Sculpture in the Expanded Field,' *The Originality of the Avant-Garde and Other Modernist Myths* (Cambridge: The MIT Press, 1986), p. 284. 2 William Tucker, *The Language of Sculpture* (London: Thames and Hudson, 1974), p. 107. 3 Estrella de Diego, *Ana Prada* (Madrid: Museo Nacional Centro de Arte Reina Sofia, 1995), p. 6. 4 Fred Orton, 'Jasper Johns: The Sculpture,' *Henry Moore Foundation Review*, no. 2 (Spring 1996), p. 11.

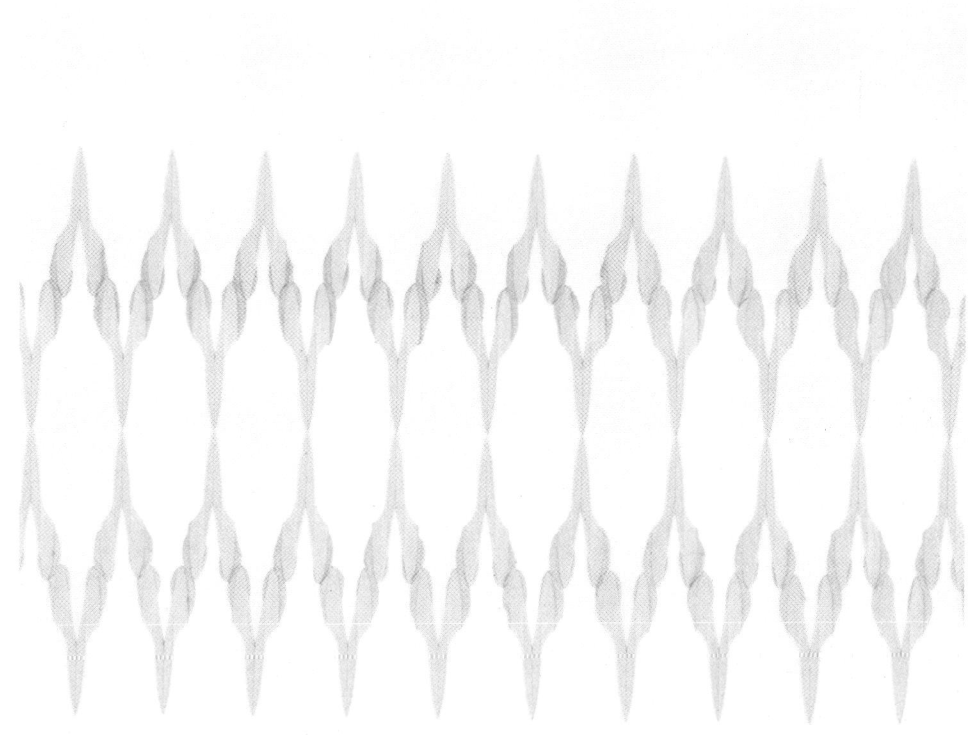

Ana Prada
Untitled, 1995 (detail)
plastic knifes and silicone
50 x 200 x 0.5 cm
collection of the artist

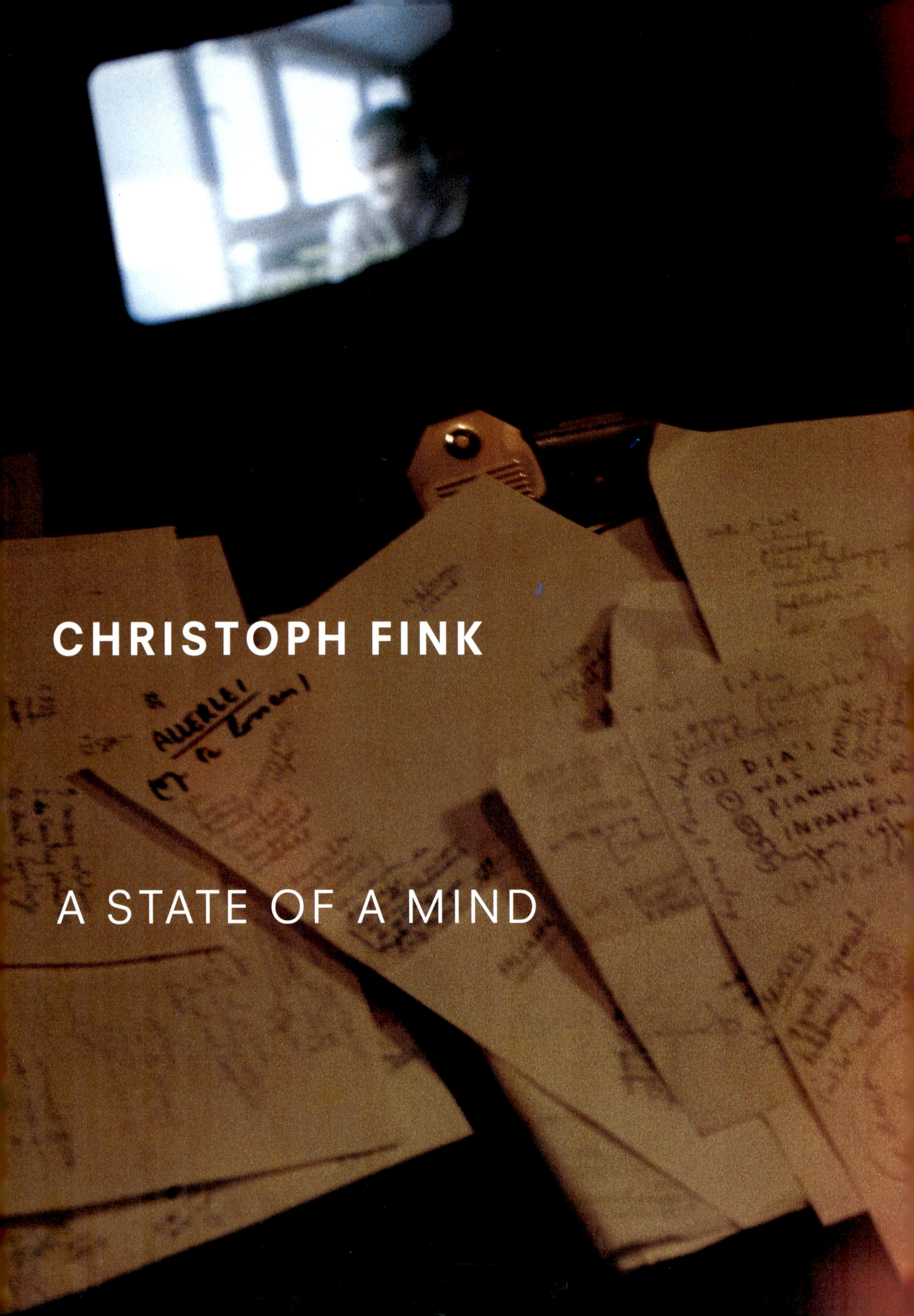
CHRISTOPH FINK
A STATE OF A MIND

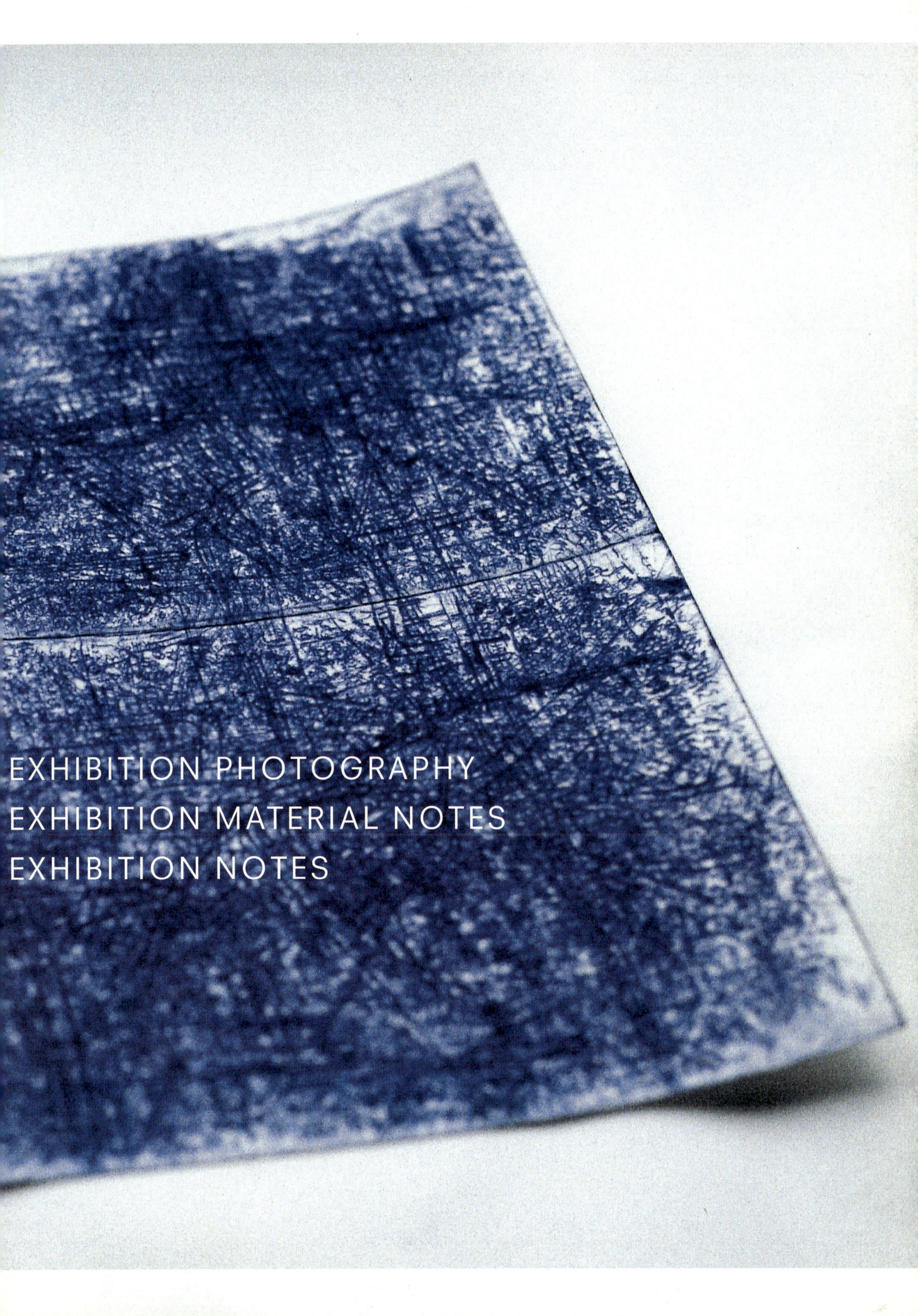

EXHIBITION PHOTOGRAPHY
EXHIBITION MATERIAL NOTES
EXHIBITION NOTES

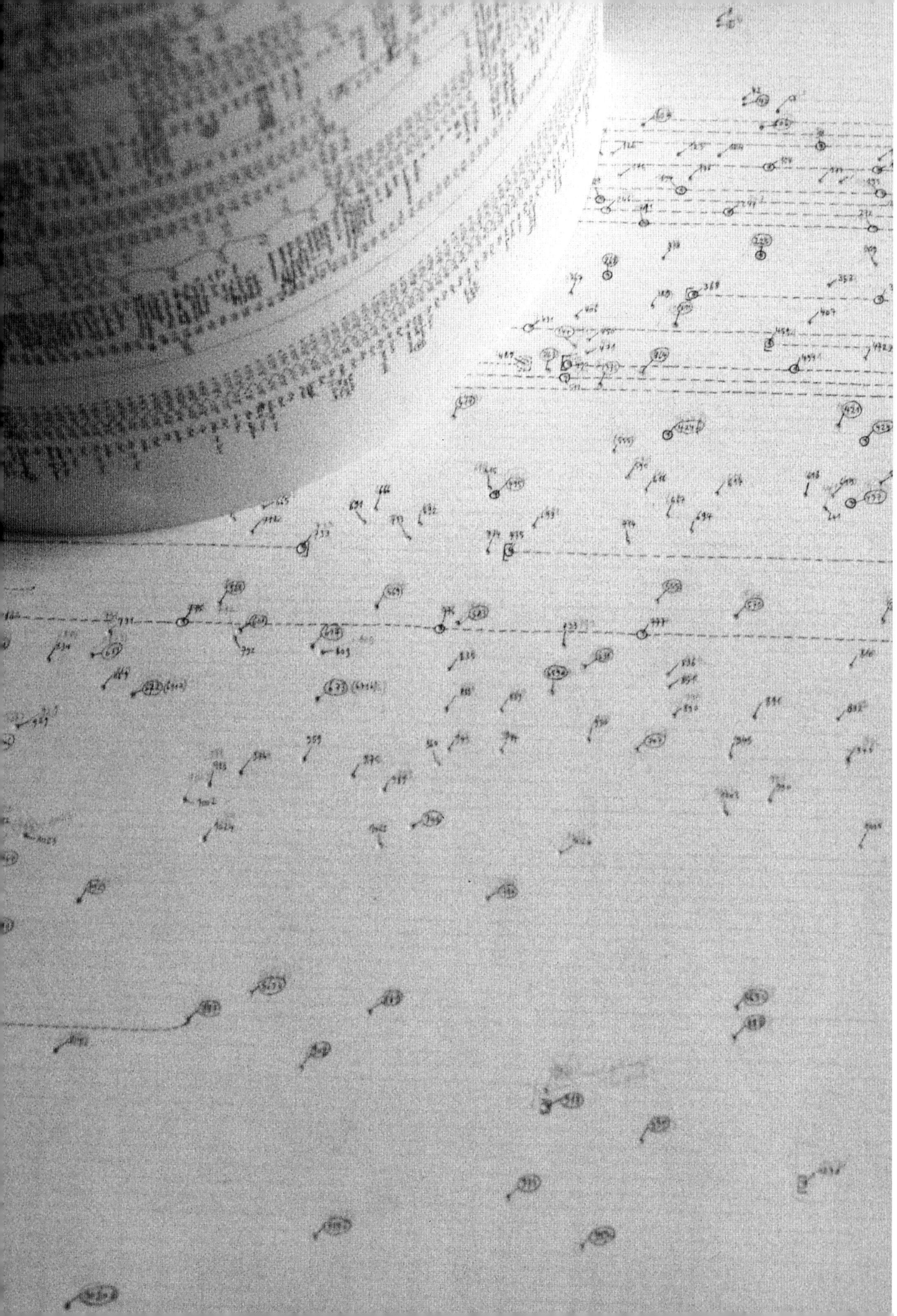

362 41'18"
364 43'50"
365 45'35"
366 46'55"
2'05"
367 0:00'00"
372 8'30"
373 11'24"
373a 14'56"
374 19'35"
375 22'35"
386 39'40"
388 43'00"
390 45'06"
394 57'47"
396 1:02'16"
398 1:03'50"
404 1:12'00"
411 1:30'10"
419 1:45'43"
421 1:48'00"
424 1:53'35"
a 1:56'20"
b 2:00'08"
c 2:01'00"
d 2:04'58"
e 2:05'35"
f 2:15'00"
425 2:16 10
427 2:17 42
429 2:19 56
430 2:20 50
a 2:21'44"
b 2:24'10"
487 4:10'40"
487a 4:19'47"
491 4:23'46"
491a 4:26'09"
492 4:28'34"
493 4:31'00"
494
495 4:34'00"
497 4:36'06"
498 4:39'05"

552 2:04'35"
0:00'00" 553 0:00'00" (dag 3 → dag 4)
37'44"
37'44" 527 37'44"
6'16"
0:00'00" 573 0:00'00"
8'00" 583 15'46"
13'54" 588 22'11"
21'33" 595 34'00"
22'53" 597 35'00"
23'46" 598 37'59"
25'20" 600 40'00"
25'54" 601 42'30"
31'28" 605 51'03"
32'35" 606 52'44"
36'20" 610 57'50"
45'31" 617 1:10'56"
53'20" 623 1:22'14"
53'50" 624 1:23'40"
1:02'05" 631 1:32'58"
1:03'43" 632 1:37'
1:04'37" 633 1:37'40"
1:07'30" 636
1:10 52 640
1:14'09 641
1:16 14
1:19'08
2:36'20"
670 2:57'58"
671 3:01'00"
672 3:01 56
678 3:03 00
2:14 48 698 4:03 27
2:19 26 704 4:20 33
704a 4:20 52
2:21 32 706 4:25 10
2:22 55 707 4:28 50
2:43 34 718 5:20
718a 5:30'
3:18 30 743 6:33'40
3'50"

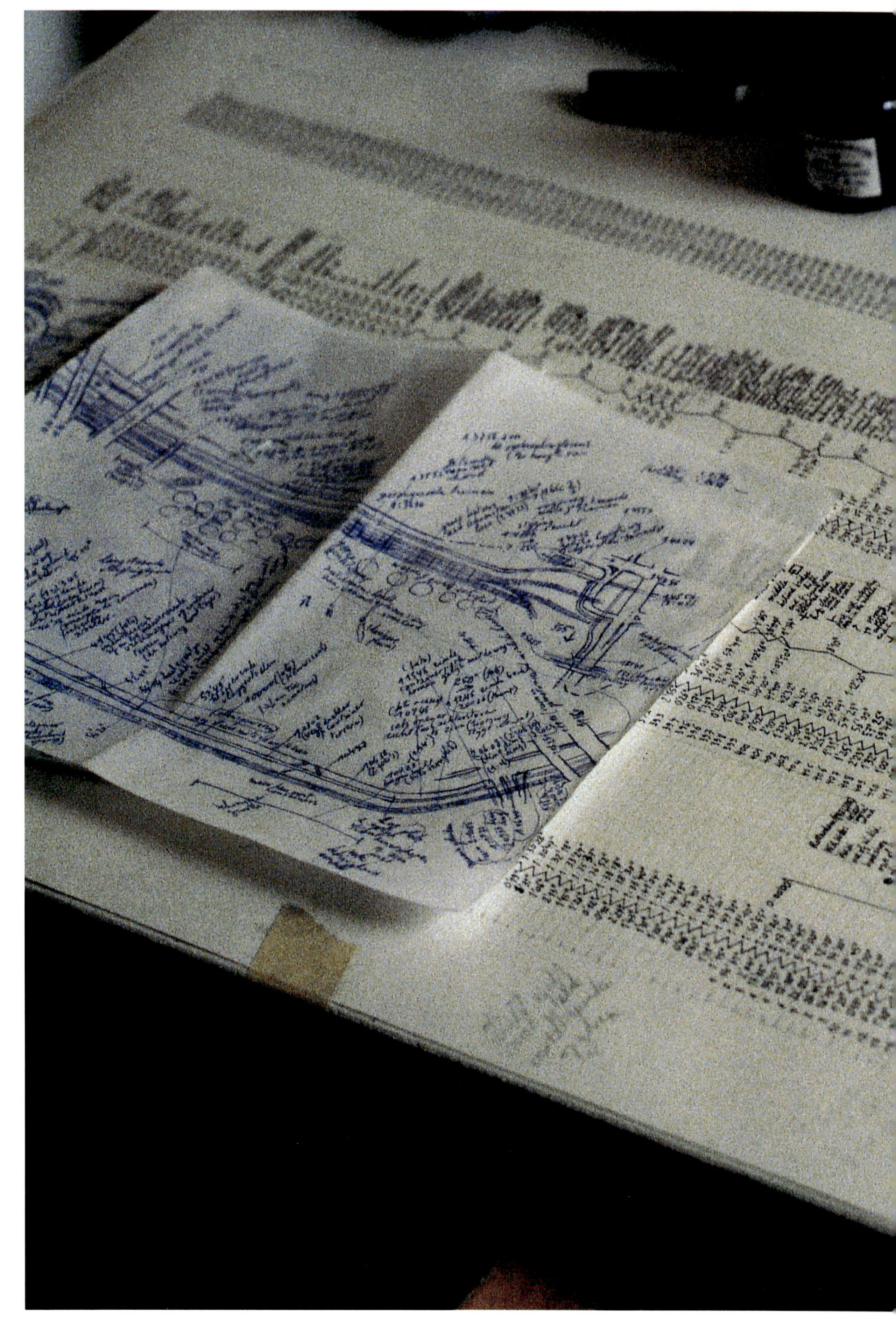

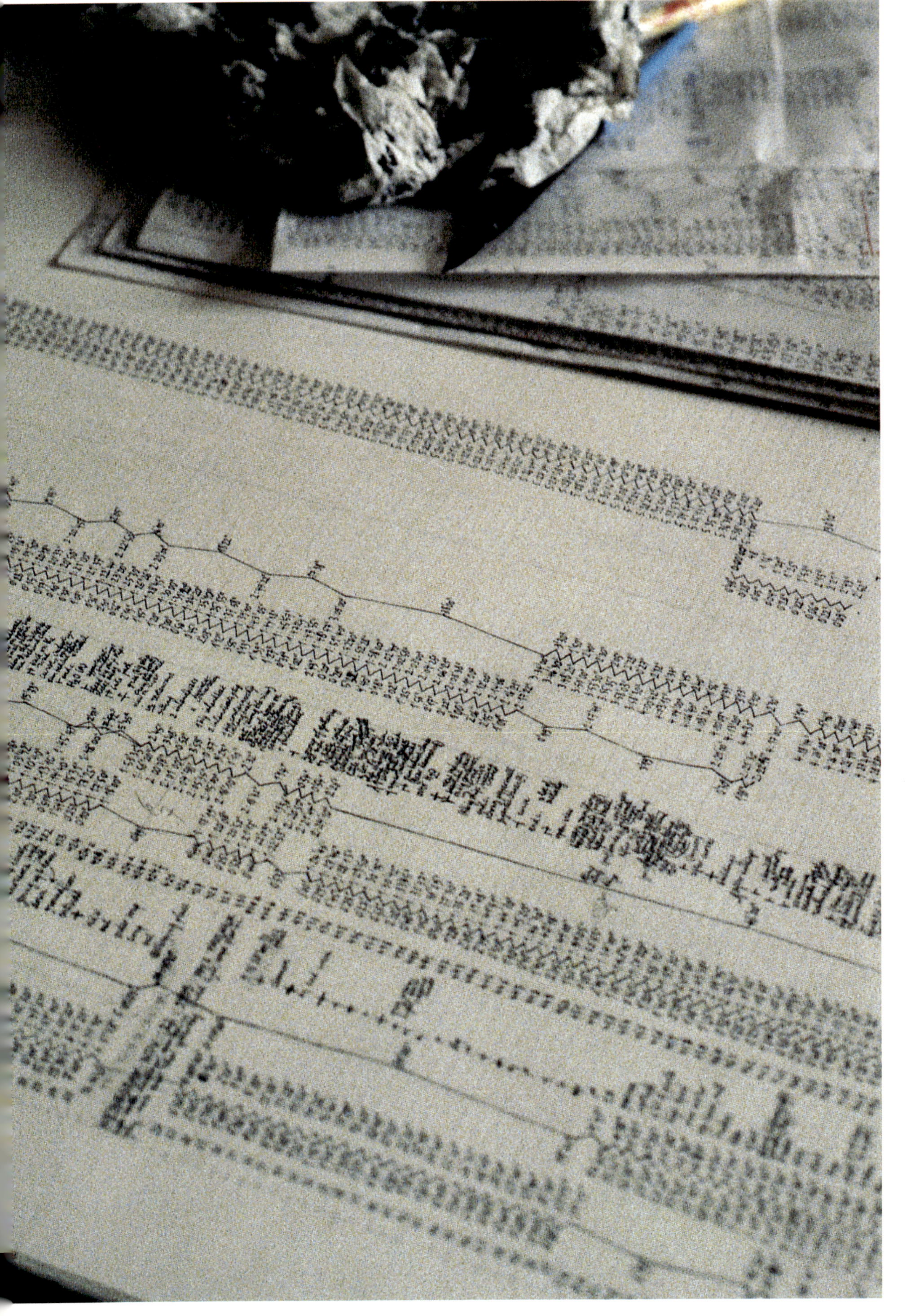

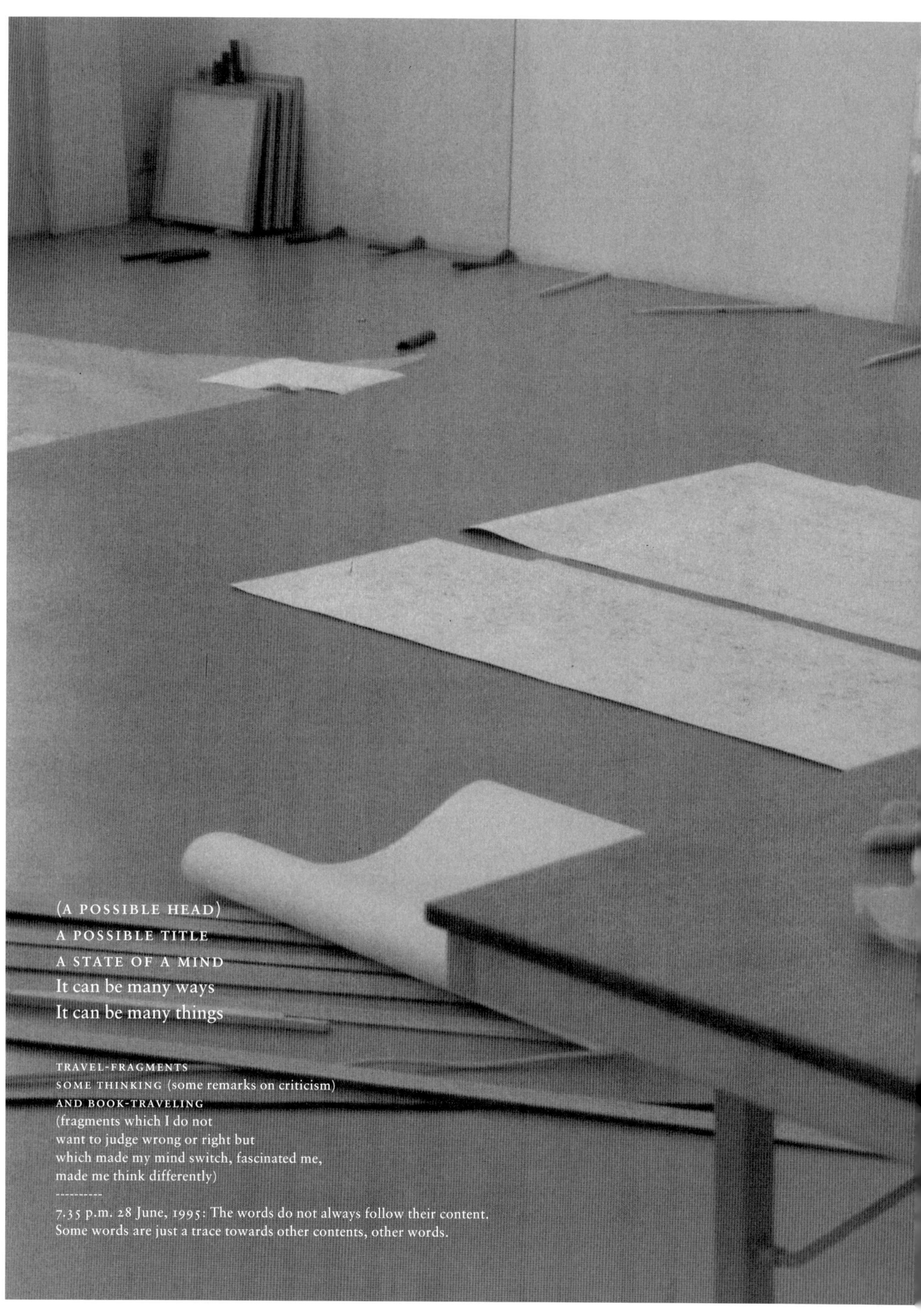

(A POSSIBLE HEAD)
A POSSIBLE TITLE
A STATE OF A MIND
It can be many ways
It can be many things

TRAVEL-FRAGMENTS
SOME THINKING (some remarks on criticism)
AND BOOK-TRAVELING
(fragments which I do not
want to judge wrong or right but
which made my mind switch, fascinated me,
made me think differently)

7.35 p.m. 28 June, 1995: The words do not always follow their content.
Some words are just a trace towards other contents, other words.

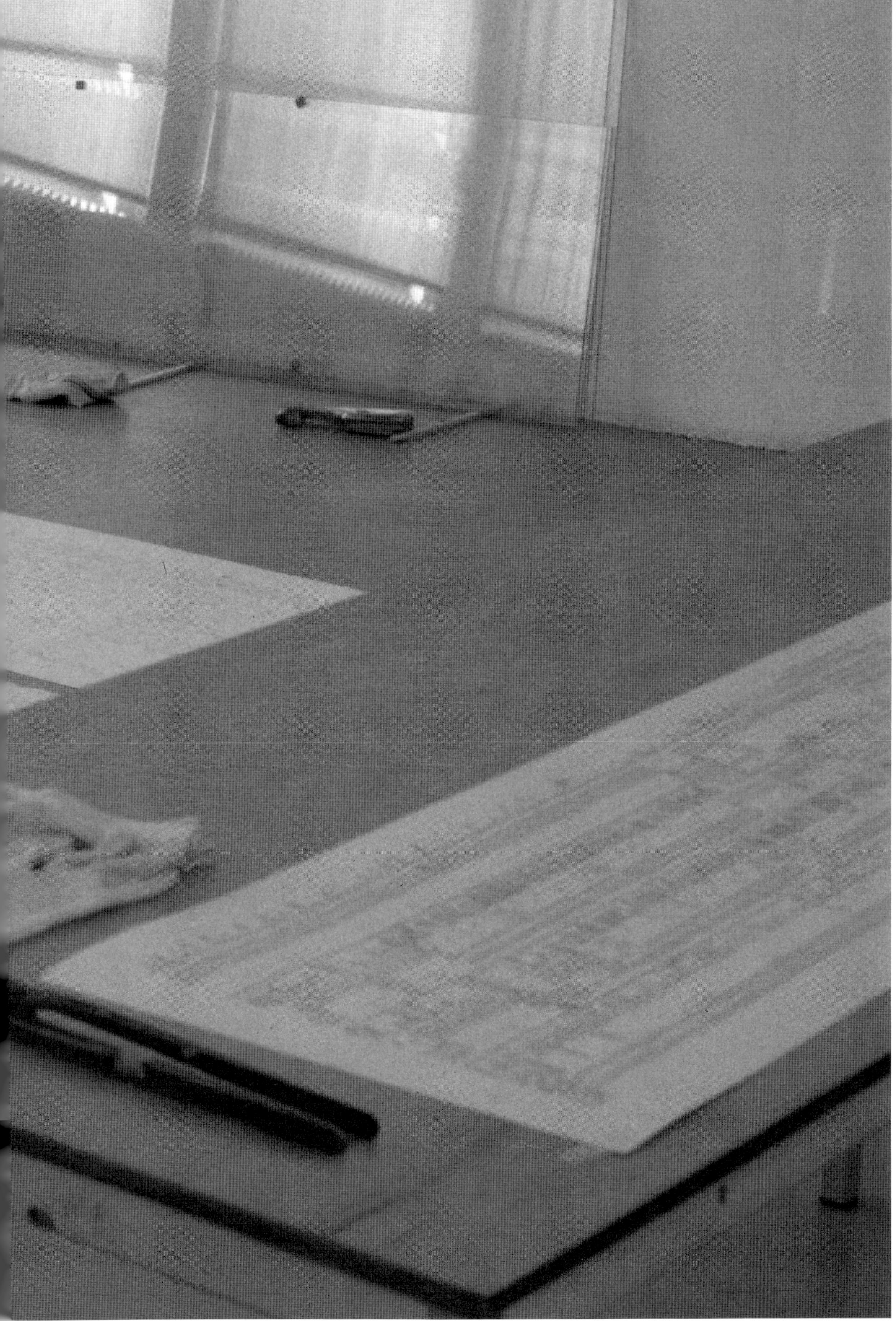

EXHIBITION MATERIALS
23 March – 19 May 1996

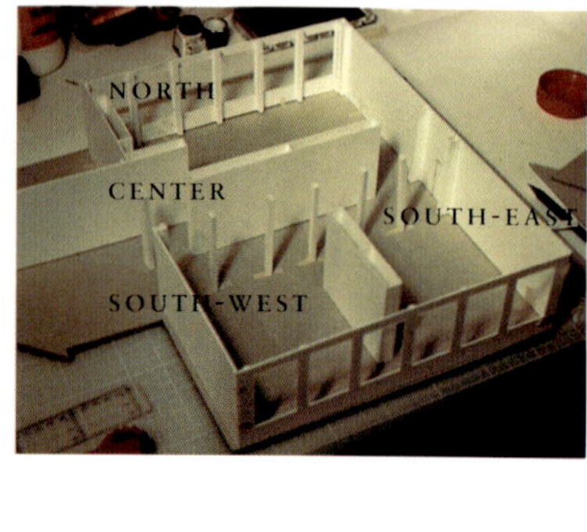

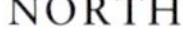

NORTH

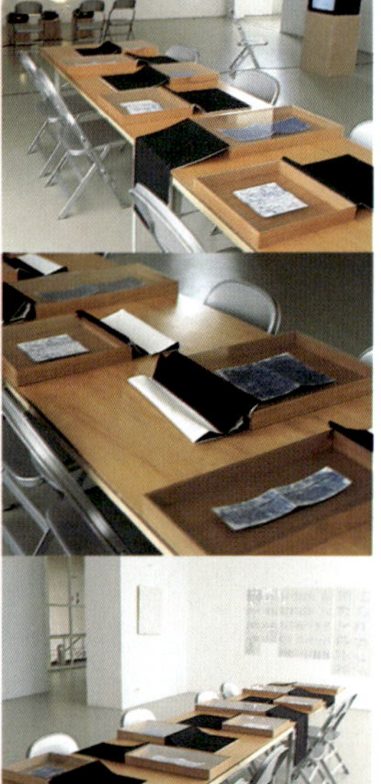

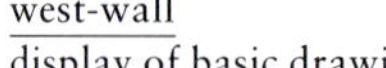

west-wall
display of basic drawings:

Venice, first trip	1 x (239 x 317 mm)
3 days walk + flights	1 x (209 x 290 mm)
	14 x (120 x 120 mm)
Venice, second trip	7 x (151 x 151 mm)
18 days walk + flights	23 x (151 x 151 mm)
Rotterdam	21 x (248 x 200 mm)
267.276 km, 7 days	

south-wall (grey)
Brussels, first movement,
187.03 km walking the main axes
I drawing by memory (= 'o'-drawing) 770 x 770 mm
15 carbon drawings + their 'fold-out' of street names,
angles, time-intervals, conditions. 500 x 500 mm
all lightproofed by curtains

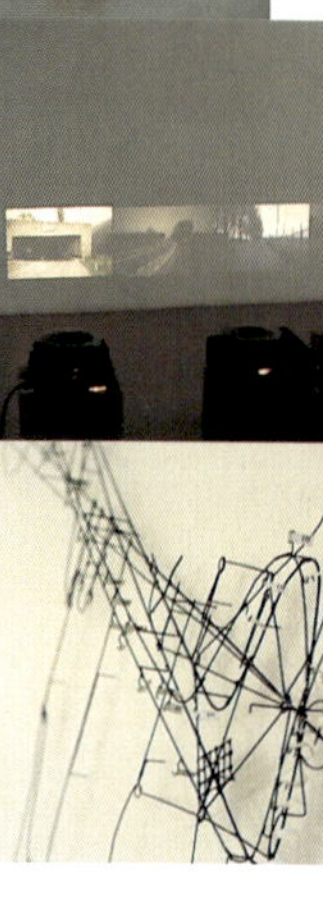

display of carbondrawings on table (8) (7) (6) (5)
(1) (2) (3) (4)

(1) Venice, first trip	120 x 120 mm
(2) Venice, second trip	151 x 151 mm
(3) Brussels, second movement	400 x 125 mm
(4) Brussels-Boston (flight)	280 x 70 mm
(5) Boston + Boston-New York	160 x 160 mm
(6) New York	170 x 170 mm
(7) New York-Brussels (flight)	280 x 70 mm
(8) Rotterdam	248 x 200 mm

all lightproofed by boxes and curtains

videocompilation, 240'
super 8 & Hi8 travelings & work processes

4 simultaneously projected slideprojections 1 | 2 | 3 | 4
interval: 4"
(1) New York, Ghent-Chamonix-Ghent (bike),
Ghent-Venice-Ghent (bike)
80 slides ('road-ahead' views)
(2) Rotterdam 80 slides ('road-ahead' views)
(3) Brussels, second movement
80 slides ('road-ahead' views)
(4) Ghent (bike-circle) 80 slides ('road-ahead' views)

sound (continiously played)
4 players, 4 languages: voice pronouncing view
directions derived from slides

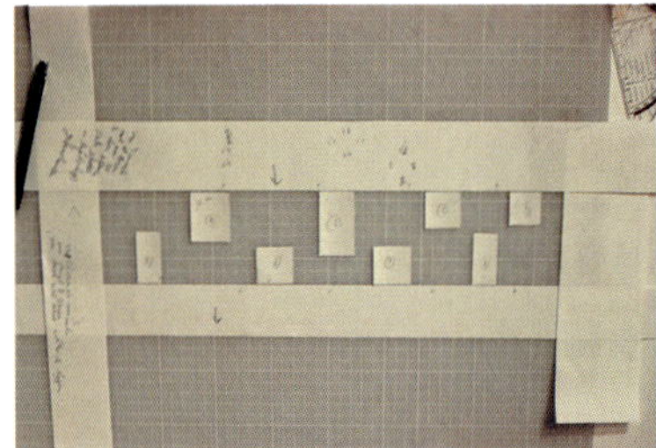

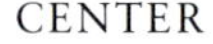

CENTER

middlewall
pencil drawing at eye level: circular-central projection of explored area's

south-side
1 wire sculpture (Venice, first trip, model to scale)
lenghth 3600 mm
1 scale drawing (Brussels, second movement)
1560 x 900 mm
1 scale drawing (Rotterdam) 760 x 1470 mm

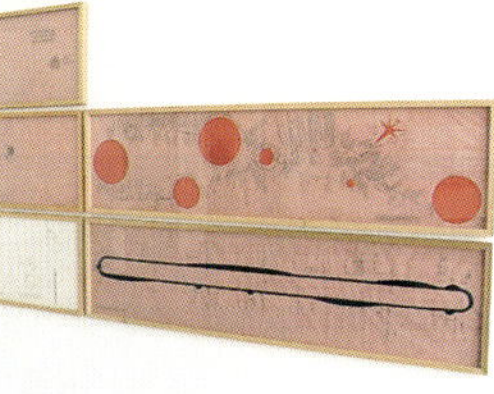

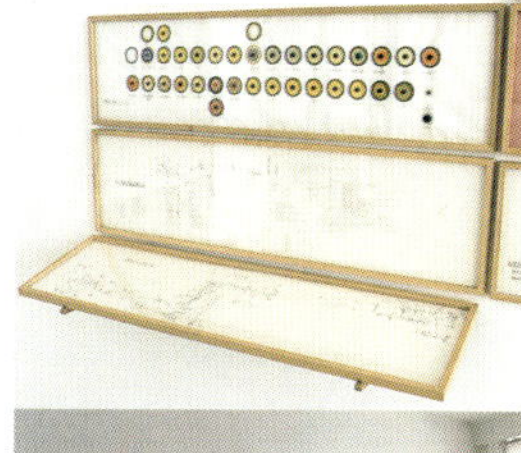

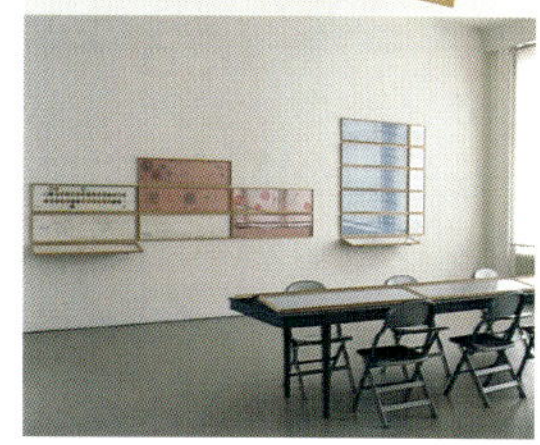

SOUTH-EAST

'Mo 05.13.1991, 4.52 p.m.-Th 06.13.1991, 2.40 p.m.'
A North-American experience, 36 drawings
31 x (1200 x 300 mm)
5 x (300 x 300 mm)
15 drawings concerning 5 flights (5 x 3 different languages & patterns)
4 drawings concerning the total time & space
2 drawings concerning the West coast time & space
3 drawings concerning details of the W.c.t. & s.
12 drawings concerning city passages

show-case with several sculptures and drawings
4 'moulds' for 'Mo 05.13.1991, ...' (ironwire)(spiral shape)
1 ironwire sculpture (cylindershape) (175 x 327 mm)
('5 cities from 'Mo 05.13.1991, ...')
photographs of '34' (34 small sculptures ('Mo 05.13.1991, ...') (zinc cubes & discs, wire forms)
several drawings (preparations for '34') 180 x 262 mm
1 artist's book drawing (Central-Europe trip)
study for 'Su 10.28.1990, 1.00 p.m.-Su 11.11.1990, 7.35 p.m.'

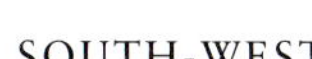

SOUTH-WEST

east-wall
Venice, first trip: 1 databank drawing 750 x 750 mm
1 chronological ordered data drawing
750 x 750 mm
Brussels, second movement: 1 databank drawing
± 107 km circlewalk in 8 segments 1705 x 420 mm
1 wire sculpture, (cylindershape)
130 x 1740 mm
Rotterdam: 1 databank drawing (vertical position)
392 x 1876 mm

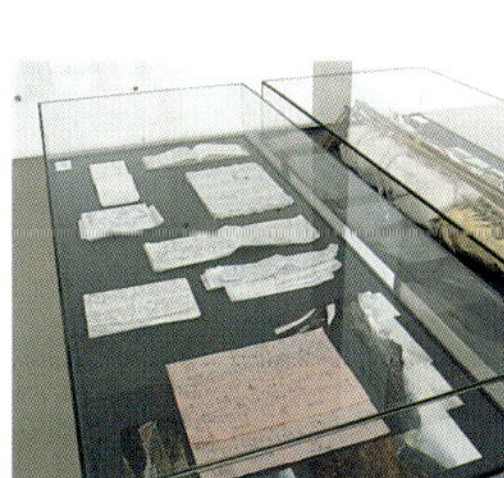

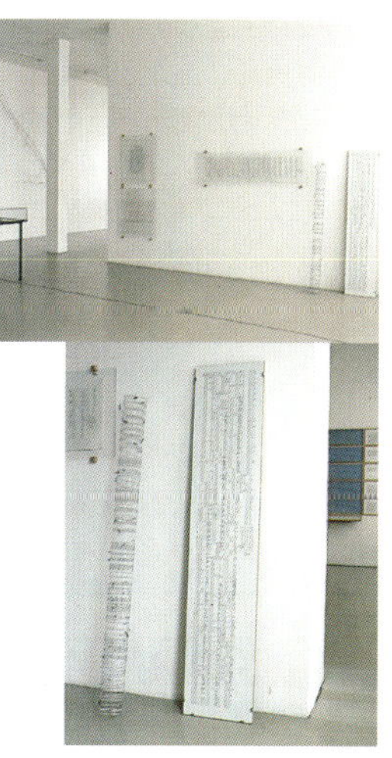

west-wall
Brussels, second movement: 1 chronological ordered data drawing
1785 x 480 mm
1 'time-perspective' drawing
1770 x 480 mm
Rotterdam: 1 chronological ordered data drawing
1780 x 752 mm
1 'time-perspective' drawing
1780 x 752 mm
1 show-case with folded-up Venice-observatory-tent + several photographs & polaroids
1 show-case with several piles of basic drawings + the bikeroute drawings (Ghent-Venice-Ghent) 2774 km, 14 days
2 x (211 x 297 mm)
sound: 1 tape (continuously played): numerical soundscape based on Brussels, second movement-data
1 tape (continuously played): numerical soundscape based on Rotterdam-data

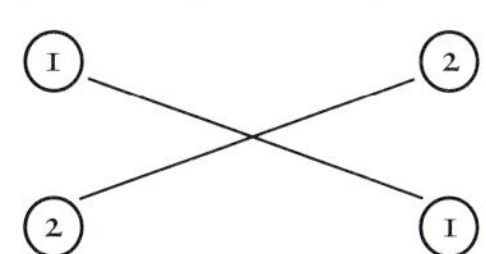

A STATE OF A MIND
It can be many ways
It can be many things

Sunday, 24 Dec., 1995
A Belgian cinematographer says he never saw a masterpiece and doesn't want to try to make one. I think that what you HAVE to try to make IS a masterpiece. The term masterpiece is not necessarily limited to an object.

I'm basically bored by chatting, theory leading to a dead-end. (How does one break the borders of language?)

It's not always clear where the work starts
... started
There is (was until now) a series of actions, which can (could) be described as such:
What I think I do is:
What I think I did until now was:
I run through an experience, a specific chosen period in the flow of life experience, which I dig out.
- concentration (I intensify the discipline of concentration)
- intuition, fascination
- ritual
All collected materials, elements (not necessarily limited to the notes (which I made during the traveling)) are reworked, reconsidered, analyzed, synthetisized, ... in an attempt to reconstruct the complexity of that experience. Ultimately the goal is not to understand exactly what happened (it is not understandable).
The total process nevertheless regenerates new experiences and from time to time something which could be called 'enlighted moments.'
As I said somewhere before: '... touching time, touching space, touching an experience: you take it, describe it, turn it around, observe it attentively, you touch it again, ... and you're completely surprised by the undescribable, the untouchable; a short moment of very intense consciousness' (a moment where you can let things go? liberating? blessed? maybe something like that).

I basically try to amuse myself (but art is not about entertainment).

'ACTING OUT OF NOT KNOWING, out of fascination.'
(Joëlle Tuerlinckx)

(The hope of being able to communicate something which could be called 'complex beauty').

The results of the whole work are certainly not limited to the materialization ① (drawings, objects).
For myself, and that's the only person whom I can speak of with a certain degree of certainty, I try to restore or reinforce the ties with existence ②. I enforce the concentration level, the level of consciousness. Spiritual enrichment. And this I hope to communicate.

How do I try to 'cancel' myself? Because the medium, the 'I' is very prominent, as I make the work. The consciousness that I am part of the total of 'experiences' means that I 'cancel' myself without fading myself out completely (as such, I'm the transmitter and part of the experience).
DOIUSETHERIGHTWORDS?
Doubting seems essential.

Christoph Fink, June 1996.

'Most people don't realize how difficult it is to make modern art – because the mind is so much in contral that it keeps people unpoetic and un-imaginative.'
'Art as an introduction to the exellence of daily life.'
(John Cage)

One question becomes more questions.
The one question is allready multiple questions (constant reflecting, rethinking).

Remark on time:
'You can work with a metronome, but time is elastic. ... Time is not metronomic ... Time breathes. It's not obvious, but it gets faster and slower, such a minute space that it's unbelievable. It's human, because we're human. We breathe.'
(Max Roach in *Drums and Druming*)

① Containers of research (of other experiences).
It doesn't touch specific goals, it is not science.
It is poetry, art.

② 'Infinitly complex network, each encountered thing is many things'
(John Cage)
'Charles Ives wrote a romantic essay about sitting in a rocking chair, on the front porch looking out toward the mountains, listening to your own symphony.'
(John Cage)

'The idea of participation instead of observation is in modern physics only recently mentioned, but everybody who studied mysticism is very familiar with that idea.
Mystical knowledge can never be obtained only by observation, but demands the fullest devotion, the participation of the whole being.
In the Eastern Philosophy of life, the idea of the 'participant' is thus essential, and the Eastern mystics developed this idea extensively, so that the observer and the observed object, the subject and object are not only undividable, but also not distinguishable.'
(Fritjof Capra in *Tao of Physics*)

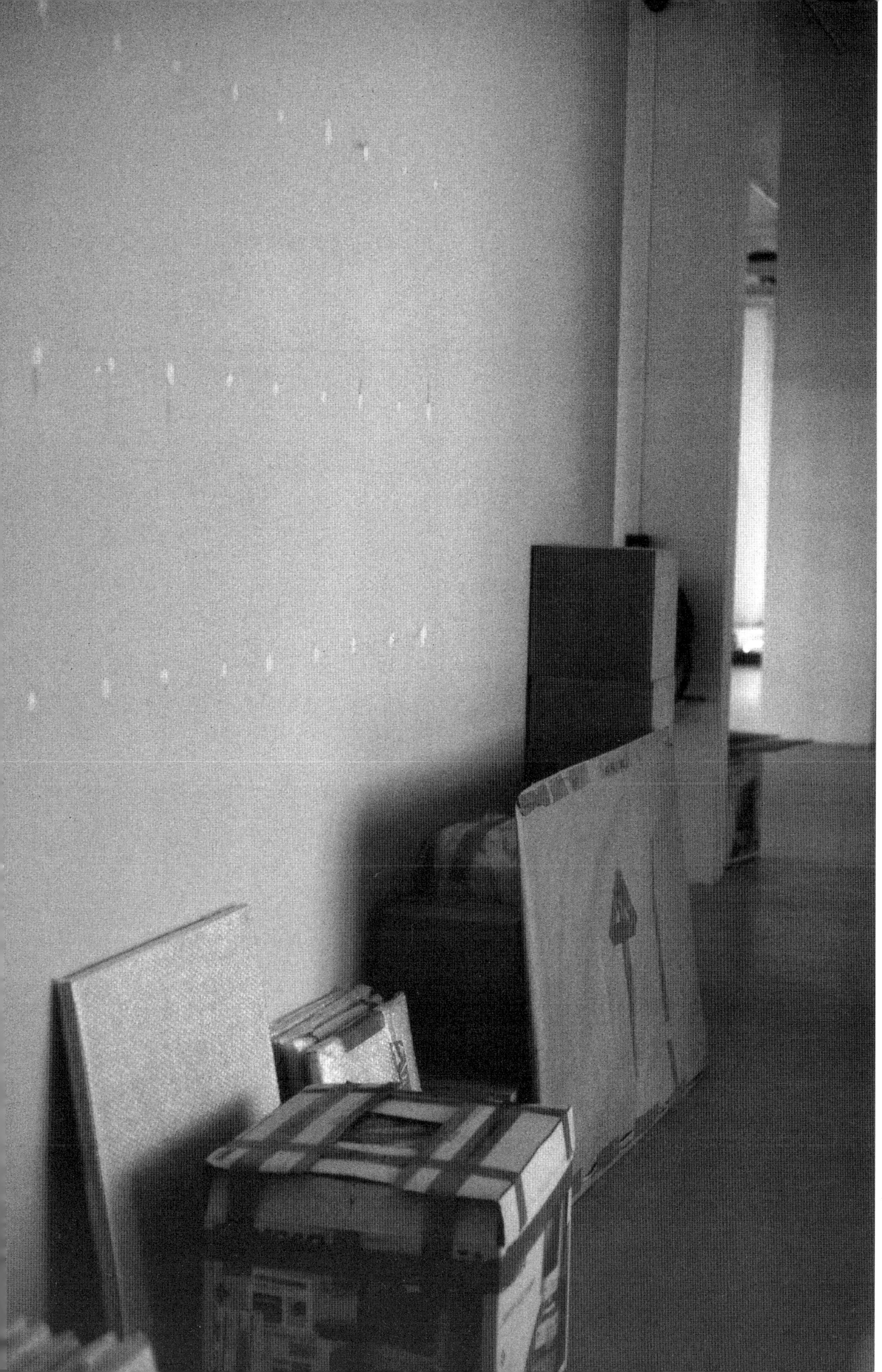

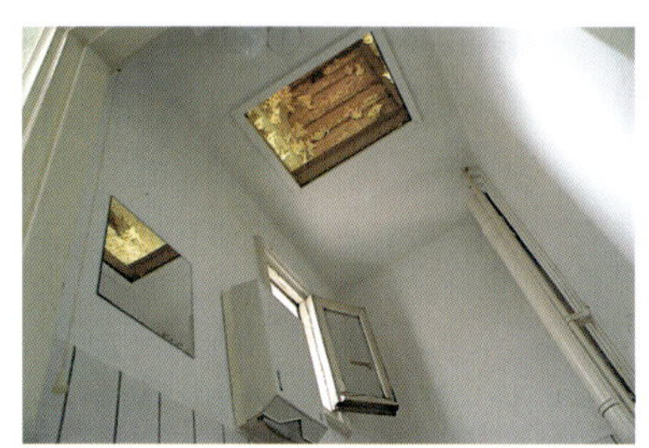

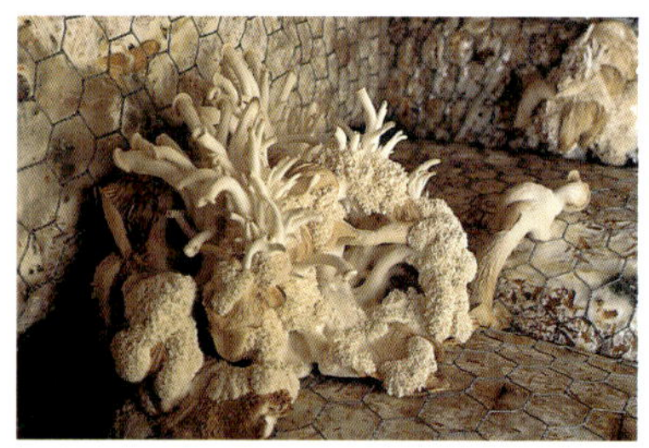

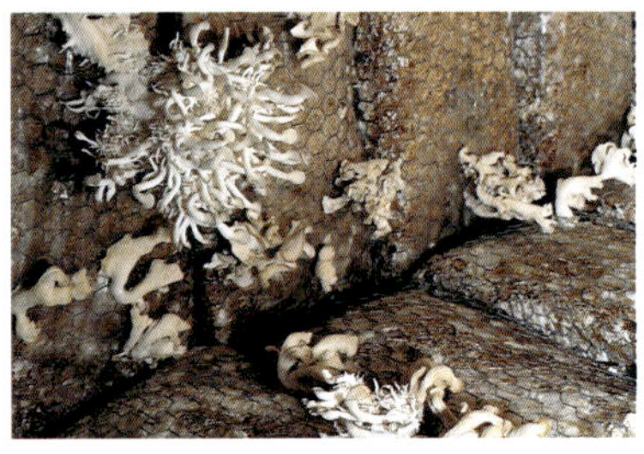

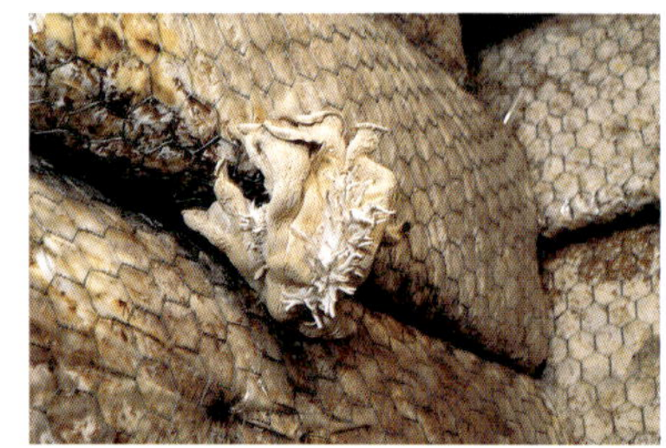

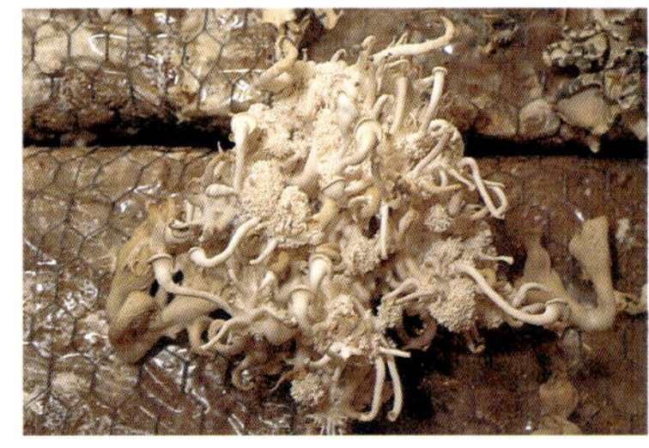

Zeger Reyers
Onder-tussen (In-between), 1996

Nutritional value of the Pleurotus Ostreatus (Oyster Mushroom)

Crude protein	10-30%
Vitamine-C	30-144 mg/100 g
Niacin	109 mg/100 g
Folic Acid	65 mg/100 g
Potassium	306 mg/100 g

'The more you know them, the less sure you feel about identifying them. Each one is itself. Each mushroom is what it is – its own center. It's useless to pretend to know mushrooms. They escape your erudition.'

John Cage in Daniel Charles, *For The Birds John Cage* (London: Marion Boyars Publishers, 1981), p. 188.

'I became aware that if I approached mushrooms in the spirit of my change operations I would die shortly.'

John Cage in Calvin Tomkins, *The Bride and the Bachelors* (London: Penguin Books, 1965), p. 123.

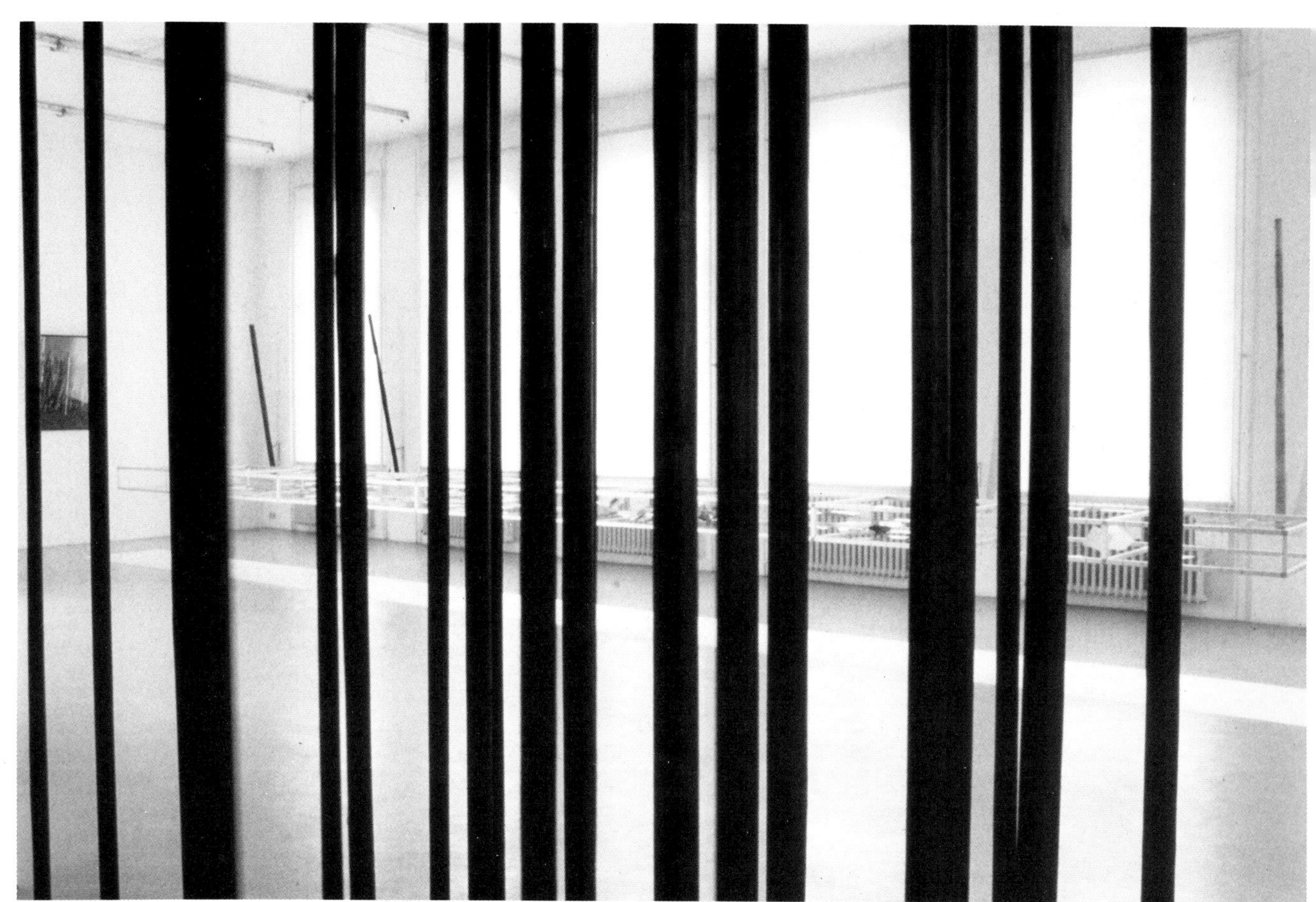

Yvonne Dröge-Wendel
Wooden Sticks, 1994-96
installation view at Witte de With
collection of the artist

I On 31 January 1992, Yvonne Dröge takes a definitive step. She enters matrimony, not with a person but with a piece of furniture, a wooden cupboard. She puts on a solemn marriage ceremony in which the priest, in the presence of gathered family members, friends and pieces of furniture, legitimizes this unusual commitment between human being and object: 'Why not the love between an object and a human being? Isn't it true that we all touch objects every day and live with objects? Without them we cannot exist. That mere fact is what distinguishes us from all other beings and makes us special. Objects make our world and without them, we are nothing.'[1] Yvonne Dröge takes the logical step in such a situation and devotes her life to that which she is most attached: things. Henceforth, she bears the brand name of the piece of furniture, Wendel, next to her own name.
This union is the affirmation of a relationship that is at the heart of Dröge-Wendel's œuvre. By way of photographs and videos, which she makes of her travels and performances, Dröge-Wendel investigates how people and things relate to each other. She considers objects as indispensable and vital extensions of the human body; they enable man to do everyday acts that he would be incapable of with his own limited capacities. In order to live as he is accustomed, man is completely dependent on his prostheses, and helpless when his artificial limbs fail. Dröge-Wendel ironically illustrated man's subordination to things in her project *La benedizione della macchina* (1994) in which she brought an old and dilapidated Renault 16 to Rome for benediction on St. Christopher's day. This pilgrimage was a con-

I Op 31 januari 1992 neemt Yvonne Dröge een beslissende stap. Zij treedt in het huwelijk, niet met een persoon, maar met een meubelstuk, een houten dressoir. Ze ensceneert een plechtige huwelijksceremonie waarbij de priester, ten overstaan van de verzamelde familieleden, vrienden en meubels, deze bijzondere verbintenis tussen mens en object legitimeert: 'Why not the love between an object and a human being? Isn't it true that we all touch objects every day, and live with objects? Without them we cannot exist. That mere fact is what distinguishes us from all other beings and makes us special. Objects make our world and without them, we are nothing.'[1] Yvonne Dröge trekt de consequenties uit dit gegeven, en wijdt haar leven aan datgene waarmee zij het meest direct verbonden is, de dingen. Naast haar eigen naam draagt zij voortaan ook de merknaam van het meubelstuk, Wendel.
Deze vereniging is de bevestiging van een relatie die in het œuvre van Dröge-Wendel centraal staat. Met foto's en video's, die zij maakt van haar reizen en performances, onderzoekt Dröge-Wendel hoe de mens en de dingen zich tot elkaar verhouden. De objecten worden daarbij beschouwd als noodzakelijke en onmisbare verlengstukken van het lichaam; ze maken de dagelijkse handelingen mogelijk waartoe de mens met zijn eigen beperkte vermogens niet in staat zou zijn. Voor de hem gewone manier van leven is hij volstrekt afhankelijk van zijn prothesen, en hulpeloos wanneer zijn kunstmatige ledematen falen. Dröge-Wendel illustreert deze onderworpenheid aan de dingen op ironische wijze, wanneer zij in het project *La benedizione della macchina* (1994) een oude en haperende Renault 16 op de heiligendag van St. Christoffel naar Rome brengt om deze te laten inzegenen. Deze

temporary variant on the journey to Lourdes by the lame, who hope to be able to move around again like healthy people: without his precious car, modern man is stripped of his ability to move about in a normal manner. In this project with an ailing car, it's the human being that proves to be the actual invalid. By choosing an object as her better half, Dröge-Wendel implies that people are not complete without objects around them. It is this vision of man being a 'well-equipped invalid'[2] that is elaborated and radicalized in the installation she made for Witte de With.

II

Wooden Sticks (1994-96) is comprised of a collection of photographs of people with a similar type of object, a stick. Some of the photographs were originally made for Dröge-Wendel's project *Off-Size Luggage* (1994) in which she traveled through the United States, the Caribbean and Botswana with a big stick as hand-

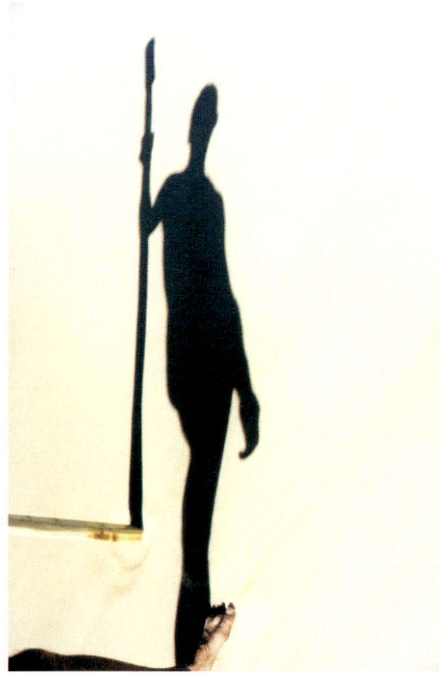

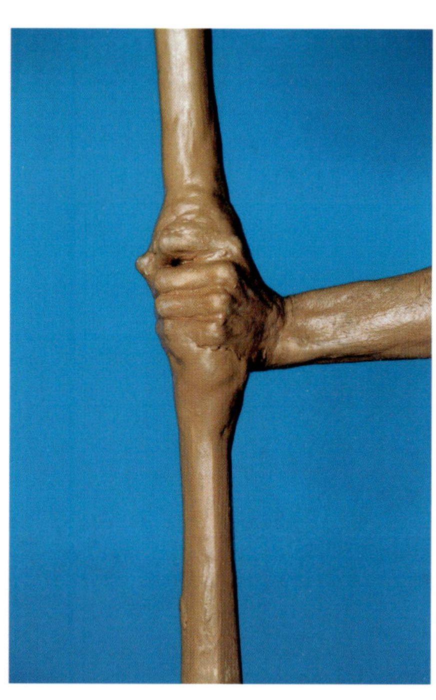

Yvonne Dröge-Wendel *Wooden Sticks*, details

bedevaart is een actuele variant op de tocht naar Lourdes door de lamme, die hoopt zich weer als ieder gezond mens te kunnen voortbewegen: zonder zijn kostbare automobiel is de moderne mens beroofd van zijn vermogen om zich op normale wijze te verplaatsen. In dit project met een gebrekkige auto, blijkt de mens de eigenlijke invalide. Zonder de objecten om hem heen, zo impliceert Dröge-Wendel met haar keuze voor een object als wederhelft, is de mens niet compleet. Het is deze visie van de mens als 'goed uitgeruste gehandicapte',[2] die in de installatie die zij maakte voor Witte de With, wordt uitgewerkt en geradicaliseerd.

II

Wooden Sticks (1994-96) omvat een verzameling foto's van mensen met eenzelfde soort voorwerp, een stok. Een deel van de foto's werd oorspronkelijk gemaakt voor het project *Off-Size Luggage* (1994), waarbij Dröge-Wendel door de Verenigde Staten, het Caribisch gebied en Botswana reisde met een grote stok als handbagage.

luggage. Every time she encountered people with a stick-like object, she photographed them and then herself imitating them with her stick. Another part of the pictures consists of reproductions of paintings from art history books, and photographs from sport magazines and newspapers in which figures are portrayed with sticks. There is a photograph of a sports star with ski poles; another of a group of poor African villagers standing around an electricity pole. In a medieval painting a king waves his scepter; in a recent newspaper clipping insurgents brandish pieces of wood. A photograph documents how Dröge-Wendel imitates with her stick a pool boy with his net; another captures an Indian at his daily chore of lighting a fire with a stick. But how do these scenes precisely correspond? What do all these sticks refer to? As soon as we try to interpret what is reproduced in these photographs, we get caught up in incomparable variables and irreconcilable categories. Actual and staged situations are jumbled. Diverse historical and cultural contexts are

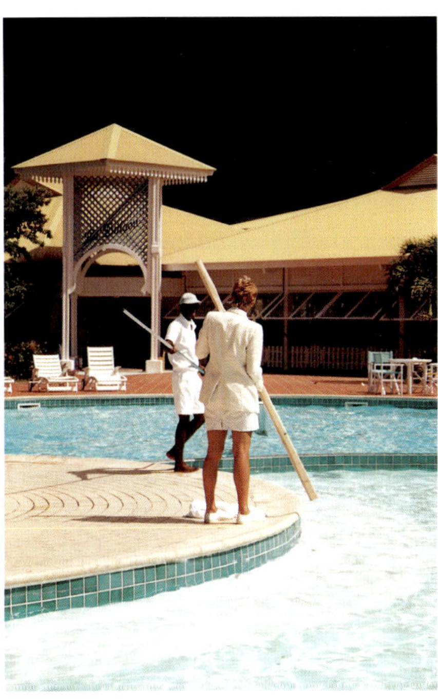

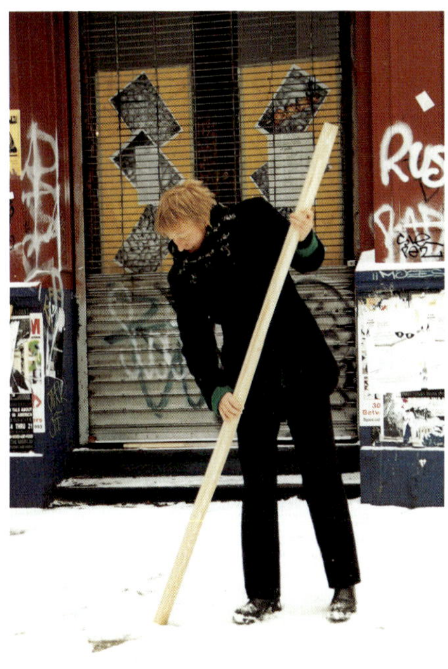

Steeds wanneer zij onderweg mensen met stok-achtige voorwerpen aantrof, fotografeerde ze niet alleen hen, maar ook zichzelf terwijl zij met haar stok eenzelfde situatie imiteerde. Andere foto's zijn reproducties uit kunstgeschiedenisboeken van schilderijen waarop figuren met stokken zijn afgebeeld, of illustraties genomen uit sportmagazines of kranten. Een foto toont een topsporter met skistokken; een andere een groep arme Afrikaanse dorpelingen rond een electriciteitspaal. Op een Middeleeuws schilderij zwaait een koning zijn scepter; op een recent krantenknipsel dreigen opstandelingen met stukken hout. Een foto documenteert hoe Dröge-Wendel met haar stok een badmeester met schepnet nabootst; een ander legt een Indiaan vast bij zijn dagelijkse gewoonte om met een stokje vuur maken. Maar wat is nu precies de overeenkomst in deze scènes? Waarop wijzen al die stokken? Zodra we de voorstellingen op deze foto's proberen te duiden, raken we verstrikt in onvergelijkbare grootheden en onverenigbare categorieën. Werkelijke en geënsceneerde situaties worden door elkaar gebruikt. Uiteenlopende historische en cultu-

placed next to one another. No difference is even made between sticks and objects that vaguely resemble sticks. The harder we try to discover the similarity that forms the base of this collection, the more differences we uncover. As we attempt to fathom the function and meaning of the sticks in the pictures, they appear to have nothing in common. What seems impossible is not what is presented in each photograph, but that they should be brought together for being similar. To our discomfort, what Dröge-Wendel shows us seems just a superficial resemblance.

III Two other exhibitions at Witte de With were similarly disconcerting for the visitor: Brandt Junceau's exhibition *Hyde Park* and Christoph Fink's presentation in *Voorwerk 5*, which also included Dröge-Wendel's installation.
Brandt Junceau presented his exhibition as a statement of genealogy and historiography, placing his own work within the tradition of two unusual predecessors, the collector and artist Elie Nadelman and the American president Franklin Delano Roosevelt, whose work he reconstructed through fragments and documents.[3] The work of both men is characterized by an unconventional attitude toward history. Junceau shows how the library complex that Roosevelt personally designed to accommodate his presidential archives was conceived as an overview of American history. Roosevelt deliberately reorganized the construction site at his birthplace at Hyde Park in Dutchess County, New York, so that the complex would comprise

rele contexten zijn naast elkaar geplaatst. Er wordt zelfs geen verschil gemaakt tussen stokken en voorwerpen die slechts uit de verte op stokken lijken. Hoe meer we trachten te ontdekken op welke overeenkomst deze verzameling is gebaseerd, hoe meer verschillen we blootleggen. Zodra we de functie en betekenis van de stokken in de foto's proberen te doorgronden, lijken zij iedere gemeenschappelijke grond te missen. Onmogelijk zijn niet de voorstellingen op de afzonderlijke foto's, maar dat zij in deze installatie als gelijksoortig zijn bijeengebracht. Wat Dröge-Wendel ons toont, lijkt, tot onze irritatie, slechts een oppervlakkige gelijkenis.

III Twee andere tentoonstellingen in Witte de With brachten de toeschouwers in een vergelijkbare verwarring: de tentoonstelling *Hyde Park* van Brandt Junceau, en de presentatie van Christoph Fink in *Voorwerk 5*, waarvan ook Dröge-Wendels installatie deel uitmaakte.
Brandt Junceau presenteerde zijn tentoonstelling als een verklaring van genealogie en geschiedschrijving: hij plaatste zijn eigen werk in de traditie van twee bijzondere voorgangers, de verzamelaar en kunstenaar Elie Nadelman en Amerikaanse president Franklin Delano Roosevelt, wiens œuvres hij met behulp van fragmenten en documenten reconstrueerde.[3] Beide œuvres worden op hun beurt gekenmerkt door een onconventionele omgang met de geschiedenis. Junceau toont hoe het bibliotheekcomplex, dat Roosevelt in 1937 eigenhandig ontwierp voor de huisvesting van zijn presidentiële archieven, werd geconcipieerd als een overzicht van de Ameri-

pre-colonial plants, seventeenth-century farmhouses and a nineteenth-century mansion. In the design, American history is not approached with historical distance; it is put on one level. The library building is an imitation of a seventeenth-century Dutchess County farmhouse, which Roosevelt had built with exact reproductions as well as authentic materials salvaged from dilapidated farmhouses. With this accumulation of old and new, original and copied architectonic fragments, Roosevelt sacrificed historicity in favor of a living evocation of the past.
History is leveled even further in the collection of plaster casts that Nadelman fabricated between 1935 and 1946. In contrast to the copies one finds in museums of antiquities, whose purpose is to fill in a collection's gaps or to complete partial sculptures, Nadelman did not faithfully model his figures after authentic examples. The *Dolls* are conversely based on reproductions in Nadelman's archeology books and on a range of clippings he compiled from history journals, newspapers and popular magazines. Pursuing the equalizing effect of reproduction, Nadelman composed his figures from fragments of different origin. He did not accentuate stylistic and symbolical differences. He concentrated rather on formal similarities, which made it possible, for example, to have a deity's crown coalesce with a little girl's hairband. Nadelman's imitations of antiquities are a degenerate progeny; they are brazenly anachronistic and absolutely unusable for scholarship. Every attempt to place or interpret them is hindered by their buildup of fragments of styles.
Both Nadelman and Roosevelt used historical sources in a spurious manner. Their

kaanse geschiedenis. Welbewust reorganiseerde Roosevelt het bouwterrein in zijn geboorteplaats Hyde Park in Dutchess County, New York, zo dat het complex ook de bestaande beplanting uit de pre-koloniale tijd, de negentiende eeuwse boerderijen van de eerste Nederlandse kolonisten en een negentiende eeuwse villa zou omvatten. De Amerikaanse geschiedenis wordt in het ontwerp niet met historische distantie benaderd, maar in ééns omvat en op hetzelfde vlak gebracht. Het bibliotheekgebouw zelf is een imitatie van de zeventiende eeuwse boerenhuizen in Dutchess County, waarbij Roosevelt niet alleen onderdelen exact liet namaken, maar ook authentieke materialen van ingestorte hoeves liet hergebruiken. Met deze opeenstapeling van oude en nieuwe, oorspronkelijke en gekopieerde architectonische fragmenten, offerde Roosevelt de historiciteit op ten gunste van een levendige evocatie van het verleden.
De geschiedenis wordt nog verder geëffend in de verzameling gipsafgietsels, die Nadelman tussen 1935 en 1946 vervaardigde. In tegenstelling tot de gebruikelijke kopieën in oudheidkundige musea, die dienen om hiaten in de collectie op te vullen of incomplete stukken te voltooien, modelleerde Nadelman zijn figuren niet waarheidsgetrouw naar authentieke voorbeelden. De *Dolls* zijn daarentegen gebaseerd op de afbeeldingen in Nadelmans archeologieboeken en op alle mogelijke knipsels, afkomstig uit zowel historische tijdschriften als uit kranten en populaire bladen. Nadelman volgde het gelijkschakelend effect van de reproductie, en stelde de figuren samen uit fragmenten van verschillende herkomst. Daarbij accentueerde hij niet de stilistische en symbolische verschillen, maar concentreerde hij zich op formele

projects imitated historical collections without taking the logic of chronological order into consideration. This subversive mimesis of historical scholarship is duplicated in the mimetic character of Junceau's own work. His exhibition at Witte de With was installed as a fictive museum; but the genealogy that he outlined in this museum would never be permitted to enter official art history. The principles of that history could not hold up to the confusion of concepts that Junceau initiated by presenting his plaster and wax casts and their molds next to Roosevelt and Nadelman's imitations, as such emphasizing the reproductive rather than the autonomous character of his work. The concept of renewal as well as the notion of authorship become untenable. These works can not be classified into a linear order: their genealogy assumes the form of an uncontrollable proliferation of split offs and multiplications.[4]

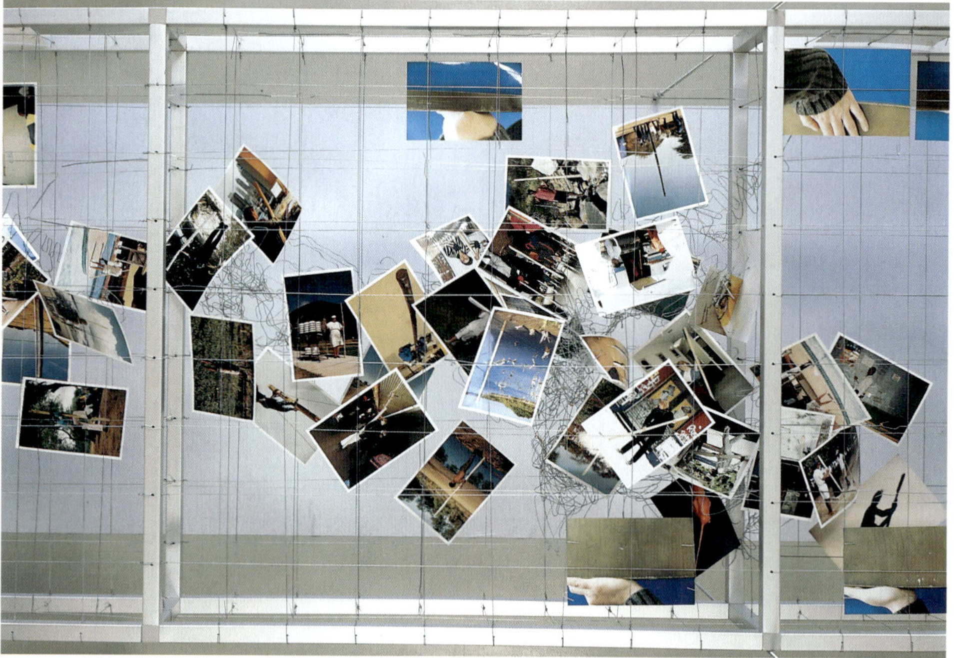

overeenkomsten, die het mogelijk maakten om bijvoorbeeld de kroon van een godheid te laten samensmelten met de haarband van een meisje. Nadelmans imitaties van oudheden vormen een verbasterd nageslacht, ze zijn schaamteloos anachronistisch, en volstrekt onbruikbaar voor de wetenschap. Elke poging tot plaatsing of interpretatie loopt stuk in hun opeenstapeling van stijlfragmenten.
Zowel Nadelman als Roosevelt maken op oneigenlijke wijze gebruik van historische bronnen; hun œuvres imiteren de geschiedkundige verzameling, maar zonder rekening te houden met de logica van de chronologische opeenvolging. Deze subversieve mimesis van de geschiedwetenschap wordt verdubbeld in het mimetische karakter van Junceau's eigen werk. Zijn tentoonstelling in Witte de With was ingericht als een fictief museum; de genealogie die in dit museum werd geschetst zou echter nooit zijn toegelaten op het terrein van de officiële kunstgeschiedenis. Haar beginselen zijn niet bestand tegen de begripsverwarring die Junceau in gang zet door zijn gipsen en wassen afgietsels en hun mallen naast de imitaties van Roose-

Christoph Fink's œuvre appears to be related to a scientific project as well. The drawings he makes during his trips through the urban landscape make one think at first of cartography. Yet Fink has expanded the territory of the itinerary. The usual place markers are supplemented by equally precise notations of less stable data: chance meetings, variable weather conditions, temporary traces of smell or sound and personal musings are also charted. The entire route is above all provided with a dimension of time: all notes are accompanied by precise time indications. While the drawings made en route still give the impression of completed city maps, Fink upsets that illusion with the series of successive revisions which he makes based on his initial notes. Before drawing he places a carbon sheet under his notebook. It becomes a single drawing reflection on the entire trip, in which all individual outlines merge into a convoluted tangle of lines. Where a customary map offers a footing by being limited to a well-organized display of highly selected markers, the carbon drawing

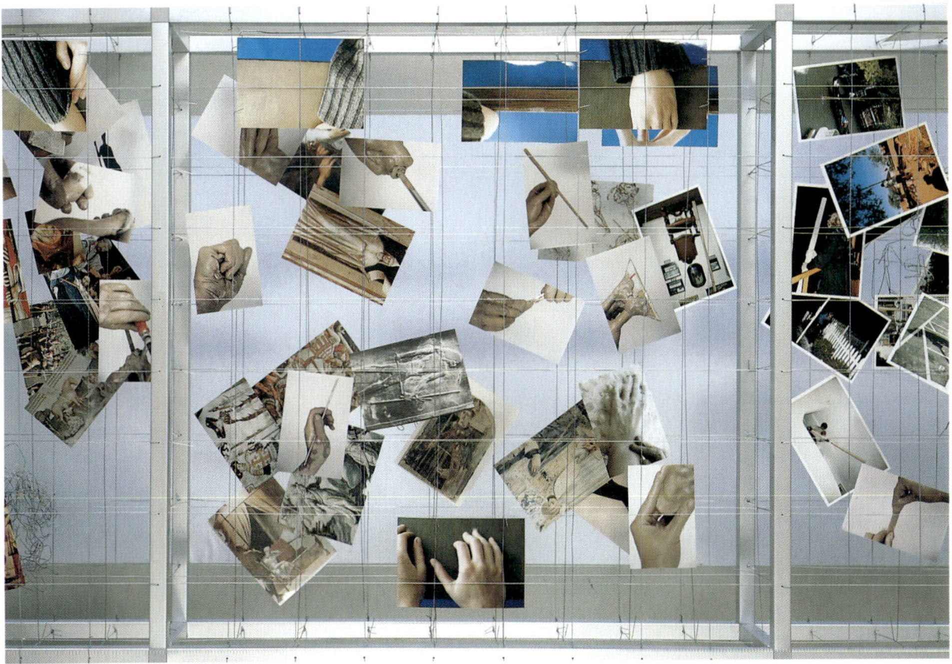

velt en Nadelman te presenteren, en zo het reproducerende in plaats van het autonome karakter van zijn werk te benadrukken. Zowel het begrip vernieuwing als de notie van auteurschap worden hier onhoudbaar. Deze werken laten zich niet in een lineaire opeenvolging rubriceren: hun genealogie neemt de vorm aan van een oncontroleerbare proliferatie van afsplitsingen en vermenigvuldigingen.[4]

Het œuvre van Christoph Fink lijkt eveneens verwant aan een wetenschappelijk project. De tekeningen die hij maakt tijdens zijn reizen door het stedelijke landschap, doen in eerste instantie denken aan de cartografie. Fink heeft het terrein van de routebeschrijving echter uitgebreid. De gebruikelijke indicaties van plaats worden aangevuld met even nauwkeurige notities van minder standvastige data: toevallige ontmoetingen, wisselvallige weersomstandigheden, tijdelijke sporen van geur of geluid en persoonlijke overpeinzingen worden eveneens in kaart gebracht. Alle notities gaan vergezeld van precieze tijdsaanduidingen. Waar de onderweg

reveals a buildup in which no individual starting point can be discerned. The so-called 'time-perspective drawing' is yet a step further removed from cartography. In this drawing Fink brings together the two sorts of time that he takes note of en route: continuous time, which puts clocked moments into chronological order, and stop-watch time, which measures the intervals in-between these points in time. In this work the itinerary seems to be calculated to the extreme. Rather than leading to a better comprehension of the territory in question, the calculation conversely generates a new landscape. The only thing to be concluded from this autonomous graph is that Fink's intentions radically depart from a cartographic scheme. Fink refuses to put the registrations of his trips to the service of bringing the landscape under control. This continuous revision of facts does not elucidate; it intensifies the travel experience. He doesn't aim to rationalize but rather pushes scientific principles as far as possible, until they exceed their own purposes and touch upon the immeasurable.

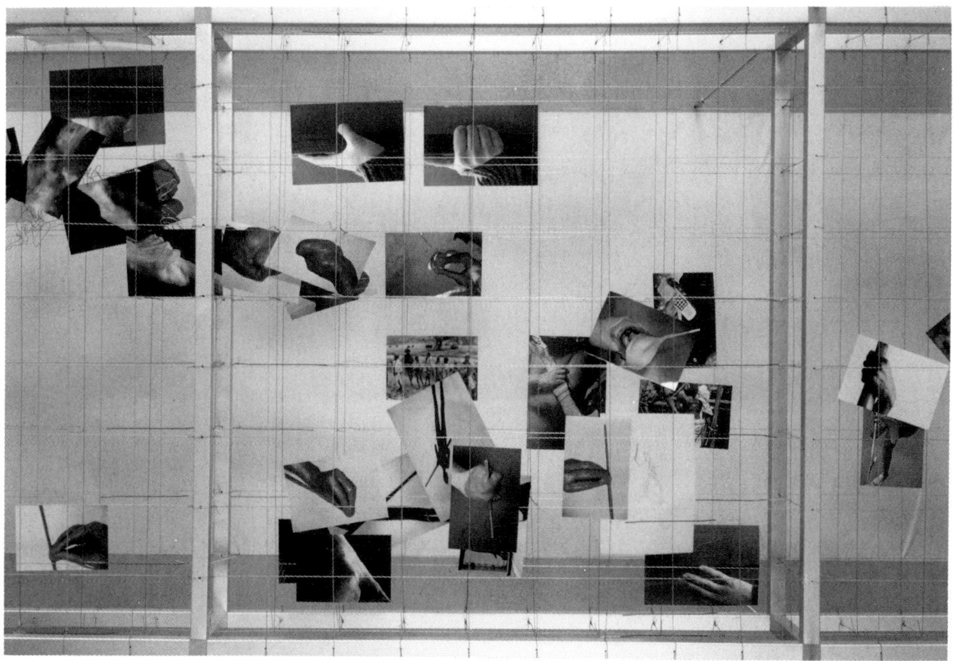

gemaakte tekeningen nog de indruk wekken van vervolledigde stadsplattegronden, verstoort Fink die illusie in de reeks bewerkingen die volgt op basis van die eerste notities. Het carbonpapier dat Fink bij het maken van zijn aantekeningen onder het notitieblok legt, geeft in één tekening de neerslag van de gehele reis, en doet de afzonderlijke overzichten opgaan in een ondoorzichtige wirwar van lijnen. Waar de gebruikelijke plattegrond houvast biedt door zich te beperken tot een overzichtelijke uitstalling van streng geselecteerde markeringspunten, toont de carbontekening een opeenstapeling waarin geen afzonderlijke aanknopingspunten meer te onderscheiden zijn. De zogenaamde tijdsperspectief-tekening is nog een stap verder van de cartografie verwijderd. In deze tekening verbindt Fink de twee soorten tijden die hij onderweg noteert: de doorlopende tijd die de geklokte momenten in chronologische volgorde plaatst, en de stopwatchtijd die de intervallen tussen deze tijdstippen meet. De routebeschrijving lijkt hier tot in het extreme te worden gemathematiseerd. De becijfering leidt echter niet tot een betere grip op het onderzoeks-

The museum and library in Junceau's work and the databanks and maps by Fink all refer to places in which our knowledge is collected and arranged. Both Fink and Junceau undermine these systems by bending their methods to their own will and by refusing to let them lead to any conclusions. The confusion they sow with this for the viewer confronts him with the limits of his systems of thought and provokes him to shift to other approaches. Precisely because their work appears to belong to a known order, Junceau and Fink upset the wavering balance of the mode of thought upon which this order relies.

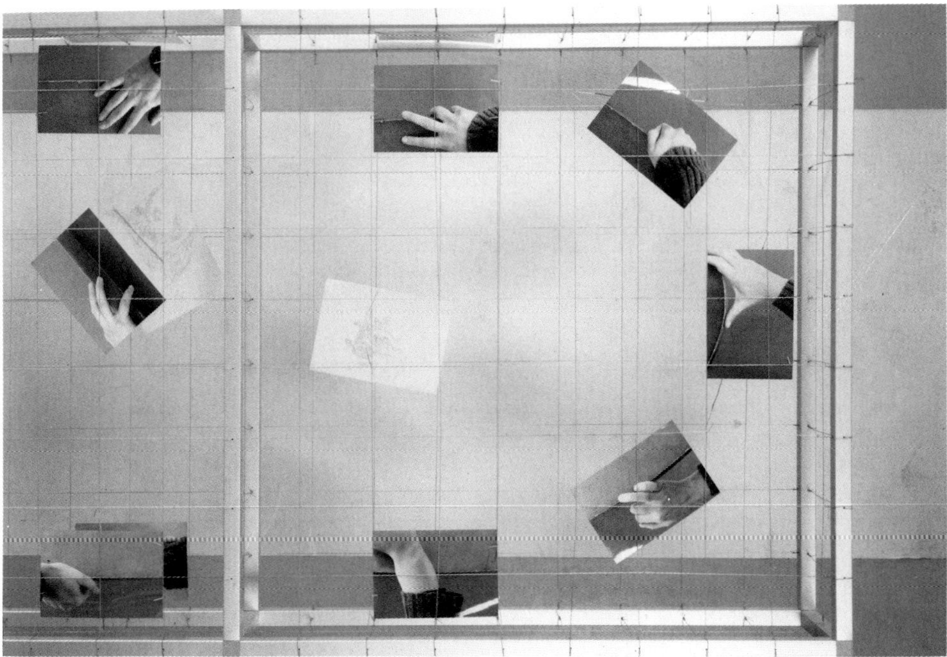

terrein, ze resulteert daarentegen in een nieuw landschap. Het enige dat zich uit deze autonome grafiek laat concluderen, is hoe Finks bedoelingen radicaal van de opzet van de cartografie afwijken. Fink weigert de registraties van zijn reizen in dienst te stellen van het beheersbaar maken van het landschap. In zijn steeds verder gaande bewerking van gegevens wordt niets verduidelijkt, maar worden de reis-ervaringen geïntensiveerd. Fink streeft in het geheel niet naar rationalisering, maar voert de wetenschappelijke principes zo ver door, dat ze hun eigenlijke doel voorbij gaan, en raken aan het onmetelijke.
Het museum en de bibliotheek in het werk van Junceau, en de databanken en kaarten van Fink refereren aan de plaatsen waar onze kennis verzameld en op orde gebracht wordt. Zowel Fink als Junceau ondermijnen deze systemen, door hun methodes naar hun eigen hand te zetten en de doeleinden waarop zij worden geacht uit te lopen te negeren. De verwarring, die zij daarmee onder de bezoeker van hun tentoonstellingen zaaien, confronteert hem met de beperkingen van zijn denksyste-

IV

Dröge-Wendel's Wooden Sticks also jolt our trusted way of thinking. The collection that makes up this installation appears rash. The concepts of the same and the other, upon which every classification is necessarily based, are completely passed by. In this installation, scenes with incongruous backgrounds are given a common ground without their origin, function or meaning being examined. Dröge-Wendel is blind to intrinsic difference. She literally keeps to the surface of what is depicted. This unorthodox indifference has far-reaching consequences: it strikes away the foundation of our entire knowledge. Modern thinking depends, as demonstrated by Michel Foucault in his archaeology of the human sciences,[5] completely on the difference between surface and depth. It presupposes that the essence of things lies under their superficial manifestation, that it hides behind the visible exterior, in a dimension that escapes sensory perception. Our thinking is focused on fathoming phenomena; understanding is reverting the visible to the invisible, to what is its deepest source and reason. The essential should be sought beyond the representation, and is only to be indirectly discovered: by way of interpretation. Dröge-Wendel defies these principles. She doesn't seem in the least bothered that things are not what they appear to be. Or that what she wants to show must not be sought behind or beyond the representation. It is rather entirely in the superficial dimension of the visible. The most important representation in the installation is thus also completely two-dimensional: a silhouette, in which every suggestion of depth is banished. This photograph is the key to the outlook upon which the whole

men, daagt hem uit om te schakelen naar andere benaderingen. Juist doordat hun werk van een bekende orde lijkt, brengen Junceau en Fink het denken waarop deze orde steunt uit zijn wankele evenwicht.

IV

Ook Dröge-Wendels *Wooden Sticks* schudt het denken waarmee we vertrouwd zijn dooreen. De ordening in deze installatie lijkt ondoordacht. Er is volstrekt voorbij gegaan aan de begrippen van 'het zelfde' en 'het andere', waarop iedere classificatie behoort te berusten. Scènes met onverenigbare achtergronden hebben, zonder dat is ingegaan op hun herkomst, functie of betekenis, in deze installatie een gemeenschappelijke plaats gekregen. Dröge-Wendel heeft geen oog voor inhoudelijk onderscheid. Ze blijft, letterlijk, aan de oppervlakte van de voorstellingen. Deze ongebruikelijke onverschilligheid heeft verstrekkende gevolgen: ze slaat de basis onder ons gehele weten vandaan. Het moderne denken berust, zoals Michel Foucault in zijn archeologie van de menswetenschappen heeft aangetoond,[5] volledig op het onderscheid tussen oppervlakte en diepte. Het gaat ervan uit dat het wezen van de dingen onder hun oppervlakkige verschijningsvorm is gelegen, schuilgaat achter de zichtbare buitenkant, in een dimensie die aan de zintuiglijke waarneming ontsnapt. Ons denken is gericht op het doorgronden van de verschijnselen; begrijpen is het terugbrengen van het zichtbare tot het onzichtbare, tot wat de diepste oorsprong en reden ervan vormt. Het wezenlijke moet gezocht worden aan gene zijde van de voorstelling, en is slechts te achterhalen via een omweg, de interpretatie.

collection hinges. Only when the other photographs are considered with the same superficiality, does it become clear what Dröge-Wendel's collection is about. In the silhouette, man and stick assume the form of one figure. It is on this figure that the other photographs are focused. Some photographs emphasize how people are always accompanied by objects. Others concentrate on the point of contact by cutting out only the hand and the object it holds. In some photographs the boundary between hand and object completely vanishes; by means of soft clay they seamlessly flow together into one whole in which it can no longer be discerned where the human body ends and the prosthesis begins. This connection is what all the representations have in common, regardless of their background. The differences in the sticks are thus of no importance. The sticks do not refer to the depths in which these differences keep hidden; they refer rather to the point where hand and object touch. The installation in which Dröge-Wendel assembled these photographs has as little depth as the representations it displays. The aluminium structure refers to a table, a flat model of arrangement in which things are placed next to each other. The structure is related to the installation *CD-Home* (1995) in which Dröge-Wendel, referring to how computers organize data, first presented photographs of the point of contact between hand and object. Both models represent a divergent way of thinking that breaks with the modern linear mode of thinking, which places things after each other. Dröge-Wendel doesn't hide a thing; she puts all her cards on the table. But we are not used to such obviousness; it's so self-evident that we overlook

Dröge-Wendel tart deze beginselen. Zij lijkt zich in het geheel niet te storen aan de conventie dat de dingen niet zijn wat ze lijken. Dat wat zij wil tonen, moet niet gezocht worden achter of buiten de voorstelling. Het bevindt zich juist geheel in die oppervlakkige dimensie van het zichtbare. De belangrijkste voorstelling uit de installatie is dan ook volledig tweedimensionaal: een silhouet, waarin iedere suggestie van diepte is uitgebannen. Deze foto biedt de sleutel tot de zienswijze waarop de gehele verzameling berust. Pas wanneer de overige foto's met eenzelfde oppervlakkigheid beschouwd worden, wordt zichtbaar waar het Dröge-Wendel in haar verzameling om gaat. In het silhouet tekenen mens en stok zich af als één gestalte. Het is deze figuur waarop ook de andere foto's zijn gefocust. Een deel van de foto's benadrukt hoe mensen altijd van voorwerpen vergezeld gaan. Andere richten zich op het contactpunt, door alleen de hand en het voorwerp dat het vasthoudt uit te snijden. In enkele foto's is de grens tussen hand en voorwerp zelfs helemaal verdwenen; door middel van zachte klei vloeien ze naadloos samen tot een geheel, waarin niet meer te onderscheiden is waar het menselijk lichaam eindigt en de prothese begint. Deze connectie is wat alle foto's, ongeacht hun achtergrond, gemeen hebben. De verschillen tussen de stokken zijn daarbij van geen belang. De stokken verwijzen immers niet naar de diepte waarin deze verschillen zich verborgen houden, maar wijzen naar het vlak waarin hand en voorwerp elkaar raken. De installatie waarin Dröge-Wendel deze foto's bijeen brengt, heeft net zo weinig diepte als de voorstellingen die zij erop uitstalt. De aluminium structuur refereert aan een tafel, een vlak ordeningsmodel, waarop de dingen naast elkaar worden geplaatst. De structuur is

it. By frustrating the automatism with which we immediately begin to interpret all representations when we see them, Dröge-Wendel, like Junceau and Fink, endeavors to prompt us into another way of perceiving. She does not offer an alternative interpretation, but wants to reveal a different way of seeing. The investigation into the relationship between people and objects that Dröge-Wendel undertook with the marriage project has nothing in common with the human sciences. Her approach is even scientifically completely irresponsible. An anthropologist would reduce the representations of the people with sticks to their origins. Following indications from the sticks, they would make interpretations about the capacities achieved by the people who produce and employ these sticks, of the needs and desires that led to the production of these objects, and of the meanings bestowed upon these objects by how they are used by man. But in *Wooden Sticks* man is no longer the subject of investigation. In this installation it's made clear what the far-reaching

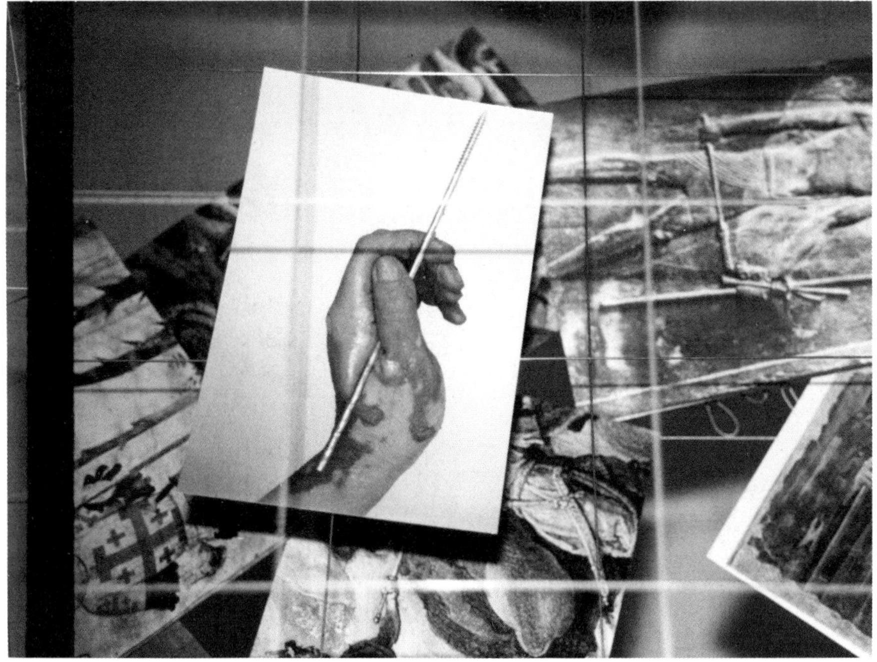

verwant aan de installatie CD-*Home* (1995) waarin Dröge-Wendel, verwijzend naar de manier waarop computers gegevens ordenen, voor het eerst foto's van het contactpunt tussen hand en object presenteerde. Beide modellen representeren een divergerende manier van denken, die breekt met het lineaire denken van de moderne tijd dat de dingen na elkaar plaatst.

Net als Fink en Junceau, tracht Dröge-Wendel ons aan te zetten tot een andere zienswijze, door het automatisme, waarmee we alle voorstellingen die we voor ogen krijgen onmiddellijk beginnen te interpreteren, te frustreren. Zij biedt geen alternatieve interpretatie, maar wil iets zichtbaar maken dat in de heersende visie noodzakelijk buiten beeld blijft. Het onderzoek naar de relatie tussen mens en object, dat Dröge-Wendel met het huwelijksproject startte, heeft dan ook niets gemeen met de menswetenschappen, waaraan haar projecten in eerste instantie verwant lijken. Haar benadering is zelfs wetenschappelijk volstrekt onverantwoord. Een antropoloog zou de voorstellingen van mensen met stokken tot hun diepste

implications are of the marriage between Yvonne Dröge and Wendel the piece of furniture. In this union what disappears from sight is man as an autonomous entity. It is because of this lack of independence that Dröge-Wendel considers men as invalids who, as the priest observed during her wedding, cannot exist without things.

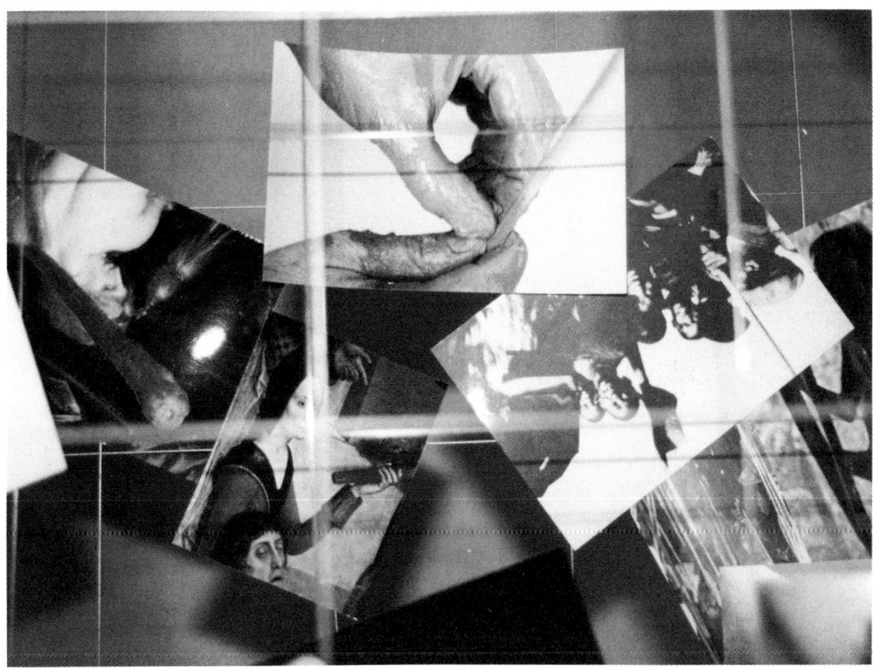

oorzaken herleiden. Volgens de aanwijzingen van de stokken zou hij interpretaties opdiepen over de vermogens die de mensen die deze stokken produceren en hanteren, hebben ontwikkeld; over de behoeften en verlangens die aanleiding gaven tot het produceren van deze voorwerpen; of over de betekenissen waaraan de mens door de wijze waarop hij deze voorwerpen hanteert uitdrukking geeft. Dröge-Wendels foto's zijn niet ingesteld op een bestudering van een handelend subject, dat zich door middel van zijn relatie met de dingen laat kennen. In *Wooden Sticks* is de mens niet langer het object van onderzoek. In deze installatie wordt duidelijk wat de vergaande implicaties zijn van het huwelijk tussen Yvonne Dröge en het meubelstuk Wendel. Wat in deze vereniging uit het zicht verdwijnt is de mens als autonome instantie. Het is vanwege dit gebrek aan zelfstandigheid dat Dröge-Wendel de mens voorstelt als een gehandicapte die, zoals de priester tijdens de huwelijksvoltrekking opmerkt, zonder de dingen niet kan bestaan.

1 *Dröge-Wendel. Objects Make Our World* (Amsterdam: Rijksacademie van Beeldende Kunsten, 1993), np. 2 The term 'well-equiped invalid' originates from the philosophy of Paul Virilio, who was a source of inspiration for Yvonne Dröge-Wendel's *La benedizione della macchina*. Paul Virilio, *L'Inertie polaire* (Paris: Christian Bourgois Editeur, 1990). 3 These reconstructions are described in: Brandt Junceau, 'The Late Style of Elie Nadelman,' *Witte de With - Cahier # 4*, pp. 103-118 and idem, 'The Franklin Delano Roosevelt Library,' pp. 119-137. 4 Roosevelt's and Nadelman's projects as well have always remained outside of official art history: they belong to a forgotten period which antedates modernism, when America first claimed its own place in art history. 5 Michel Foucault, *The Order of Things* (London: Travistock Publications, 1974). [Originally: *Les mots et les choses* (Paris: Editions Gallimard, 1966).]

Yvonne Dröge-Wendel
Universal Pattern, 1994-96
collection of the artist

1 Dröge-Wendel, *Objects Make Our World* (Amsterdam: Rijksacademie van Beeldende Kunsten, 1993), geen paginering. 2 De term 'wohlausgerüstete Invaliden' is afkomstig uit de filosofie van Paul Virilio, die voor Yvonne Dröge-Wendel een inspiratiebron voor *La benedizione della macchina* was. Paul Virilio, *Rasender Stillstand* (München/Wenen: Carl Hanser Verlag, 1992), p. 51. [oorspronkelijk: *L'inertie polaire* (Parijs: Christian Bourgois Éditeur, 1990)]. 3 Deze reconstructies worden beschreven in: Brandt Junceau. 'The Late Style of Elie Nadelman', *Witte de With - Cahier # 4*, pp. 103-118, en Brandt Junceau, 'The Franklin Delano Roosevelt Library', idem, pp. 119-137. 4 De eigenaardige œuvres van Roosevelt en Nadelman zijn dan ook altijd buiten het terrein van de officiële kunstgeschiedenis gebleven: ze behoren tot een vergeten periode, die voorafging aan het modernisme waarmee Amerika voor het eerst een eigen plaats in de kunstgeschiedenis opeiste. 5 Michel Foucault. *De woorden en de dingen* (Baarn: Uitgeverij Ambo, 1973). [oorspronkelijk: *Les mots et les choses* (Parijs: Editions Gallimard, 1966).]

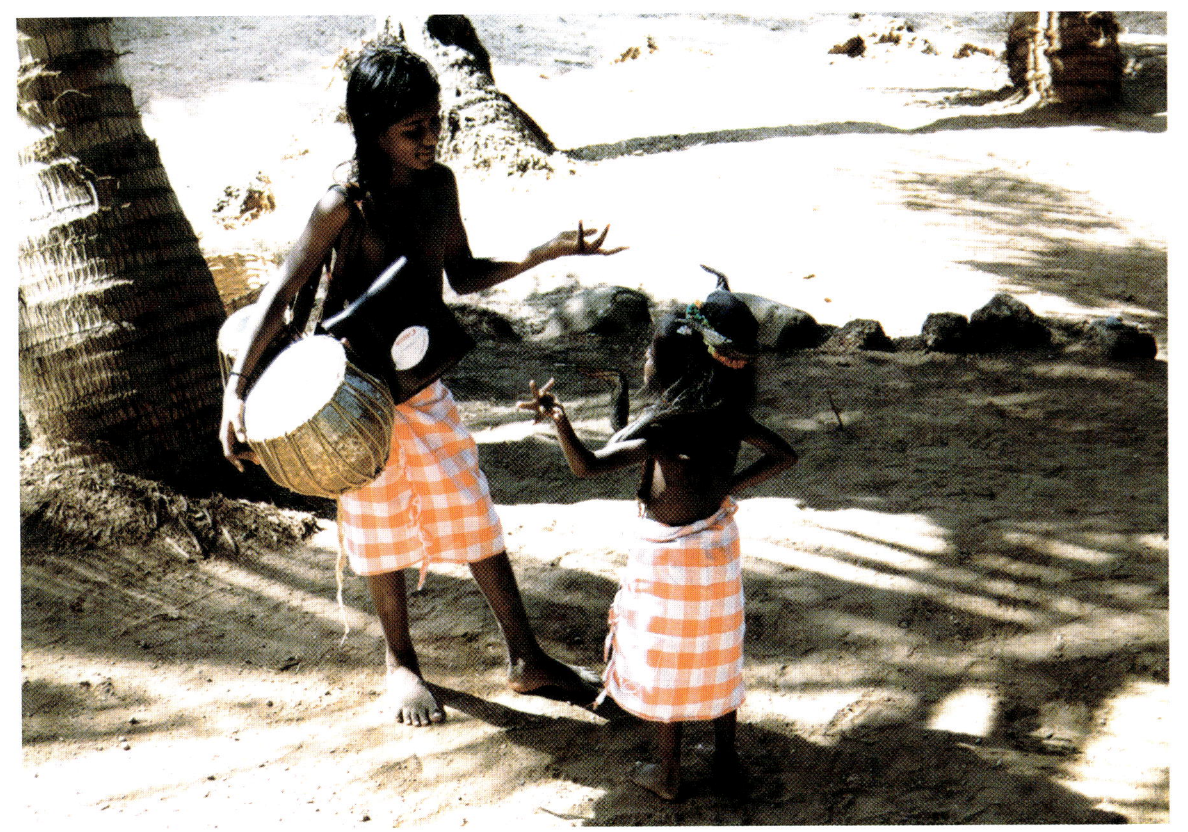

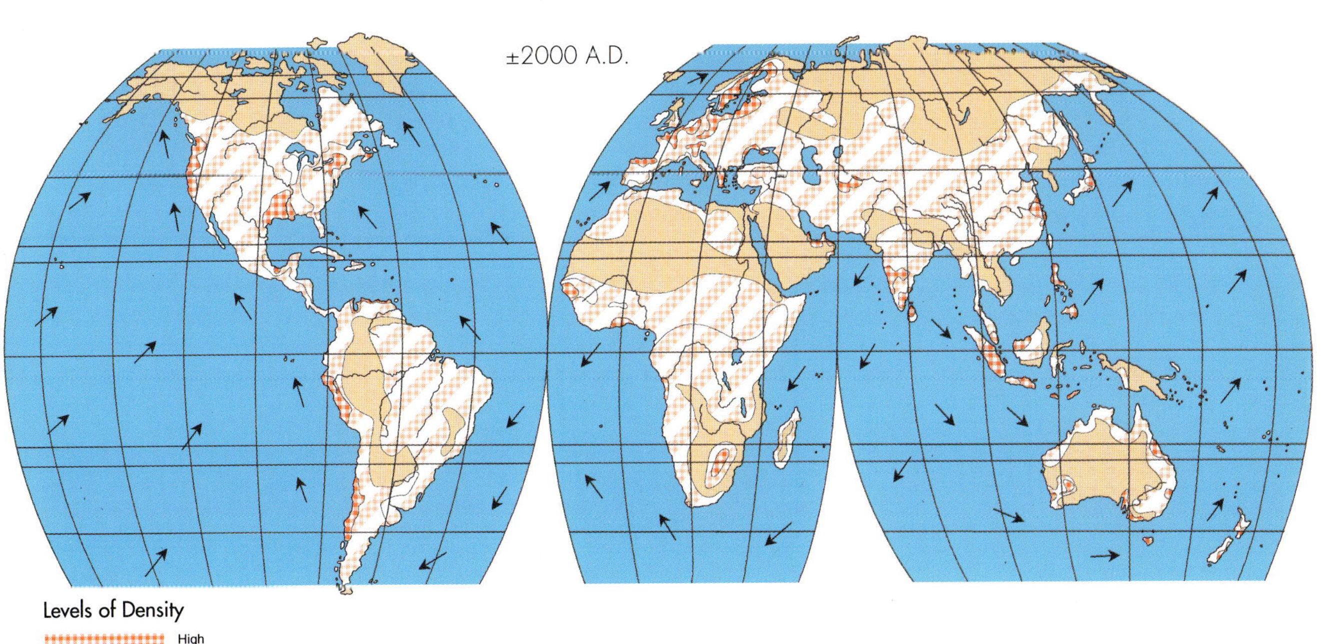

Levels of Density

High

Medium

Low

Density of Universal Pattern

Dröge-Wendel

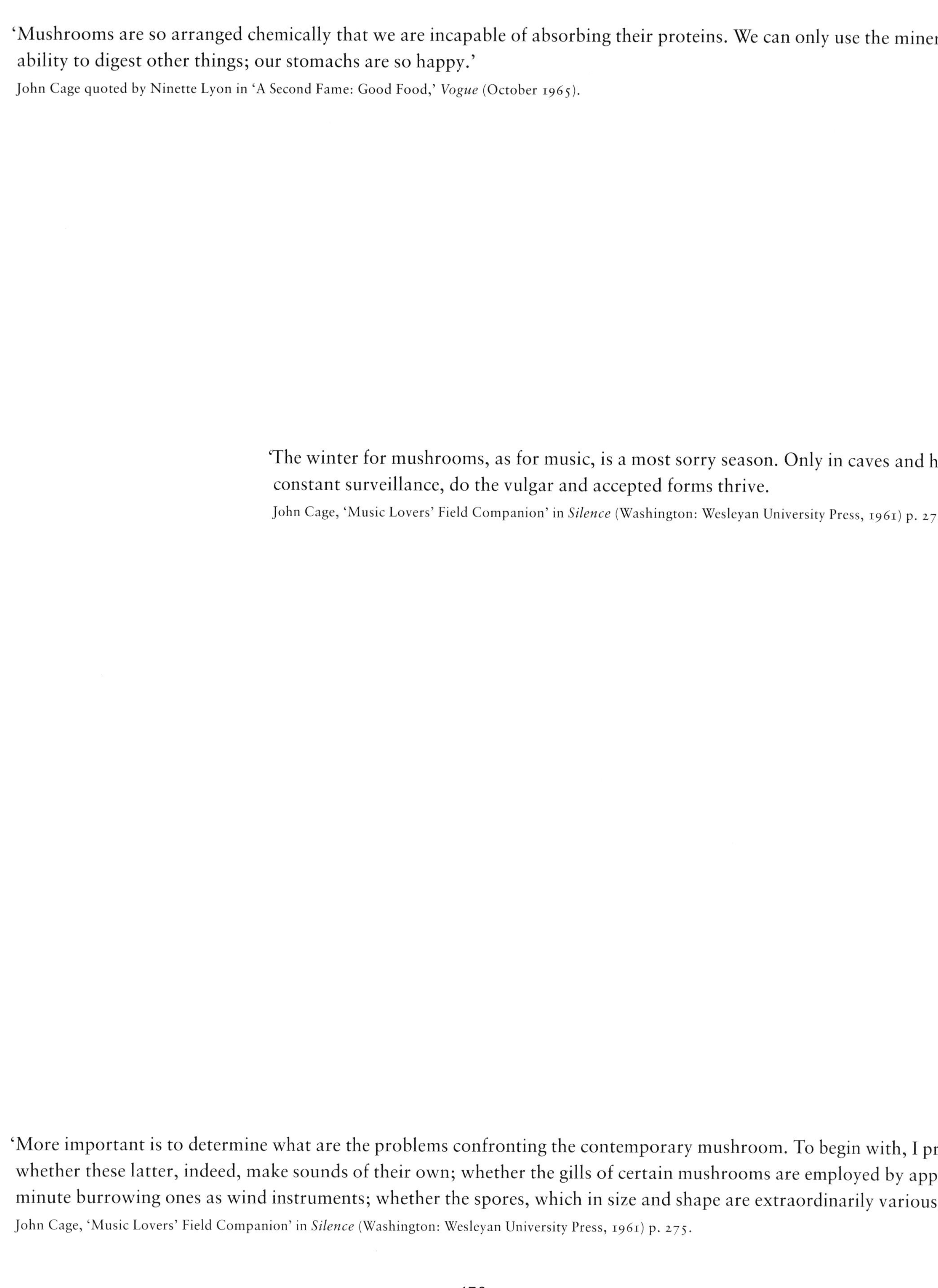

'Mushrooms are so arranged chemically that we are incapable of absorbing their proteins. We can only use the miner
ability to digest other things; our stomachs are so happy.'

John Cage quoted by Ninette Lyon in 'A Second Fame: Good Food,' *Vogue* (October 1965).

'The winter for mushrooms, as for music, is a most sorry season. Only in caves and h
constant surveillance, do the vulgar and accepted forms thrive.

John Cage, 'Music Lovers' Field Companion' in *Silence* (Washington: Wesleyan University Press, 1961) p. 27

'More important is to determine what are the problems confronting the contemporary mushroom. To begin with, I pr
whether these latter, indeed, make sounds of their own; whether the gills of certain mushrooms are employed by app
minute burrowing ones as wind instruments; whether the spores, which in size and shape are extraordinarily various,

John Cage, 'Music Lovers' Field Companion' in *Silence* (Washington: Wesleyan University Press, 1961) p. 275.

ins, and the water, which is not sufficient. But they taste so good they increase our

natters of temperature and humidity, and in concert halls where matters of trusteeship and box office are under

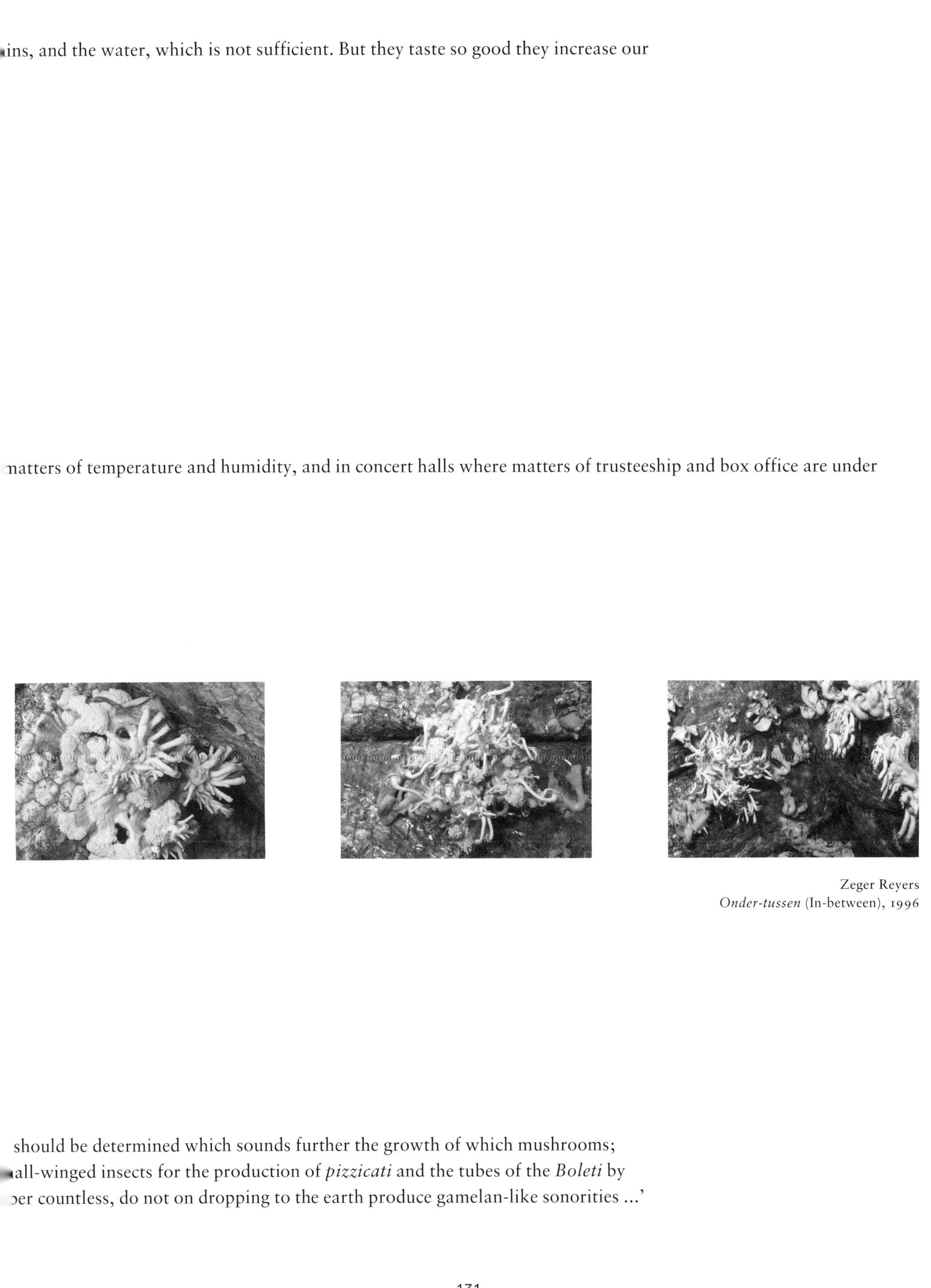

Zeger Reyers
Onder-tussen (In-between), 1996

should be determined which sounds further the growth of which mushrooms;
all-winged insects for the production of *pizzicati* and the tubes of the *Boleti* by
per countless, do not on dropping to the earth produce gamelan-like sonorities ...'

Jean-François Chevrier

Territory is associated with survival, intimacy, struggle. A territory is also a land, an inhabited landscape. Before it was taken up by sociology, the notion marked the meeting point of geography and ethology. When the land corresponds to a political identity, and particularly to the definition of a national entity (the nation-state of the nineteenth century), the territory defines a legal space of community belonging – and the stakes are effectively political.
I have consistently found this dimension at work, in various ways, among the artists I have met during my visits to Israel. The historical and political influence seems almost too obvious, as though it conditioned the visitor's perception, as well as the artistic activity itself. But to consider Sigalit Landau's work, I must examine this 'conditioning.'

Cultures with a pictorial tradition have consistently produced an imaginary translation of their territories, corresponding more or less directly to that first domestication of nature which is the cultivation of the soil. Since the days of Brunelleschi and Masaccio, the mosaic of cities and countryside that is Italy knit itself together through its painting, forming what Federico Zeri calls a 'visual myth' before actually constituting a nation (whose political and cultural unity remains fragile). In the painting of

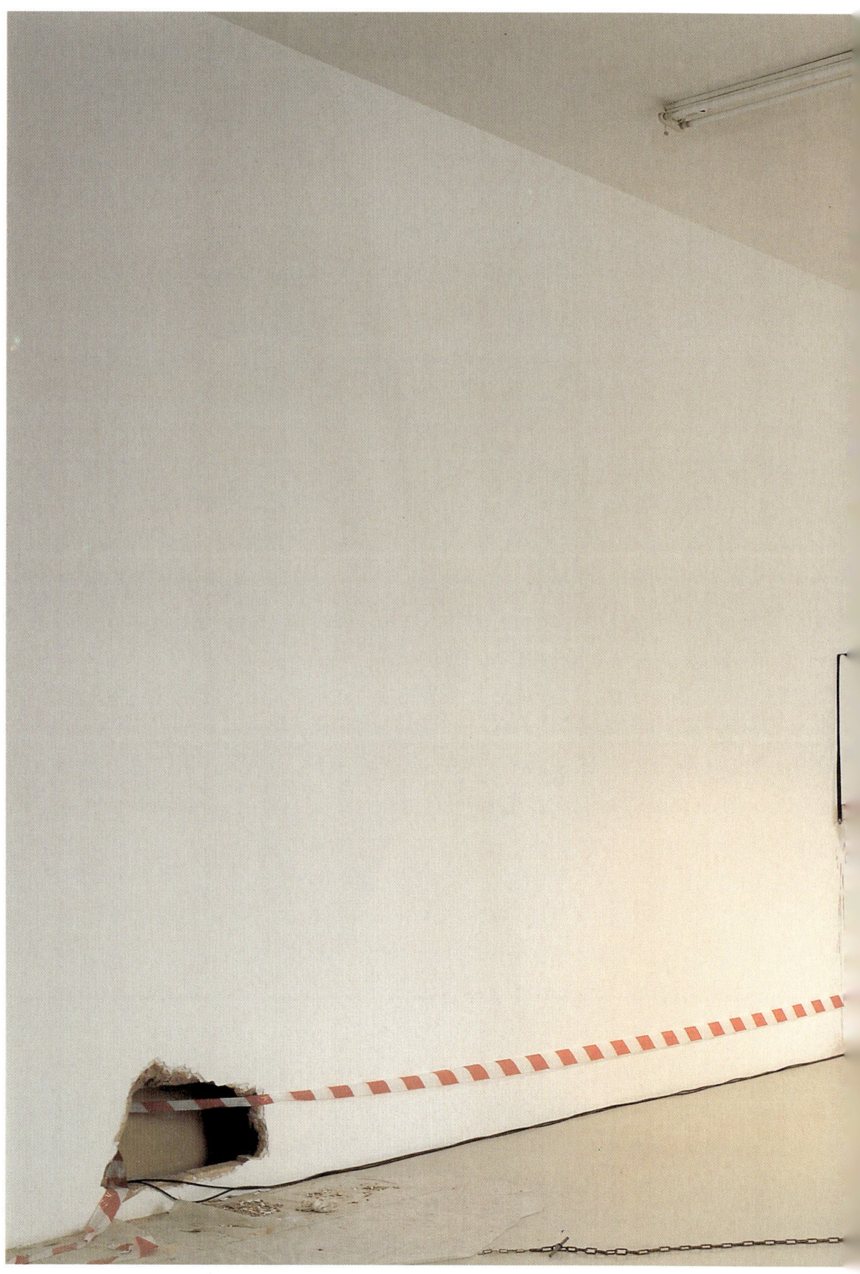

Sigalit Landau

Sigalit Landau
Sandblasting Lighthouse, 1996
mixed media
collection of the artist

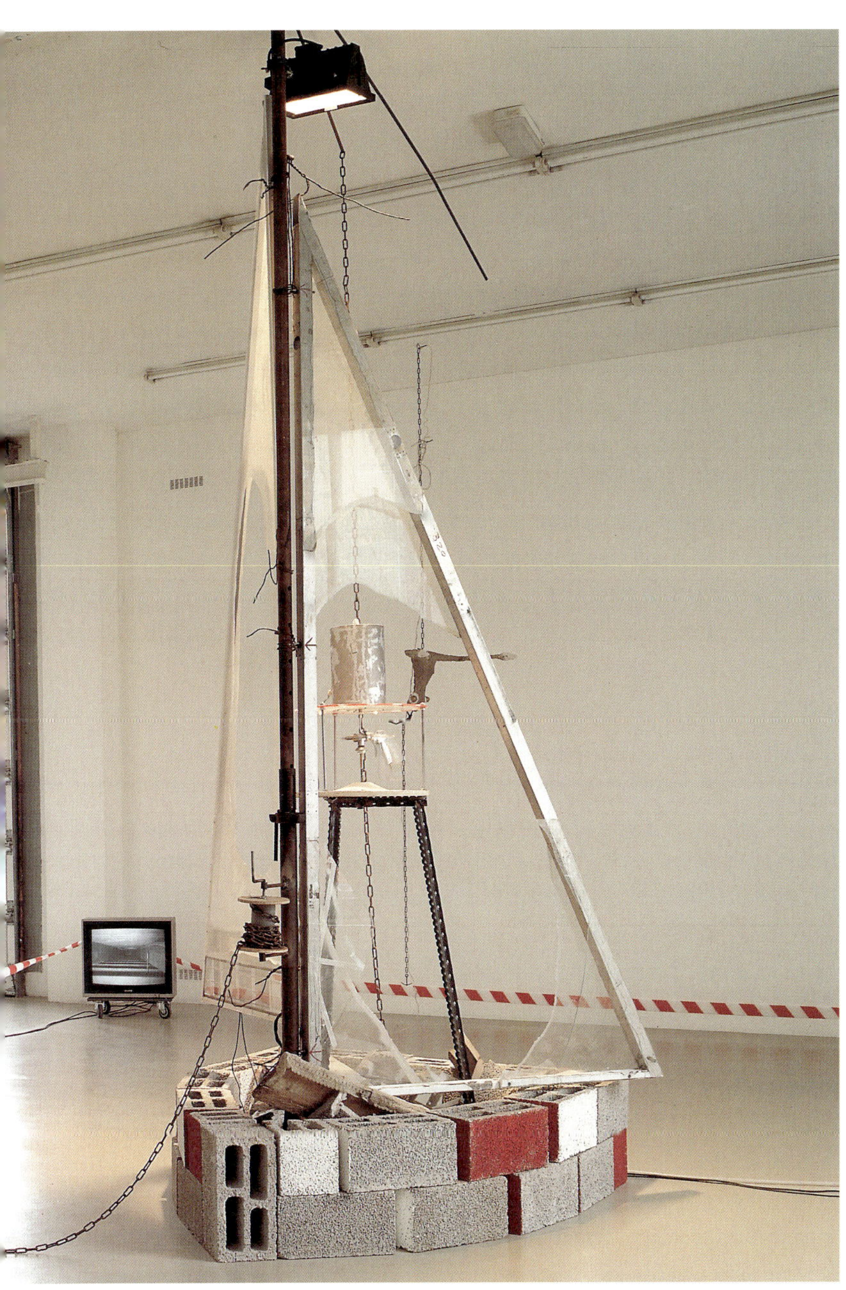

Au territoire sont associées la survie, l'intimité, la lutte.
Le territoire est aussi un pays, un paysage habité. La notion, reprise par la sociologie, se situe d'abord à la rencontre de la géographie et de l'éthologie. Quand le pays correspond à une identité politique, et particulièrement à la définition d'une entité nationale (l'État-nation du XIXe siècle), le territoire définit un espace légal d'appartenance communautaire et un enjeu effectivement politique.
Je n'ai cessé de retrouver cette dimension à l'œuvre, sur des modes variables, chez les artistes que j'ai pu rencontrer lors de mes visites en Israël.
La détermination historique, politique, semble presque trop évidente, comme un conditionnement qui s'exercerait sur la perception du visiteur autant que sur l'activité artistique elle-même. Mais, si je considère le travail de Sigalit Landau, je ne peux qu'examiner ce 'conditionnement'.

Les cultures dotées d'une tradition picturale ont produit systématiquement une traduction imaginaire de leurs territoires, correspondant plus ou moins directement à cette première domestication de la nature qu'est la culture de la terre.
A travers sa peinture, la mosaïque de pays et de villes qu'est l'Italie s'est rassemblée, depuis Brunelleschi et Masaccio, en un 'mythe visuel', selon l'expression de Federico Zeri, avant de constituer une nation (dont

Masaccio, the description of an urban site and of the population inhabiting it forms an archetype of the theatricality that defines the ideal locus of community in the European tradition. Pictorial description is an image of pacification, transforming the conflictual space of the territory into a landscape; thus in *Sauve qui peut (la vie)*, Jean-Luc Godard speaks of '*des pays sages comme des images*,' lands as tranquil as pictures. The pictorial form of the *tableau*, whether painted or photographic, is in itself, structurally, a form of pacification: it condenses, frames, knits together, composes. (In French the word '*composer*' also means to 'come to terms': with an enemy, with adversity, etc.)

The representation of nature in the West has been infused, at least since romanticism, by the recurring temptation of quietism, which identifies harmony with the absence of conflict. But this temptation is never more than an extreme form of dedramatization. In narrative paintings, the drama often contrasts with the peaceful (and indifferent) beauty of nature. Bertolt Brecht remarked exactly that in Bruegel's *Fall of Icarus*: 'The particular beauty and gaiety of the landscape during such a horrible event.' The gap has to do with the 'distancing effect': 'No painter, perhaps, has painted such a beautiful world as Bruegel, nor at the same time represented the frenetic activity of men as being so illogical. To his clumsy, ignorant, lost men, he has bequeathed a peerless world.'[1]

This pictorial tradition, associating the distance of the represented landscape with an imaginary pacification of the territory (in contradiction to drama), is precisely what Jewish-Israeli culture lacks. Here, as in many Western lands – not to speak of other civilizations – contemporary art cannot be the transformation of an indigenous pictorial heritage. The image-models come from elsewhere, from other cultural horizons or from more recent domains: the media, the cinema. Because it is situated between the fine arts and the media, photography can constitute an alternative to pictorial space. Until abstract expressionism, the American pictorial tradition was essentially photographic (in the nineteenth century, Carleton Watkins is more interesting than the painters of the sublime landscape). But it is understandable that this solution should appear as a kind of substitute, which does not give the artist a sufficient grasp of the environment. One problem is that photography has more to do with seeing than with making. Another is that the photographic image tends to be forced unequivocally to the side of the media, when it cannot somehow place itself within a well-established pictorial tradition. Still more, when the picto-

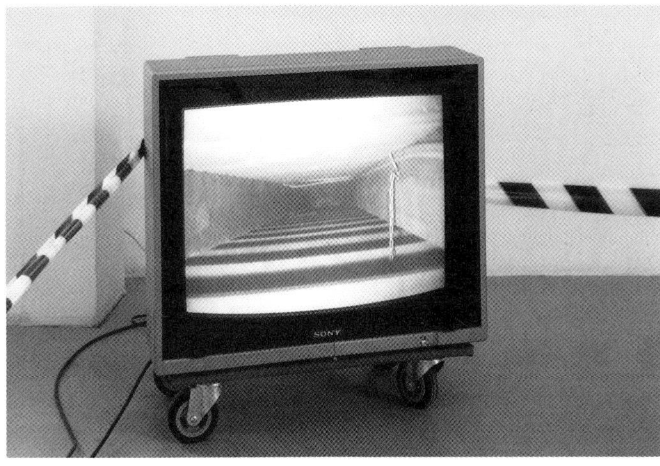

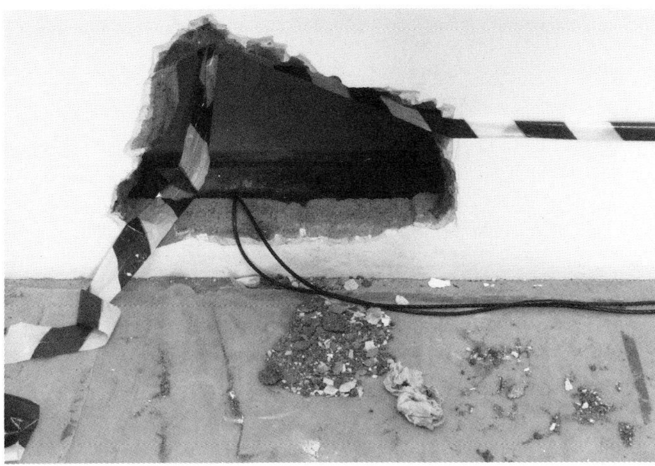

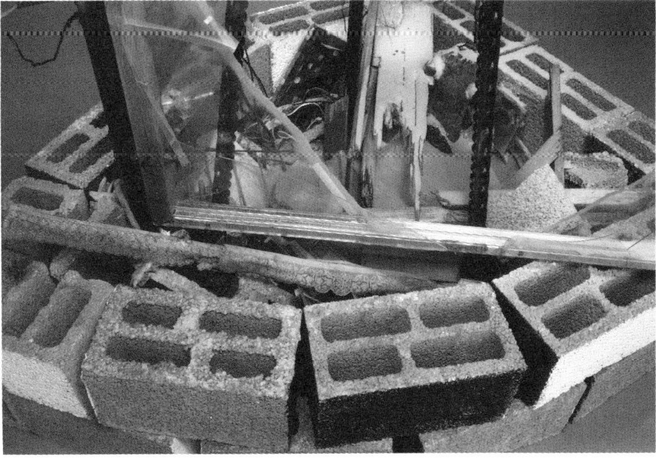

Sigalit Landau
Sandblasting Lighthouse, details

l'homogénéité politique et culturelle reste d'ailleurs fragile). Chez Masaccio, la description d'un site urbain et de la population qui l'habite forme l'archétype de cette théâtralité qui définit, dans la tradition européenne, le lieu idéal d'une communauté. Transformant l'espace conflictuel du territoire en paysage – 'des pays sages comme des images', dit Jean-Luc Godard dans *Sauve qui peut (la vie)* –, la description picturale est une image de pacification. Le tableau, peint ou photographique, est en lui-même, structurellement, une forme de pacification: il condense, il cadre, il rassemble, il compose. On peut dire en français 'composer' pour 'pactiser': composer avec l'ennemi, avec l'adversité, etc.

La représentation de la nature en Occident est hantée, au moins depuis le Romantisme, par une tentation du quiétisme, qui identifie harmonie et absence de conflit. Mais cette tentation n'est jamais que la forme extrême d'une dédramatisation. Dans les tableaux narratifs, le drame contraste souvent avec la beauté paisible (et indifférente) de la nature. Bertolt Brecht le remarquait à propos de *La Chute d'Icare* de Bruegel: 'Beauté et gaîté particulières du paysage pendant un aussi horrible événement.' Cet écart ressortit à 'l'effet de distanciation': 'Aucun peintre, peut-être, n'a peint le monde aussi beau que Bruegel ni

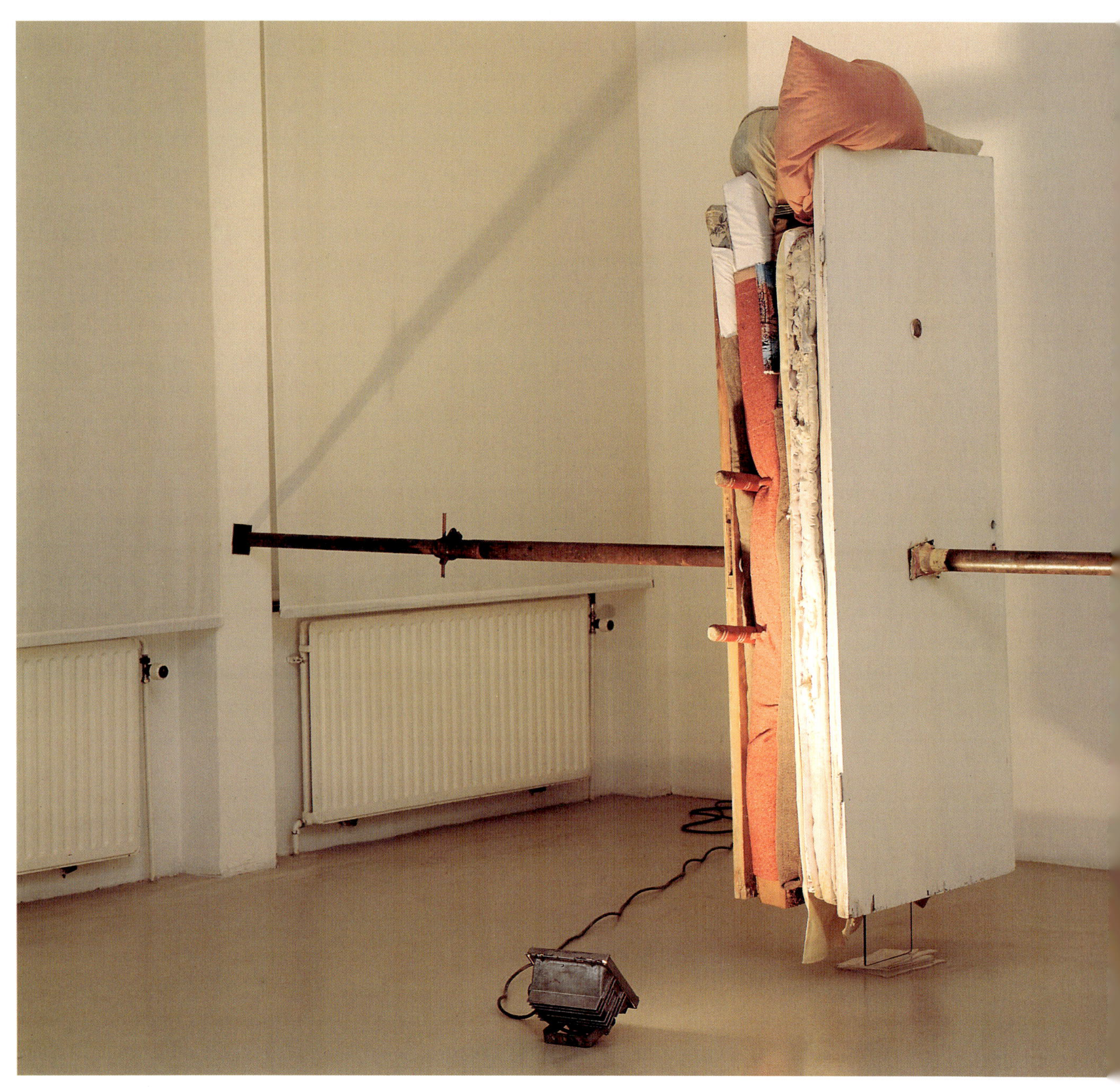

Sigalit Landau
Compressed Household, 1994
220 x 560 x 90 cm
mixed media
collection of the artist

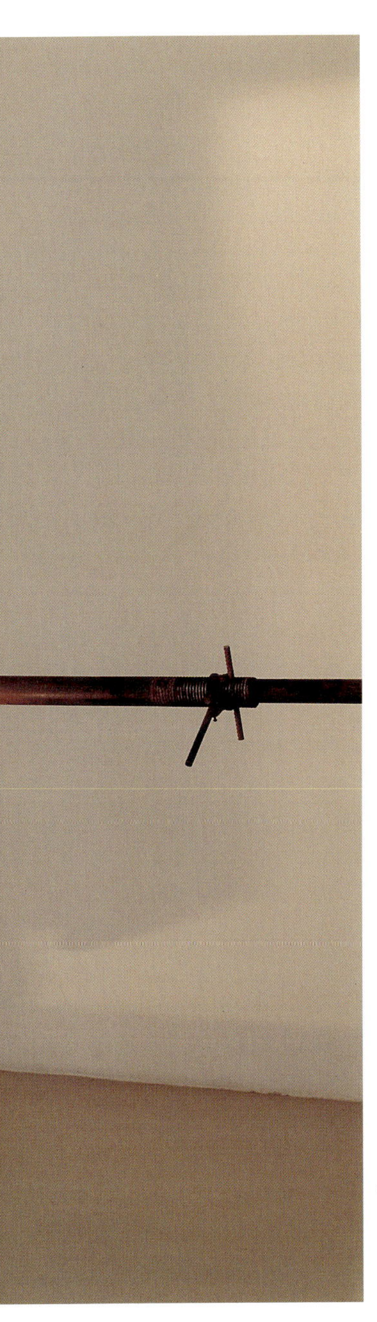

représenté en même temps l'agitation des hommes comme aussi illogique. Il a transmis à ses hommes gauches, ignorants, égarés, un univers superbe.'[11]

Cette tradition picturale, qui associe la distance du paysage représenté à un imaginaire pacifique du territoire (qui contredit le drame), est précisément ce qui manque dans la culture juive israélienne. Ici, comme en bien d'autres contrées occidentales, pour ne pas parler d'autres civilisations, l'art contemporain ne peut être la transformation d'un héritage pictural autochtone. Les images-modèles viennent d'ailleurs, d'autres horizons culturels ou d'autres domaines plus récents: les médias, le cinéma. Parce qu'elle est située entre les beaux-arts et les médias, la photographie peut constituer une alternative à l'espace pictural. Jusqu'à l'Expressionnisme abstrait, la *pictorial tradition* américaine est essentiellement photographique (au XIXe siècle, Carleton Watkins est plus intéressant que les peintres du sublime paysager). Mais on peut comprendre que cette solution apparaisse comme une formule de remplacement, qui ne donne pas à l'artiste une prise suffisante sur son environnement. D'une part, la photographie ressortit au voir plus qu'au faire. D'autre part, l'image photographique tend à être rejetée unilatéralement du côté des médias si elle ne peut se placer, d'une manière ou d'une autre, dans une tradition picturale suffisamment établie. Plus encore, quand le tableau, comme forme picturale, manque, et avec lui, l'idéal d'un espace autonome de la représentation, l'activité artistique doit constamment produire ses propres limites. Cette obligation a reçu toutefois une légitimité du soupçon jeté par les avant-gardes sur les idées de représentation et d'autonomie. A défaut d'une tradition picturale, Sigalit Landau hérite d'une tradition du soupçon. Elle invente des territoires, en semblant refuser toute résolution imaginaire du conflit.

Dans l'histoire de l'art moderne, le principe constructif et le modèle du montage, déduit du cinéma, se sont largement substitués à l'idée de composition. Mais la difficulté subsiste de penser la construction sans la représentation, à moins de sacrifier la dimension expressive et dramatique à une norme fonctionnaliste, qu'il faut alors soumettre à une critique, qui tend elle-même à se normaliser par un effet d'institutionnalisation presque automatique.
Le maître de Sigalit Landau, Nahum Tevet, connaît cette difficulté. Il exposait en 1991 au Tel Aviv Museum of Art, sous le titre *Painting Lessons, Sculptures 1984-1990*, des paysages-assemblages qui mêlent avec exubérance des éléments constructifs non figuratifs et des objets trouvés fonctionnels (tables, chaises, etc.). Comme

rial form of the *tableau* is lacking – and with it, the ideal of an autonomous space of representation – artistic activity must constantly produce its own limits. This necessity has gained a legitimacy from the avant-garde's suspicion toward the ideas of representation and autonomy. In the absence of a pictorial tradition, Sigalit Landau has inherited a tradition of suspicion. She invents territories and appears to refuse any imaginary resolution of conflict.

In the history of modern art, the constructive principle and the model of montage derived from cinema have largely replaced the idea of composition. But a difficulty remains, that of understanding construction without representation – lest the expressive and dramatic dimension of art be sacrificed to a functionalist norm, which then must be submitted to critique, which itself tends to be normalized by an almost automatic effect of institutionalization. Sigalit Landau's teacher, Nahum Tevet, has met this difficulty. In an exhibition entitled *Painting Lessons, Sculptures 1984-1990* in 1991 at the Tel Aviv Museum of Art, he presented landscape-assemblages with an exuberant mix of non-figurative constructive elements and found functional objects (tables, chairs, etc.). Like Guy Bar-Amotz, who also studied with Nahum Tevet and with whom she exhibited at the Israel Museum in Jerusalem, Sigalit Landau prefers to turn away from the lessons of painting and to introduce the dramatizing procedures of performance into assemblage. But where Bar-Amotz conceives his environments as integrated circuits whose range of expansion is strictly limited within the exhibition space, Landau occupies the space with a profusion of obstacles and involutions, shot through with breaches and thresholds. This double bid toward regressive accumulation and transgressive breakout was manifest in the exhibition at Witte de With. Each visitor could experience the artist's rage of intervention: the introversion of the constructive assemblages and the will to break out, to literally pierce through the limits of the institutional frame. Far from Israel, in a prosperous and relatively peaceful European city, the installation flung down the image of a conflictual territory.

As the insistent motif of shelter bears witness, this territory is also and above all a territory of intimacy. But it is an intimacy constructed in the terms of conflict, as seen among communities which cannot achieve social integration and are left adrift in urban, capitalist modernity. The *Sandblasting Lighthouse* (1996), without any rotating lantern and cut off from communication with the mainland – for its radio is broken – has washed up on the beach like a

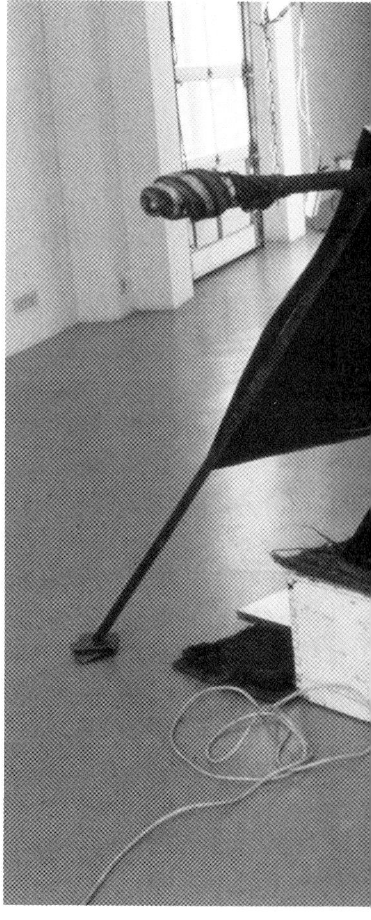

Sigalit Landau
Door Tent with Threshold Creature, 1994-96
300 x 210 x 122 cm
mixed media
collection Amos Natan, Jerusalem
collection Amir Weinberg, Tel Aviv

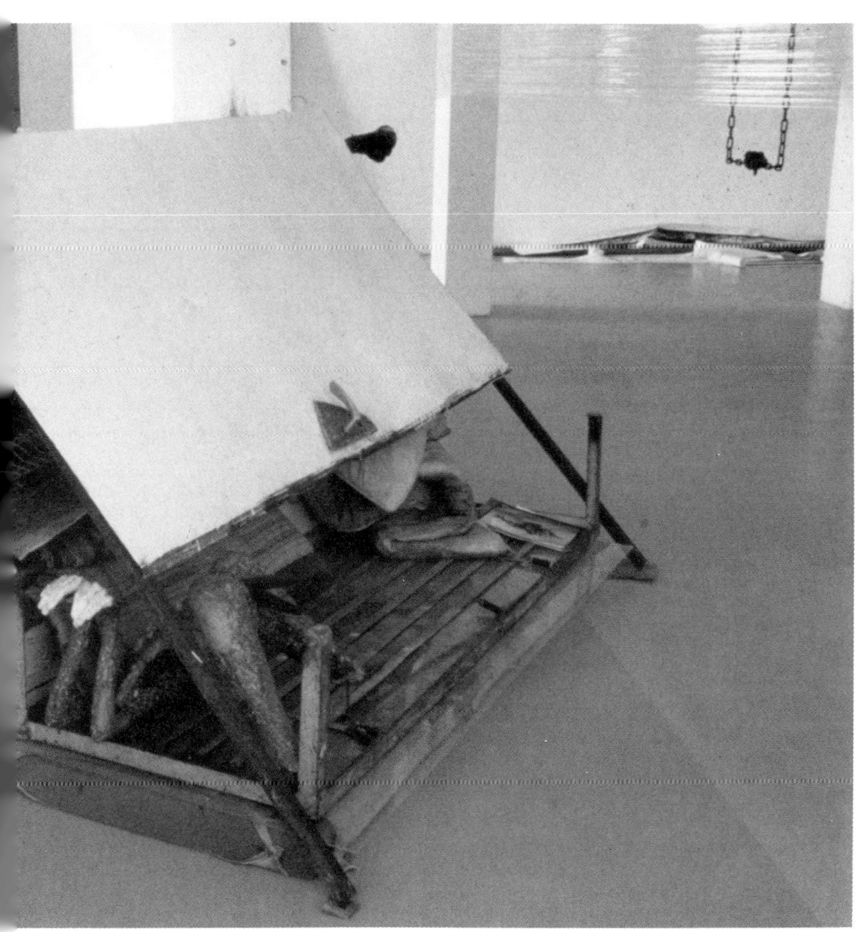

Guy Bar-Amotz, qui s'est formé également auprès de Nahum Tevet et avec qui elle a exposé au Israel Museum à Jerusalem, Sigalit Landau préfère ignorer l'enseignement de la peinture pour introduire dans l'assemblage les procédures de dramatisation de la performance. Mais, tandis que Guy Bar-Amotz conçoit ses environnements comme des circuits intégrés, dont l'aire d'expansion est rigoureusement délimiteé dans l'espace d'exposition, Sigalit Landau investit des lieux en multipliant les obstacles et les replis, autant que les percées et les franchissements. Ce double parti pris d'accumulation régressive et d'effraction transgressive était manifeste dans l'exposition de Witte de With. Chaque visiteur pouvait éprouver la rage d'intervention de l'artiste: l'intrusion des assemblages constructifs introvertis et la volonté de rompre, de percer, littéralement, les limites du cadre institutionnel. Loin d'Israël, dans une ville européenne prospère et relativement paisible, l'installation précipitait l'image d'un territoire conflictuel.

Comme l'atteste suffisamment l'insistance du motif de l'abri, ce territoire est aussi et d'abord celui d'une intimité. Mais une intimité qui se construit dans les termes du conflit, comme celle des communautés en rupture d'intégration, dans les sociétés en dérive de la modernité urbaine capitaliste. Le phare

stranded bark. Sand shot from a pistol-grip used for cleaning façades has invaded the hull of this lighthouse metamorphosed as a boat; ants tunnel through the drifts. The lighthouse is no longer a landmark but a shelter wrenched open, 'exposed' (exhibited). In the adjoining gallery, a tent, bent from a battered door of rusted metal – rather than a folded canvas – forms another shelter, more enclosed, but pierced nonetheless by five small eye holes, and filled with monstrous heaps (rugs, blankets, various accessories). Protection and accumulation are associated in this symbol of survival, the pile, so often found in assemblage art. This act of piling is analogous to the idea of the wrapper-man (*homme-emballage*) in the theater of Tadeusz Kantor, inspired by the sight of the homeless: 'the *itinerants*, circulating outside society in a perpetual wandering, without hearth and home, fashioned by their maniacal urge to *wrap up* their bodies in coats, covers, and shredded sheets, steeped in the complicated anatomy of clothing, in the mysteries of the packages, sacks, shopping bags, straps, and strings that serve to protect their bodies from the sun, the rain, the cold.'[2]

In 1994, during the weeks of *Art Focus*, Sigalit Landau occupied one of the empty spaces of a shopping center nearby Tel Aviv's new central bus station. She chose the most reclusive,

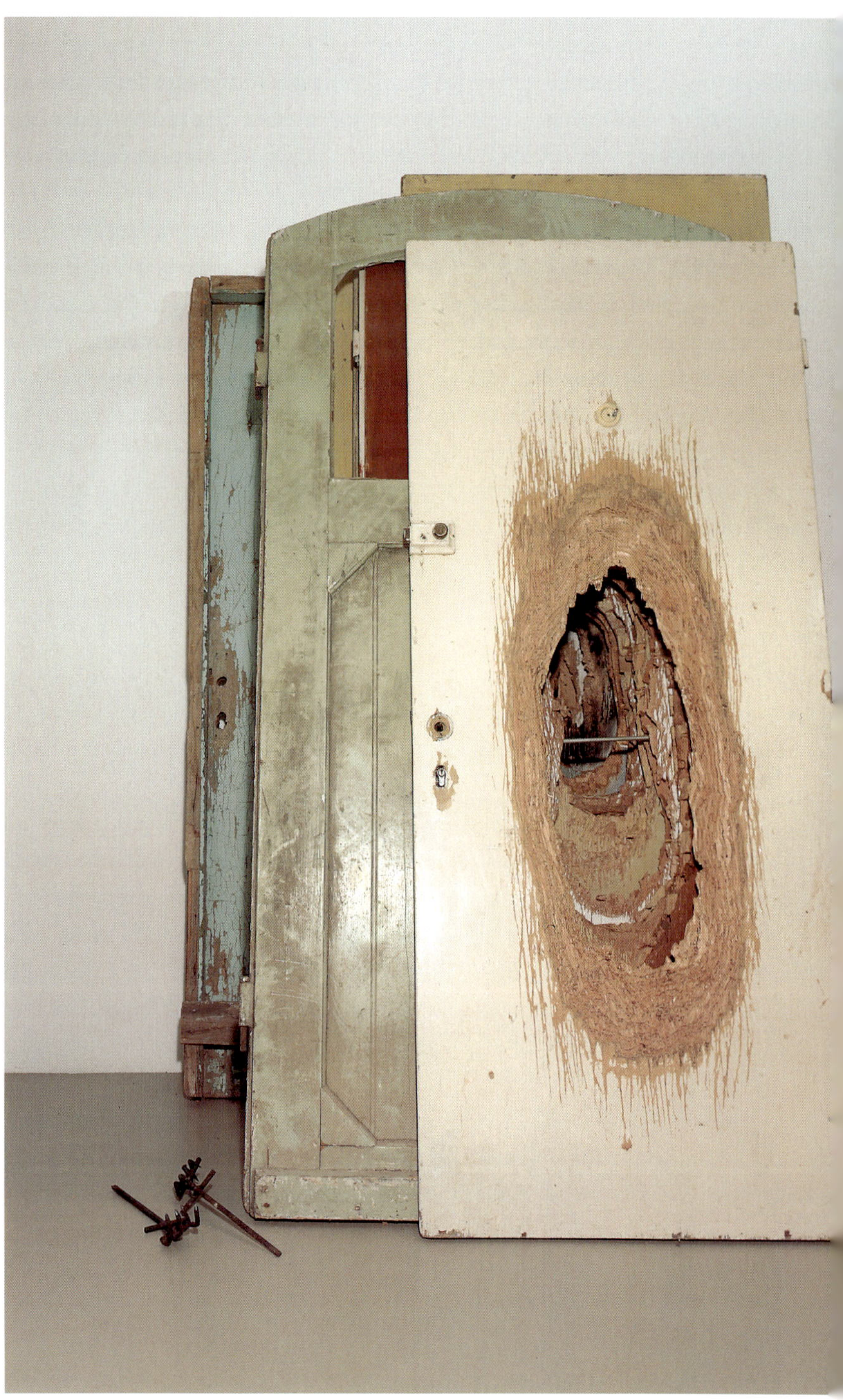

Sigalit Landau
Many Scratched Doors, 1994
210 x 100 x 100 cm
wooden doors
collection of the artist

(*Sandblasting Lighthouse*, 1996), sans signal lumineux, et sans possibilité de communication radio avec la terre ferme (la radio est cassée), s'est échoué, comme une barque ensablée: le sable projeté au pistolet pour nettoyer les façades a envahi la coque du phare métamorphosé en barque, où évoluent maintenant des fourmis. Le phare n'est plus un repère mais un abri trop ouvert, 'exposé'. Dans la pièce contiguë, une tente, constituée du pliage d'une porte défoncée en métal rouillé – plutôt que d'une toile dépliée – est un autre abri, plus fermé, percé toutefois de cinq oeilletons, et monstrueusement encombré (tapis, couvertures, accessoires divers). Protection et accumulation sont associées dans une sorte d'entassement symbolique de survie, comme on en trouve souvent dans l'art d'assemblage. Cet entassement est analogue à l'idée de l'homme-emballage dans le théâtre de Tadeusz Kantor, qui s'était inspiré de la vue des sans-abris: 'les *hommes itinérants*, circulant en dehors de la société, dans une perpétuelle errance, sans feu ni lieu, formés par leur folie maniaque d'*emballer* leurs corps dans des manteaux, couvertures, pièces de drap, plongés dans l'anatomie compliquée du vêtement, dans les mystères des paquets, des sacs, des cabas, de courroies, de ficelles qui doivent protéger leurs corps du soleil, de la pluie et du froid.'[2]

En 1994, pendant les semaines d'*Art Focus*, Sigalit Landau avait investi l'un des espaces vacants du complexe commercial adjoint à la nouvelle station centrale d'autobus de Tel Aviv. Elle avait choisi l'endroit le plus reculé, le plus secret, pour en faire un abri qui fût aussi un atelier semi-public. Deux éléments de cette installation ont été transportés à Rotterdam: *Compressed Household*, la compression de matelas suspendus entre deux tubes d'échaffaudage (tendus d'un mur à un autre) et *Many Scratched Doors*. Les portes superposées forment un volume feuilleté dans lequel un grattage obsessionnel, animal, a creusé une béance obscène. Une profondeur sans issue s'est définie dans l'épaisseur des panneaux de bois, qui déjoue à la fois le passage et l'obstacle associés au motif de la porte. Cette figure peut être interprétée comme une allégorie ironique de l'illusionnisme pictural, apparentée, sur un mode également ironique, au dernier environnement, voyeuriste, de Duchamp (*Etant donnés*, 1946-66). La trivialité compulsive et la patiente brutalité du procédé participent surtout d'une imitation du comportement animal, qui nous renvoie à l'interprétation éthologique du territoire.

Une autre pièce présentée à Rotterdam, plus évidemment allégorique, traite explicitement du territoire: un territoire 'blessé' (*Wounded Territory*,

secret spot to construct a shelter which was also a semi-public studio. Two components of this installation were transported to Rotterdam: *Compressed Household*, the mattresses compressed by two scaffolding tubes (jammed between the walls) and *Many Scratched Doors*. The stacked doors form a layered volume in which an obsessive, animal gnawing has hollowed an obscene hole. This exitless depth hewn into the thickness of the wooden panels plays simultaneously against the twin suggestions of passage and obstacle contained in the motif of the door. The figure can be interpreted as an ironic allegory of pictorial illusionism, comparable in an equally ironic mode to the final, voyeuristic environment of Duchamp (*Etant donnés* [Given...], 1946-66).
The compulsive triviality and patient brutality of the process is above all an imitation of animal behavior, referring us back to the ethological notion of territory.

Another, more clearly allegorical piece presented in Rotterdam deals explicitly with this theme: *Wounded Territory* (1995), a damaged land of refuge for *Life under a Stone*, the life of animalcula, the parasite crowd of the *Fungus* which infects the domain of the sacred (symbolized by an evocation of Temple Mount) and corrupts the work of art. While the other works of comparable size are conceived at the scale of the body, this one is presented as an imaginary landscape in relief, laid out at the visitor's feet. Even though it is constituted of heterogeneous elements, it is composed as much as it is assembled, because it combines figures through a metaphorical slippage, rather than assembling symbols: the checkerboard base of the landscape is formed of mouse pads, the mouse is transformed into soap (for purification), while the fungi become figures of a virus infecting the computer network. It's a funny montage. But this play of metaphor is less convincing than a violence that proliferates as it roams from place to place, unappeased, with no outlet.

1
Bertolt Brecht, *Sur le réalisme* (Paris: L'Arche, 1970), pp. 70-71.

2
Tadeusz Kantor, *Métamorphoses* (Paris: Chêne/Hachette, 1982), p. 56.

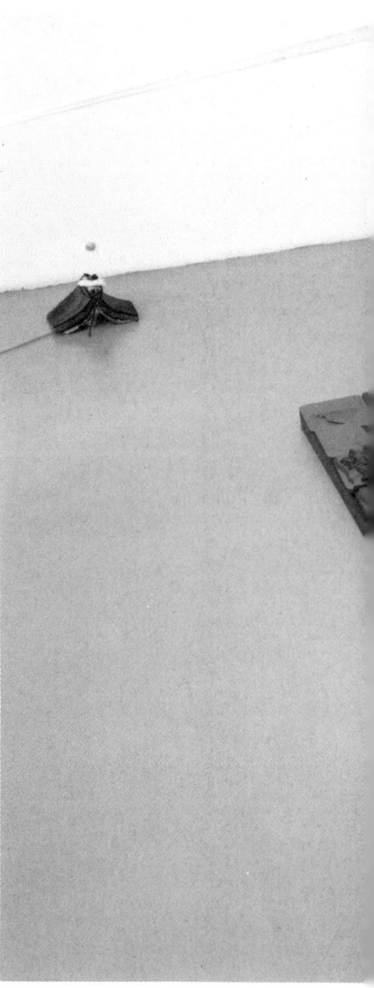

1995), où la vie s'est réfugiée sous les pierres (*Life under a Stone*) comme celle des animalcules, comme la foule parasite des moisissures (*Fungus*) qui infecte le domaine du sacré, symbolisé par l'évocation du Mont du Temple, et corrompt l'œuvre d'art. Tandis que les autres pièces d'importance comparable sont conçues à l'échelle du corps, celle-ci se présente comme un paysage imaginaire en relief, étendu aux pieds du visiteur. Même si elle est constituée d'éléments hétérogènes, elle est composée autant qu'assemblée, car elle combine des figures, par glissement métaphorique, plus qu'elle n'assemble des symboles: la base en damier du paysage est formée de *mouse pads*, la souris est transformée en savon (pour la purification), et les moisissures figurent donc les virus introduits dans le réseau. Le montage est drôle. Mais ces jeux métaphoriques sont moins convaincants qu'une violence qui se déplace et prolifère d'un lieu à un autre, sans apaisement et sans issue.

Sigalit Landau
Wounded Territory and Life under a Stone: Computer Mouse-pads, Fungus in Cage and Macintosh Soap, 1995
244 x 215 x 18 cm and 43 x 32 x 21 cm
mixed media
collection of the artist

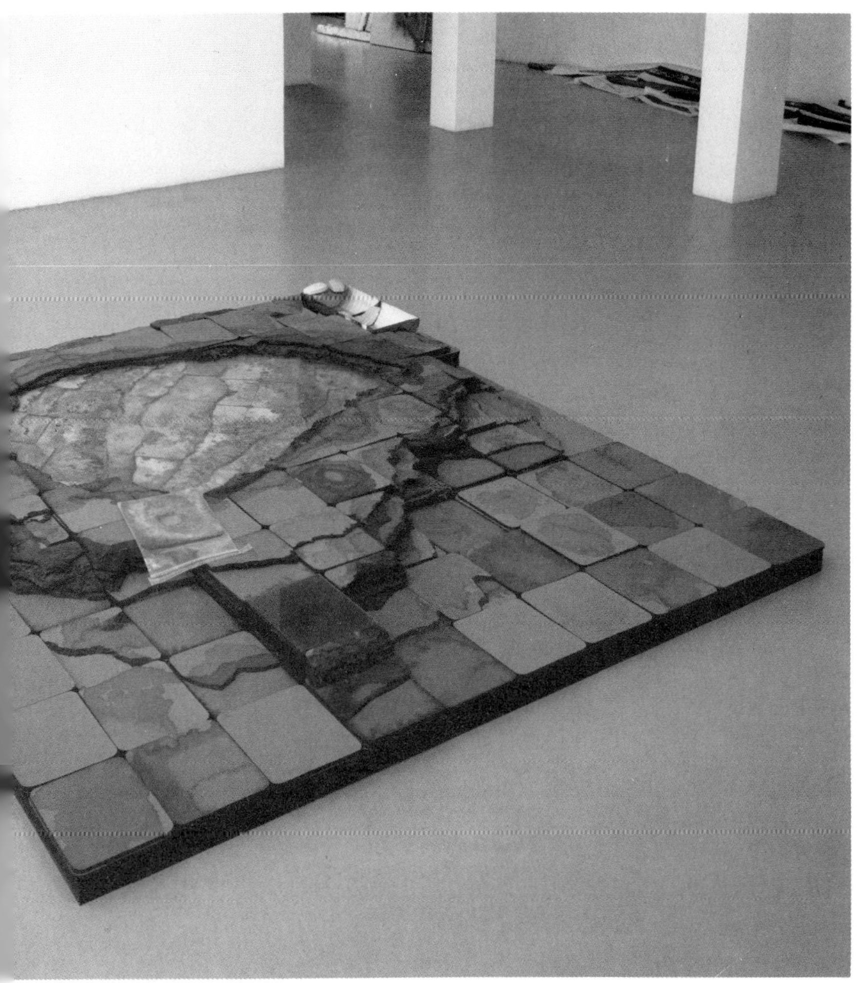

1
Bertolt Brecht, *Sur le réalisme* (Paris: L'Arche, 1970), pp. 70-71.

2
Tadeusz Kantor, *Métamorphoses* (Paris: Chêne/Hachette, 1982), p. 56.

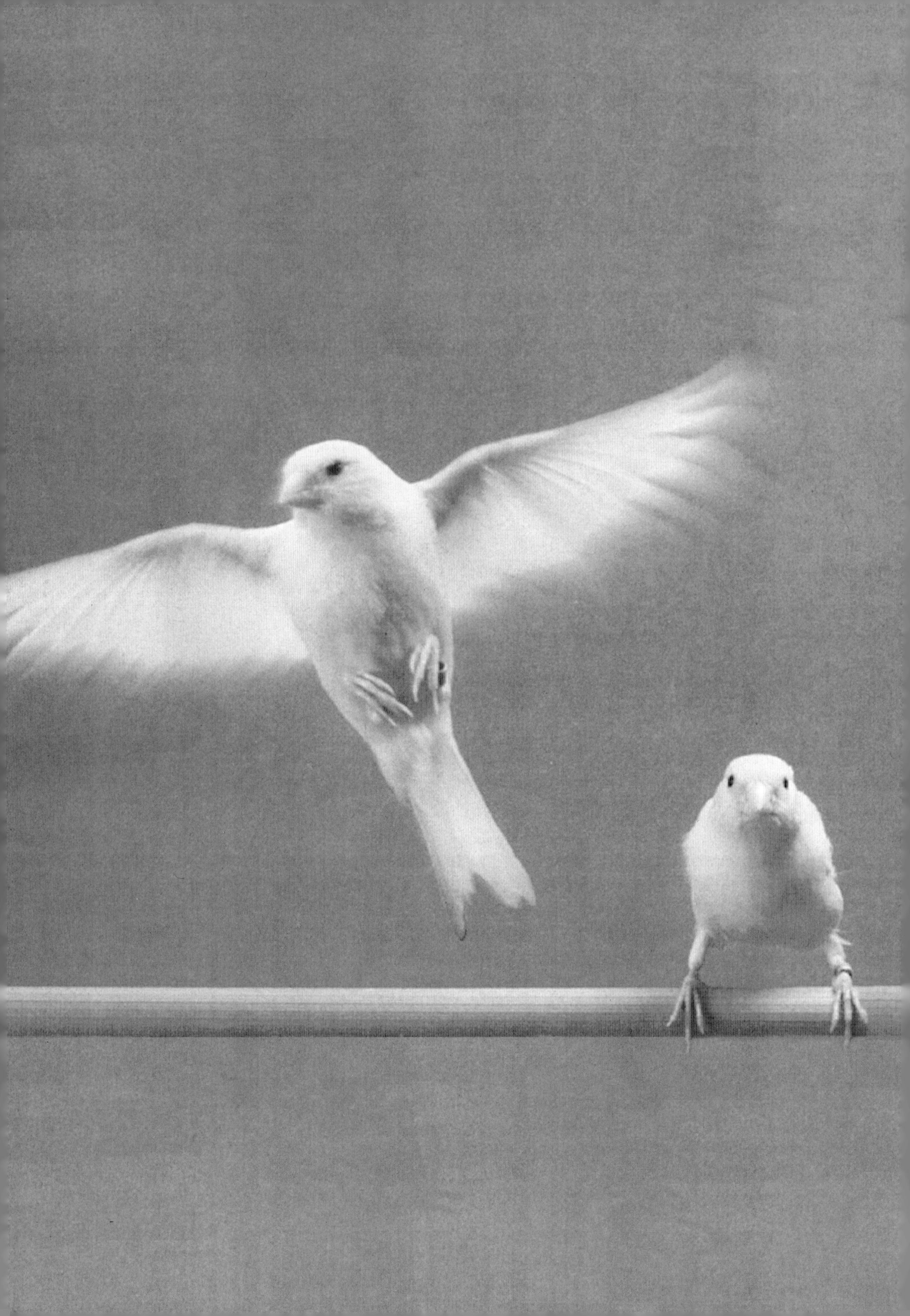

‘Migration as a Point of Departure’ was a Witte de With initiated discussion on migration, the theme of the exhibition presented at Witte de With by the curators of Manifesta 1. Manifesta is a new European biennial that aims to create a novel biennial structure. Each edition of Manifesta will take place in a different European city and will be organized by a different team of independent curators. Manifesta 1, held from 9 June until 19 August 1996 in various cultural institutions throughout Rotterdam, was curated by Katalin Néray, Rosa Martínez, Viktor Misiano, Andrew Renton and Hans-Ulrich Obrist.

Discussion participants were curators Rosa Martínez, Viktor Misiano, and Hans-Ulrich Obrist; artists Carl Michael von Hausswolff, Hale Tenger, and Jenny Marketou; Rasheen Araeen was the chairman.

04 MANIFESTA 1

Migration – as a Point of Departure

Anke Bangma (Witte de With staff member): The tradition of large manifestations on contemporary art has mainly been defined by *documenta* in Kassel and the *Venice Biennial*. These two manifestations have determined the conventional models for group exhibitions: they represent either the expression of the vision of one curator, or an unconnected assembly of national presentations. *Manifesta* intends to develop an alternative model for exhibitions of contemporary art. Witte de With could relate to this experimental set up. It can be compared to the exhibition *WATT* (1994), in which Witte de With investigated the possibilities of the group show by exhibiting the work of 29 artists in two separate institutions. We decided to support *Manifesta 1* by making our entire exhibition space available and by giving the curators carte blanche in selecting artists and conceptualizing the exhibition.

The theme of the exhibition presented by *Manifesta 1* in Witte de With is migration. It is a term which seems to point in many directions. The curators of *Manifesta 1* have presented it as a theme which wants to do justice to the cultural diversity in contemporary Europe, as well as an exhibition model which seeks to promote interaction between artists, and a basis for a dialogue about the state of European art. As a biennial without any fixed location or identity, *Manifesta* itself might even be considered to be a migrant. The theme of the exhibition at Witte de With therefore turns out to be the point of departure for the entire manifestation. But what exactly is the meaning of the migration that is reflected and promoted by *Manifesta 1*? It seems striking that *Manifesta* has been carried out, almost in opposition to its theme, as a strictly European biennial. With this discussion, Witte de With wants to analyze the meaning and potential of migration within these boundaries.

Rasheed Araeen: I would like to raise some questions about the concept of migration, historically, as a basis for dialogue. Particularly in the context of *Manifesta*'s proclaimed point of departure: that the present nature of European culture is cultural diversity. We should ask ourselves why migration has become such an important theme for dialogue, and we have to consider whether this dialogue is just illusion or reality.

Of course, the idea of migration is not new. Human beings have always moved from one place to another, in search of food and shelter. We can find literature going back to the ancient Greeks that expresses those experiences. But it has been unusual in the visual arts to make migration a theme. Nonetheless, artists have always migrated from one city to another, in search of a place to live and practice their art. Take, for example, some of the artists who participated in the large migration wave of the twentieth century: Picasso from Spain, Brancusi from Romania, Mondriaan from Holland, Kandinsky from Russia. They were looking for a metropolis where it would be possible for them not only to establish themselves as artists but to establish a dialogue with other artists within an intellectual framework that suited them. When Picasso and Braque met in Paris, they found they had something in common. It was dialogue, not differences, that brought them together. This doesn't mean Picasso did not go through the trauma of migration. But they wanted to transcend personal experience for something which they thought was a greater idea: exploring the artistic field to see if a common dialogue was possible.

This was not a unique experience; in fact, avant-garde movements such as surrealism and dadaism openly called for artists from all over the world to

A discussion

communicate with one another, to transcend nationalities. At that time however, the framework for dialogue between European artists and artists from 'the colonies' did not exist. After the Second World War the situation changed. There was a mass migration of intellectuals from the ex-colonies to Europe. Until recently, these artists were not concerned with the issue of migration in their work either. Now migration is becoming a common theme of exhibitions all over the world. Take, for example, the last *Sydney Biennial* and the next *Johannesburg Biennial*, both of which have migration as a theme. Considering its nominal role in art history, why is it that migration has become so important today? Why should it be the basis of dialogue between artists of different nationalities, cultures and races?

Jenny Marketou: You define Braque's and Picasso's migration as migrating to a center. I also migrated; I was born in Greece and now live in New York. Artists today raise rather the issue of the experience of what happens between point A and B. We don't really need to go to a center; we can be in any place to work and still communicate with each other. I think the sudden interest in migration results from the mode of communication and mobility that technologies such as the Internet have allowed us. Because we can move around much easier, we have become more and more conscious of this and it has become part of our artistic process.

Hale Tenger: Maybe I can add something to this from my personal experience. In 1988, I was studying in England for my M.A., and by the time my scholarship ended, I really didn't want to go back to Istanbul. But I did go back, and after settling down with my work, my social environment etc., I started feeling that I didn't want to live somewhere else. I want to live in Istanbul but be able to do the things that I would have been able to do if I had migrated elsewhere. I did not have any guarantee this would be possible at that time, because nobody knew what was going on there. The last biennials in Istanbul changed this.

Rosa Martínez: Maybe nowadays migration is really becoming a major issue because the social and economic conditions, as well as the distribution of work in our capitalist societies, make this problem very present. A form of migration is when one leaves one's country for another in order to find a better intellectual space or a new creative outlet. The other much more tragic form of migration is when one is forced to flee one's country for survival or political reasons. So perhaps we are much more aware of these things because we are on the defensive. I like the Moroccan sociologist Fatima Marnisi, who uses the harem as a metaphor to explain the differences between men and women, between public and private life, between the Western world and Islam. She finds Europe to be like a harem because she always has to have a visa to come here, and she feels as if she has to get the permission of the caretaker of the harem to go in and out. She thinks that Europe, even if we consider it a place of tolerance and inclusion, is still sometimes a place of exclusion. We have to deal with this ambivalence, with our wish to be open to the other and the necessity to close frontiers to feel safe. For me, these are fundamental issues in contemporary life and art.

Hans-Ulrich Obrist: I think this distinction between voluntary and involuntary migration is very important. In current discussions one often talks about voluntary migration, glorifies migration, and yet totally forgets all the involuntary migration which is going on. Adding to what Jenny Marketou was saying about communication, I really think that the Internet hasn't had an effect on migration. In her research on urban development, Saskia Sassen came to the very interesting conclusion that the Internet doesn't make cities superfluous. Most Internet connections, e-mail, etc., happen within big cities; and people still move to the cities. Until very recently, there was always the idea of the absolute center. In the eighties, cities like Cologne and New York were considered the absolute centers of contemporary art. During our research for *Manifesta* we observed what I think has become a very strong phenomenon over the last five years, that there is a multiplication of centers. For example, suddenly things started to happen in Glasgow. At the moment there is a similar feeling in many European cities. These cities are very self-confident that they can become centers too. Many art students I meet migrate through five, six different cities during their studies, which to me indicates that a very profound change is occurring. The centers are multiplying.

Andrew Renton: What occurs to me is that in the multiplicity of centers there may indeed be a disappointment at the point of arrival at this so-called center. You get there, but it isn't somewhere you can actually focus upon. You can't use it as a space for dialogue, as Picasso and Braque did. That doesn't exist anymore. The center isn't there. What happens upon arrival, then, is that rather than finding a new home base, a place to identify with, we are forced to retrace our steps in the light of that failure, and reconstruct our identity from something we vaguely remember from before. It is very interesting that *Manifesta* should take place in a city like Rotterdam, incidentally, because one of the disconcerting things about the city is that you can keep walking and never find its center. When it was rebuilt from scratch it could never grow organically around a center. It kept on shifting. I think this is how *Manifesta* has evolved, too.

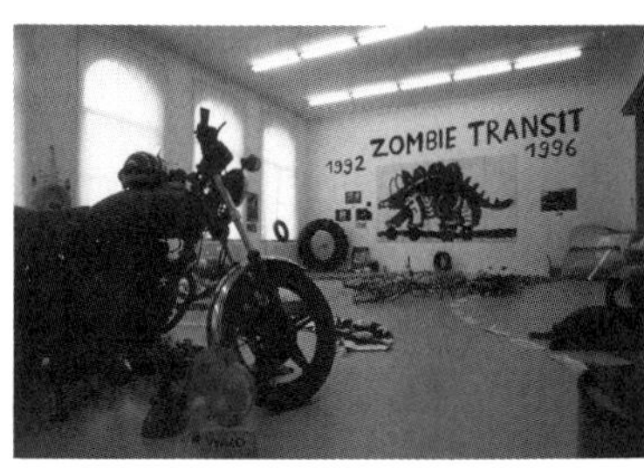

1

Bartomeu Marí (director of Witte de With): Another reason why migration is recently becoming more of an issue in the arts is because it is growing as a political problem. In countries like Germany or France there is social unease provoked on the one hand by the rise of fascism and on the other by serious economic and social problems. The politicians, who apparently do not know how to resolve their problems, have turned to the artists and intellectuals for help. Thus the French minister of culture has asked his country's art institutions and schools to come up with projects to address this social rupture.

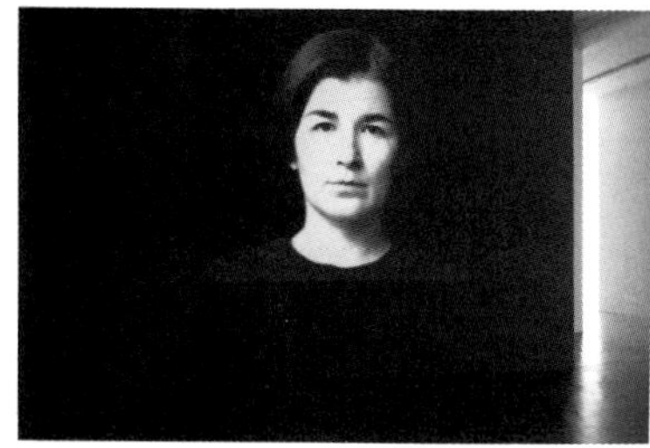

Hans-Ulrich Obrist: Paul Virilio in an interview I did with him for the *Manifesta* catalogue, makes a distinction between external and internal migration. External migration refers to immigrants coming to Europe from abroad. Internal migration refers to a movement necessitated by the short-term contracts, resulting from computerization and new technologies and the mass unemployment they have caused; it refers to people moving within Europe, giving up the need of a stable habitat for the need of a six-month job. While foreign migration can be enriching, Virilio feels internal migration can be dangerous to Europe.

Carl Michael von Hausswolff: Artists go somewhere because they want to do their work. But there is also this social, financial issue: they want to get famous! But when they have

done that, they could go somewhere else. It has very much to do with gaining power all the time. I left Götenberg. I did that city, I conquered it, and I am now conquering Stockholm. Then I'll go on.
But there is a new way of gaining power now: digital technology – you no longer have to physically go somewhere to gain power.

Viktor Misiano: All these new technologies like Internet and so on, for me, represent a new Utopia. For example, I edit a magazine in Moscow for which we are now creating an Internet version. We researched possible servers and we found the most convenient to be in New York. Though we keep underscoring this idea of a multiplication of centers, we should not forget that the art scene still exists within the structure of the art system, which is a structure of power. Artists from different regions of Russia come to Moscow, try to conquer the big city and next they will try abroad. Migration is a symbol of success! And within the system, it is a mechanism of symbolical exchange. But is that exchange a dialogue? Is the dialogue authentic or not?
For these migrants, a very precise game is involved: selling their identity on the art market. The more clever your sales pitch, the greater your success. This logic implies that a really authentic dialogue does not exist. If it exists, it is something very particular, very complicated and very risky.

Rasheed Araeen: Until recently, art institutions have been oblivious to the existence and histories of sixteen million migrants from Asia, Africa, and Latin America. Suddenly these institutions want to establish a dialogue on migration. But if they really want to establish a dialogue, they have to start by recognizing these ignored histories.

Jenny Marketou: I think artists always have been aware of the political time and space in which they exist; and the empowering institutions have always appropriated the displaced, the 'other' within the framework of 'multiculturalism' and self-representation for marginalized communities.
In my work, I examine the relationship between the experience of cultural displacement, migrations, and cultural identity. Now I find myself entrenched by 'politically correct' art which I find has become dogmatic, didactic, and too much about turning theory into art, and which confines the artist's aspiration to distancing or assimilation instead of a form of 'critical independence.' A good example of these kinds of works were shown in the 1993 *Whitney Biennial*. This is why I am interested in making art that, although it addresses issues of identity, questions of audiences and communities, and migrations across borders, focuses on the 'migrating,' 'volatile,' 'hybrid,' 'nomadic,' and 'participatory' qualities of the art object itself. This challenges our perception of the traditional art object, our desire to possess it, and the state of the institution. Because new technologies have played a key role in reshaping circulating cultural symbols, perception, mobility, and possibility, more and more artists have been involved with the Internet in making art projects. The Internet could become the escape from the patriarchal role of the art establishment. It enables interaction beyond the institutions and can be accessible in many places at once.

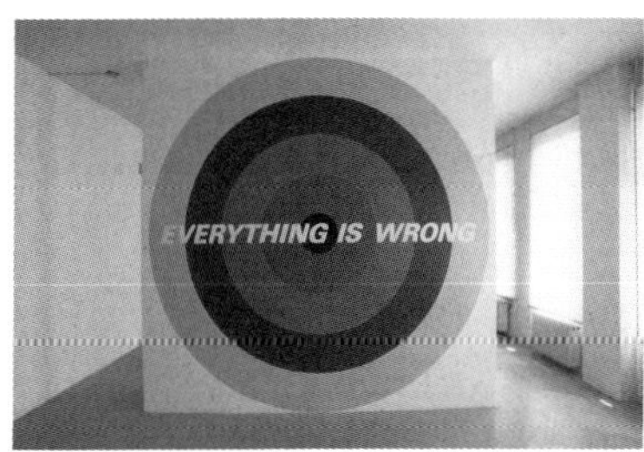

3

Rasheed Araeen: What worries me is that many artists are making statements on migration, are trying to have a dialogue, without taking into account the role of the institutions.
I am not saying that we can escape that control but I think it necessary that those controls be questioned and challenged rather then believing in the naive idea that human beings can communicate and transcend that control.
What is Europe? What is European culture? Is the migration

notion really a dialogue within the specific situation which exists today in Europe? When Europe was still a colonizer, artists from other countries came here with the idea that something common had been brought out by the globalization of modernism. They abandoned their particular visual arts and their particular traditions. They adopted modernism, thinking that it was something progressive, that their own culture would also shift from traditionalism into modernity. After World War II, artists from India, Africa, China, and the West Indies came to Europe, but somehow did not find the institutional framework which they expected, within which they could develop a dialogue with the European artists. This is why we do not know today the history of these artists of the last 45 years. If you are a white artist, (I don't want to use the word white, but I have no other choice) going through an experience of migration, you are aware of your history and that history is commonly known. But do we know the artistic contribution of the so-called immigrant community in Europe? The present doesn't exist without the past. I think that is the fundamental issue for all of Europe. Without knowledge of each other's histories we cannot construct any platform for dialogues on migration, or displacement, hybridity, or communication.

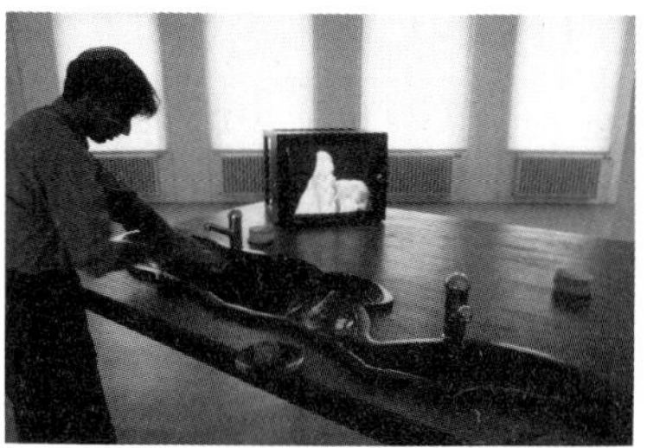

4

Carl Michael von Hausswolff: I trust my genes more than I trust any history. And I think that is true for quite a lot of people, especially young people who do not want to live in the past.

Rasheed Araeen: No, you cannot ignore the history. One must know one's own history.

Jenny Marketou: Nomads did not write their history; it was always passed on orally. The more I become aware and understand Western history, the more I don't want to read it. I don't believe in official history anymore, from which I have always been excluded. I want to define my own history.

Anke Bangma: I'd like to ask the curators a question. *Manifesta* is making art history, right now. It is defining how we will look at artists in the future and which artists will be part of art history. Don't you find it problematic that on the one hand, you are making a new basis for dialogue, implied by a theme like migration, but at the same time *Manifesta* is being presented as a European Biennial? I am not sure whether it was the choice of the curators, but the word Europe is in every sentence of the *Manifesta* brochure.

Rosa Martínez: We, the curators, didn't choose to put this name on the exhibition. We also rejected emphatically the first subtitle to be put under the word *Manifesta*: 'the pan-European manifestation,' because we found it could be understood as a new kind of colonialism. It is part of reality that we have to live with the tension of always trying to define our identities. I wish we could play with our identities and to live them not as an essence but as an interchange game. Therefore, I compare exhibitions with love stories. They share the fact that they are part of existential transits, which hardly ever occur in a pure form but tend to merge and even become confused.
In the field of love, a migration takes place between two people. To love is to emerge from oneself and to move towards the other, and such a journey, while trespassing on the other's territory, affords the only chance of forfeiting one's identity to generate a common space. For me, this notion of the love story was very important in curating the exhibition; I wanted to make clear that you can move from one identity to another, and enable experiences of such transformation.

Audience: How exactly does this notion of migration translate to an exhibition, and in particular to this exhibition?

Andrew Renton: I think we aspired to an exhibition that was about the processes which went into making of works of art. I see this as an unfinished exhibition. We looked for a solution that would not be obscure or abstract, and decided to show how things come to be where they are.
We felt that one of the failings of large-scale exhibitions is that they are only about packing crates and removal vans.
We hope that something different has happened here. Many of the projects that have emerged here in the past couple of weeks are projects offering a type of personal generosity, they have to do with the city, with talking, with passing notes from one person to another, with passing food around a table. This is what I mean by process. It is open-ended, and there is a place for the person who comes to look.

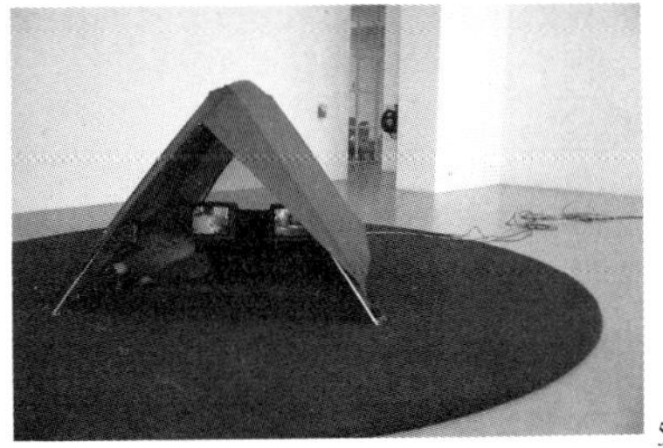
5

Hans-Ulrich Obrist: *Migrateurs*, an ongoing series of exhibitions, seventeen so far, that I organize for the Musée d'Art Moderne de la Ville de Paris, reflects on the issues of migration. *Migrateurs* (the French word for migrating bird) is a mobile platform, there is no fixed space for it in the museum, it is re-defined for each presentation according to necessity. To give you some examples, Felix Gonzalez Torres made a portrait of an airline that evoked memories of real and fictive journeys. There was a promenadology project by Paul Armand Gette and Lucius Burckhardt (promenadology is the term Burckhardt invented for his science of walking) and also a small retrospective of Bas Jan Ader which led us to the journey of Arthur Cravan, Emilia Ehrhardt, and Lew Welch. Douglas Gordon's project migrated in its different forms through the whole museum. If there is signification of the object it is relational, it is signification for the other.

Rasheed Araeen: I would like to make a distinction between migration and tourism. What is going on now is tourism; and that for me is a pleasure trip which is contrary to the painful experience of migration.
I would like to quote one of the artists in *Manifesta*, Huang Yong Ping, who really underwent that trauma of migration: 'I consider "Departure" as the beginning of life and activity, while "Arrival" represents the end and death.' Now, can the artists in *Manifesta* share this pain?

Audience: Do you really believe that *Manifesta* has to do with the pain of migration? In the context of a United Europe, isn't migration much more of an economic topic? *Manifesta* wanted to get rid of the national presentations of the *Venice Biennial*, and their political and economical connotations, but doesn't *Manifesta* run the risk of becoming a new kind of state art for the United Europe, this time representing typically European instead of national topics?

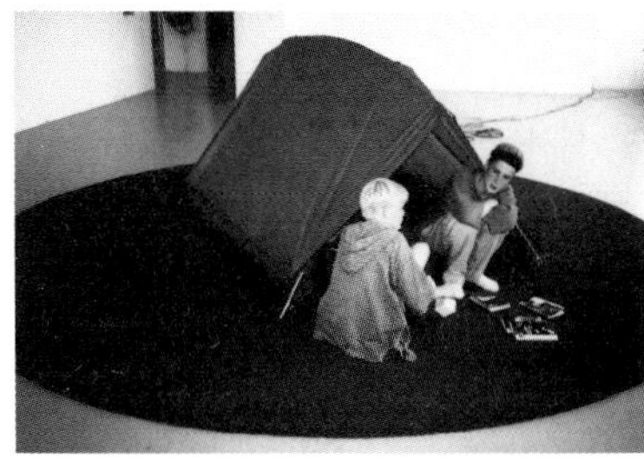
6

Andrew Renton: I think we should try to home in on some specific artworks that are visible in Rotterdam now, and the artists who have come to work here – because all aspects of this theme of migration which we have been discussing are quite evident within this exhibition. So much of Uri Tzaig's work faces the anxiety of migration by carrying the traces of where he has been. Even the gesture of hand washing with soap made from Dead Sea mud is a nostalgia for a place which is always, by definition, elsewhere. Think of his *Universal Square* video – it's not just about a center, it's about our desire to be centered, to have a place. Jenny Marketou encourages a spiritual nomadism by inviting the visitor to engage directly in this *Translocal* camp site. That distinction between tourism and migration, which has been emphasized in this debate, is addressed by Hale Tenger in her video installation *Cross Section*. Her discourse makes it uncomfortably clear where the boundaries between free and restricted movement through Europe lie. If she, as a Turkish person, wants to cross these borders, her movement is politicized. It's not simply tourism. Even the canaries which Carl Michael von Hausswolff has flying through the exhibition are involuntary migrants from a colonial history. The domesticated canaries have adapted so well to their captivity that they don't even know how to live in freedom, and seem to prefer their familiar prison. I was worried about the birds coming here at first, and now I'm worried about them leaving. They've settled down here – even laid some eggs ...

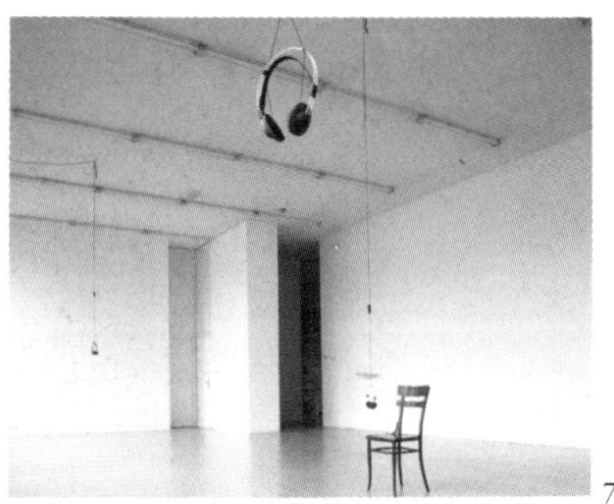

7

Rasheed Araeen: I think it is up to the artists to communicate with one another through their art. But we must also take into consideration the fact that the status of the art object does not arise on its own. The object and artistic practice operate within a culture as a whole. And if the culture as a whole is institutionalized, then our own existence, our own practice, is also institutionalized. It is important to question those structures; art must be critical.

Audience: I'm an immigrant to the Netherlands, and it is my experience that it is hard to find information on non-western art. I doubt whether the art world is really aware of this. The European art world is just too self-oriented. I don't understand your problems. You know everything. You have the instruments. You have the Internet. Europeans are much too busy with their own identity. To me, this is purely intellectual masturbation.

Carl Michael von Hausswolff: You are right. There is no real interest in the immigrants, no real effort to make room for them in our culture. Instead of opening up, Europe is completely self-centered. It is scared of loosing a static identity, scared of this change of culture. People were imported from Africa and Asia to work in Europe and when they are not needed any longer, they are just sent out.

Andrew Renton: What we have done here is absolutely not dry intellectual indulgence. It is something that really is participatory. You get inside the tent, you wash your hands, you go into the cafeteria, you go to the bar. You use your body to have a direct relation and dialogue of some kind in some particular way. My belief is that within the context of art we have the possibility of a language more or less common to all of us. It is probably called Western history. But let's be optimistic and say that there is something useable within it that we might adapt to our purposes. I think that is what we have been trying to get at today, and that there are very specific, even surprisingly generous, gestures in terms of the works to be found here. I think they prove that it is actually possible to enter into dialogue.

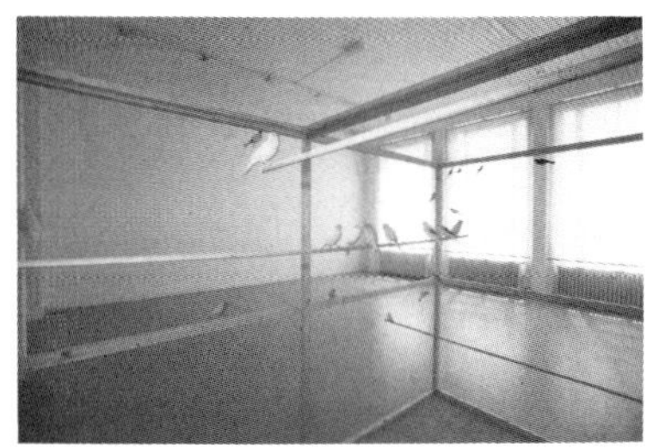
9

1 Susann Walder
Zombie Transit, 1992-96

2 Hale Tenger
Cross Section, 1996

3 Henrik Plenge Jacobson
Everything is wrong, 1996

4 Uri Tzaig
Untitled, 1996

5 Jenny Marketou
TRANSLOCAL, 1995-96

6 Jenny Marketou
TRANSLOCAL, 1995-96

7 Róza El-Hassan
Guard of Time, 1996
courtesy of Knoll Gallery, Budapest

8 Eva Marisaldi
Steady-girl, 1996

Title-page & 9 Carl Michael von Hausswolff
1. *The Selfportrait as a Natural Filter*
2. *'Colonialism is the Fruit of Centralist Thinking'*
3. *'Who runs may read'*
4. *Serinus Canarius Domesticus*
5. *Yellow*
1996
courtesy of Andréhn-Schiptjenko, Stockholm

10 Susann Walder
Zombie Transit, 1992-96

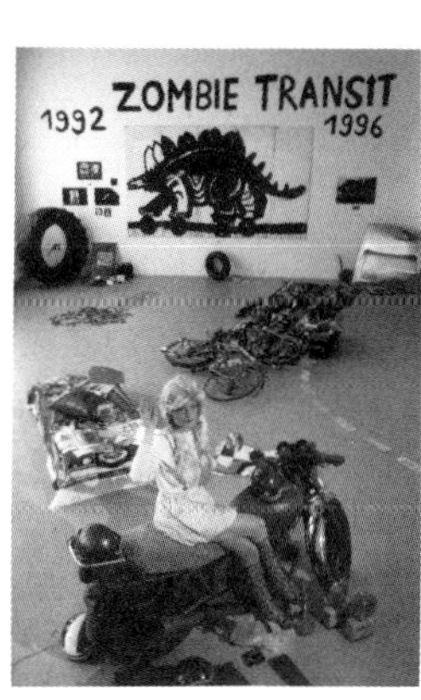

10

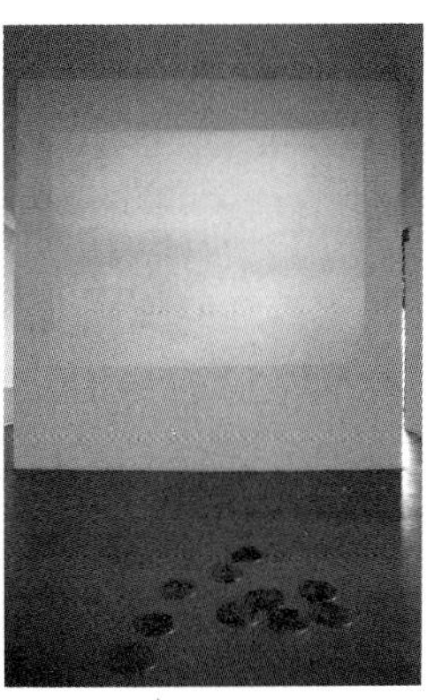
8

05 ON AN ANTID

New communication techniques are being used by an increasingly large public worldwide. In 'On an Antidote,' Witte de With invited media professionals involved in the arts who are using and experimenting with the new media to relate their experiences with these new tools. Though often presented as revolutionary, the questions that these new media raise on the relationship of art and its public and about the role of art in culture in general are similar to those that were topical when the 'old' media, such as radio and television, were introduced.

ICC.
INC.
CLIC
DEMO
CO

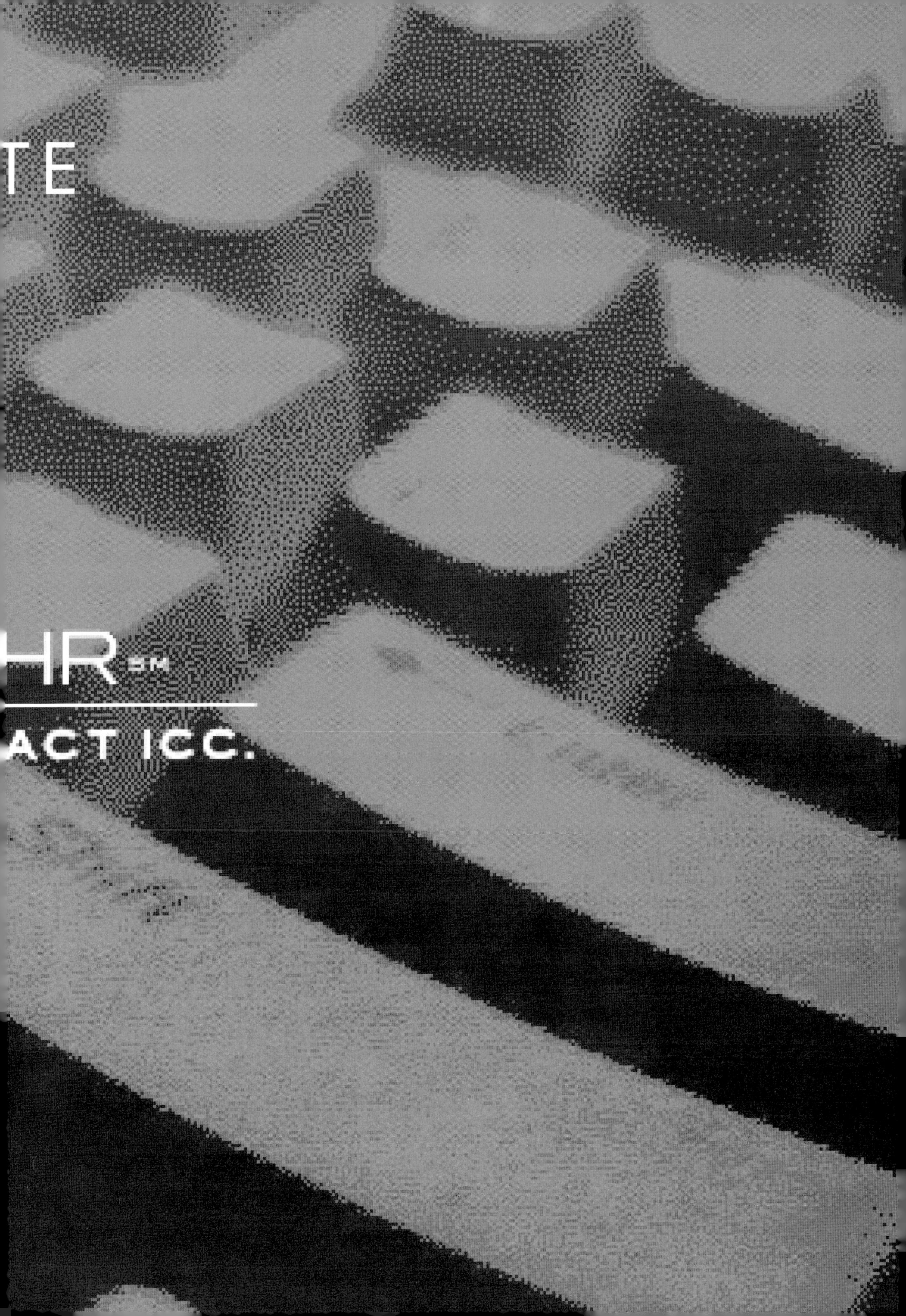
TE
HR SM
ACT ICC.

The Modem and the Mouse: Reflections on On-line Publishing and Art Criticism

Robert Atkins

A Medium

'We become what we behold....We shape our tools and thereafter our tools shape us.' (**Marshall McLuhan**)

In Understanding Media, (New York: McGraw-Hill, 1964), p. 122.

While watching the 1944 version of Jane Eyre the other night, my thoughts wandered from old movies to new media. The film opens with a literal image of the cover of Charlotte Bronte's book. The novel/movie's title is quickly replaced by views of pages inscribed with the film's credits, followed by a voice-over that sets the scene. In breathtakingly quick succession the formulaic opening of this movie conflates the history of the modern, narrative media: novel, silent film, radio, and sound-film. I was reminded of the theoretical donnée that no medium disappears; the function of every old medium is simply taken up by a new medium as its developmental point of departure. (And sometimes there is not even much development: Consider, for instance, how little separates the 'reading' of the news on radio and television.)

Closer to home, I was also reminded of TalkBack! A Forum for Critical Discourse (http://talkback.lehman.cuny.edu/tb) the on-line art 'journal' that I edit, which I founded last year. I increasingly wonder about the nature of this hypertext-based 'site' 'on' the World Wide Web. The orgy of quotation marks in the previous sentences signifies my discomfort with the problematic use of old labels and metaphors to deal with new media and forms. Why the territorial and spatial metaphors of a 'site' 'on' the Internet if not to stake out an ideological turf that corresponds to the ownership of actual, physical property? Likewise for the media-construction of the Net as anarchic frontier, rather than the repressive gulag it has so quickly become. So before 'we become what we behold,' we exist in a world generated by language. (Let me note, in passing, that this dangerous media-construction of the Net as an anarchic frontier helped enable an unprecedented assault in late-1995 and early-1996 on Net-based communications, which criminalized content often legal in print and broadcast media. Given that the network is both unitary and international, what's criminalized in China, Singapore, the United States and Germany is essentially off-limits everywhere.)

The problem with language isn't simply ideological, though. It also reflects the ubiquitous tendency to look at new phenomena through old eyes.

As Peter Lyman, the librarian of the University of California at Berkeley, recently told New York Times reporter **Sylvia Donato**: 'We always talk about new technology using old vocabulary. "Electronic publishing," "digital library," "information highway": To our grandchildren these terms will sound as peculiar as "horseless carriage".'

'New Libraries,' New York Times (April 29, 1996), p. 21.

What's at stake in such designations? Almost everything – at least at the outset of new technologies. The CD-Rom medium, for example, has been largely commandeered by book publishers, instead of video-game or other entertainment producers. The result? An enterprise virtually still-born. Blinkered by paradigms of book-production, distribution, and author-publisher relationships that have almost nothing to do with making a CD-Rom, book publishers have been unable to establish the CD-Rom as a commercially viable medium. In fact, their publishing project requires an entirely different model that reflects the collaborative realities of multi-media production, a modus operandi familiar to denizens of the entertainment and performing-arts worlds, rather than the book or visual-art realms. This paradigm shift is slowly beginning to take hold, but four years (and countless projects, many by artists) have been lost in the interim. The medium – in this case, an inherently collaborative one – may not be the (only) message, but to ignore it is to place yourself in peril.

What about 'publishing' a 'journal' of 'art criticism' on-line? Is thinking about the Internet also inappropriately couched in the linguistic models of publishing? Yes and no, although the situation hardly parallels that of multimedia. Bear in mind that in the beginning, the Internet was the word. This medium consisted primarily of text from its U.S. Defense-Department-inspired inception in 1969 until Tim Berner Lee's creation of the hypertext-based World Wide Web in 1990. (The Web's success wasn't really insured until the National Center for Supercomputing Application released software to navigate – or browse – it in 1993.). In some ways, it's remarkable how much art has been posted on the Net, given that sophisticated sound- and image- (or hypermedia) technologies are only now being developed and becoming widespread.

The hypertext medium on which the Web is based, offers a number of features that distinguish it from the linear model of the print-medium. These include the ability to quickly and efficiently search materials or data bases, to open multiple windows on a screen, and to create links. Many commentators – myself included – regard the (interactive) link as the essential characteristic of the medium. On-line publishers have tentatively begun to explore the creation of links, but rarely to exploit the communications-potential of interactivity created by these links. (More on this subject later.) Instead, links are frequently used to cross reference or illustrate material. But just as a periodical-reader may be temporarily diverted from the linearity of a text by an image – especially in an art publication – so, too, will the on-line reader be diverted from a seamless, linear read. Does this non-linearity contradict the essential quality of the essay itself – a form predicated on persuasion, on the (linear) argument? (When it comes to fiction, the branching hypernovel demonstrates the plausibility of offering the reader multiple paths though the works – as does multi-narrator, multi-viewpoint writing by novelists like William Faulkner, whose works long pre-date the advent of digital media.) Of course the demands of linear writing have always haunted the process of translation necessary to evoke, analyze and criticize in language a work of art. Although in some ways recent art increasingly utilizes language-related strategies (especially neo-conceptual and media art), such works also accentuate the distinctions between art and writing as very different forms of knowledge. Such tensions also surface in terms of reception. Essay reading and installation-viewing, for instance, are totally different activities. The site-specific-installation viewer takes in numerous sights in an unprogrammed sequence. These sights often comprise more than views of objects: the objects are also likely to be complemented by sound or projections, all created for a specific historical or autobiographical context central to the meaning of the installation. On the Net, works by such hybridizing, neo-conceptual and media artists currently predominate.

A Publication

'Internet is an open space where the difference between 'art' and 'not art' has become blurred as never before in XX century. That's why there are so few 'artists' in this space.... What is WWW art? Is it public art? Advertising? More data noise? Does it have anything to do with galleries and critics? Do we want it? WWW Art Medal. We give it to web-pages that were created not as art works but gave us definite "art" feeling'. (**Alexei Shulgin**)

Shulgin is a photographer and web-site operator in Moscow. I received this e-mail message from him on April 17, 1996.

TalkBack! A Forum for Critical Discourse arose from my conviction that on-line art was being ignored by the art world. In mid-1995, I presented the idea to Susan Hoeltzel and Douglas Davis, co-directors of the City University of New York's Center for Long Distance Art and Culture, who enthusiastically endorsed it. Although little funding has been available, the center has offered me invaluable technical support and server space.

One of TalkBack!'s stated mandates was to cover on-line art because such art, having no commercial rationale, was not being covered by the 'trade' publications. (The flurry of attention it drew in early 1996 represents an interest in novelty more than a commitment to a new, non-commercial form.) Nor have there been many cross-over journals dealing with digital or even media art in the ever-more-Balkanized art world(s). (In this regard, on-line art resembles the ghetto realms of public art or graffiti.) I also wanted to cover social issues because such coverage suits my sensibility as a non-formalist critic, journalist, and censorship-chronicler. If I had any models in mind, it was the tradition of the early twentieth-century 'little magazine,' publications such as Arthur Cravan's Maintenant, Wyndam Lewis' Blast!, Or Marcel Duchamp's Blind Man. These journals showcased art and critical essays and functioned as the fulcrum of dialogue among small circles of **committed readers**. But at the same time, I felt that the 'forum' in TalkBack!'s title encouraged both interactivity and an investigation of the new, on-line form itself.

The question of audience is complex. One might assume that the economically advantaged audience for art - in the first world, at least - increasingly overlaps with the households with on-line capacity. This is true as far as it goes, but the demographics of the Net suggest that the 50-65 year olds are among the least likely of any adults to be on-line. This is likely to change quickly as on-line access become ubiquitous.

The first issue, which went on-line in December 1995, was devoted to the archive-as-artwork. (If you were reading on-line, you'd click HERE to see TalkBack!, instead of reading my description.) In brief, it encompassed in-depth examinations of artworks (Muntadas' File Room, Cati Laporte's Almanac of Disasters, and graffiti on-line) as well as meditations about on-line publishing paradigms and the nature of the library, past and future. Other regular departments complemented the features (or 'Centerpieces') section: manifestos ('The Beef'); a guide to on-line art sites and zines ('Out There'); commentary about shows and trends, as well as interviews with William Gibson and Susan Sontag, among others ('Scene & Heard'); previews of on-line, public-art-projects ('The Buzz'); artworks ('The Gallery'); AIDS-related images by artists such as Barbara Kruger and Glenn Ligon and opportunities for petitioning policy-makers ('AIDS Memorial'); an ongoing chronicle of the cyber-machinations of governments, corporations and social 'milestones' such as the establishment of the first on-line Girl Scout troop (the 'On-line Timeline'), and a bulletin board ('Talk back to TalkBack!')

When I reflected on this debut issue, it struck me as a hybrid, like so much art on the Net. In attempting to fill voids in available information - as well as commentary - I'd created everything from a consumer guide ('Out

There') to a data base (the 'On-line Timeline'). I was happy to do so. But I was worried that fairly lengthy pieces about individual artworks seemed slightly flat and even out of place – reflecting, as Shulgin put it, the 'blurred,' art/non-art status of Net art. Put another way, the traditional focus on individual artworks seems a matter of focusing on details when the larger panorama itself urgently requires explication. This larger panorama is on-line culture. It has become increasingly apparent to me that on-line art exists as part of a cyberculture fast becoming the premier site of conflict for the actual, physical culture or RL (real life). As **Sherry Turkle** suggested to me, 'The Net dramatizes, concretizes, makes it more urgent to confront what's true [in RL] anyway.'

In an interview with the author conducted on February 8, 1996. An edited version of this interview appeared in TalkBack! # 2. Sherry Turkle, Life on the Screen: Identity in the Age of the Internet (New York: Simon & Schuster, 1995).

Issue # 2 – being completed as I write this – partly reflects that shift. Its theme is identity. This concern is playfully evoked with increasing frequency, as in the New Yorker cartoon showing one dog telling another that 'on the Internet, nobody knows you're a dog,' or in a story I recently heard poet Ann Lauterbach tell about a five-year-old who spells his name D-A-V-I-D-ENTER. But we all know that humor is often a wake-up call alerting us to serious, sometimes divisive, social issues. While TalkBack! # 2 hardly abandons on-line art – it features articles about Stelarc, cyber-exhibitions, curatorial practices, and an examination of the on-line art market – it also contains interviews with cybertheorists Sherry Turkle and Sandy Stone, an investigation of on-line anonymity and complex works of on-line art about identity. One happy likelihood is that it will appeal to a wider range of readers interested in cyberculture than did issue # 1.

It also features two large sections that would seem incongruous in an off-line or print, magazine- or journal-context. One is the exhibition catalog for the Fashion Moda exhibition seen this past winter at the Lehman College Art Gallery, the location of the City University of New York's Center for Long Distance Art and Culture. The show examined the historic Bronx alternative space that pioneered graffiti and hip-hop, in the process raising complex issues about urban identity and artworld appropriation of street content – and content producers.

The second is the Appropriated Corpse which would be virtually impossible – and pointless as an experiment in interactivity – in print. A play on the surrealist parlor game, the Exquisite Corpse, this modified, digital version invites site visitors to download images by nearly two dozen artists, modify those images, and e-mail them back for (possible) on-line exhibition. The Appropriated Corpse at least raises the crucial question of what might constitute meaningful (on-line) interactivity in a medium that encourages interactivity and a culture-of-couch-potatoes that simultaneously discourages it. Is this a bold experiment in interactivity or a banal gesture? It's unclear to me how this open-ended project will turn out or even what criteria of evaluation – beyond that of offering participants genuine choices – are appropriate to it. In part, this depends on the response the project generates. More than simply the status of a work of art is blurred by the Internet.

An Inquiry

'Now the world is ready to jump into cyberspace. Whether the rich, interactive marketplace that has created – and been created by – 800 service [free phone calls for consumers] will translate to the on-line environment is largely up to people like all of us [telecommunications executives.]'
Quoted by David Bennahum in 'Tolling the Bell,' New York (18 March 1996), pp. 22-27.
(**Robert Allen**, Chief Executive Officer, AT&T)

'Ultimately we have to decide whether we are no more than an economy sharing a common currency in which the primary social glue binding us together is the business transactions we do with one another, or if we are still a society in that we have special obligations to one another as citizens.'
Quoted by David Bennahum in 'Tolling the Bell,' New York (18 March 1996), pp. 22-27
(**Robert Reich**, U.S. Secretary of Labor)

Anyone who has spent much time on-line realizes that the development of new forms of interactivity is what ultimately will distinguish on-line commu-

In a lecture at the Museum of Modern Art on 8 April 1996.

nication from what's come before. As **Jane Veeder** – a computer graphics artist and director of the Digital Cinema Laboratory at San Francisco State University – succinctly noted: 'Everyone understands that digital culture means interacting with everything.' Veeder's formulation raises – and begs – the key questions: What kind(s) of interactivity will that be? And whose interests will be served?

As I write this in the spring of 1996, contradictory signals about the commercial colonization of the Internet are appearing in the financial pages. Well-positioned software developers and service providers are having a field day – witness the explosive stock offering of the search engine, Yahoo, for instance – while some of the luster has apparently worn off the Internet for non-cyber, commercial concerns. Expensive web sites currently offer few prospects of short-term financial gain, at least not until the perception of secure credit-card billing is widespread. (This is imminent.) Web-site designers, in turn, are unable to charge the high prices their services commanded just last year. But even a temporary lull in the gold-rush mentality enveloping commercial development of the Net offers at least a moment to reflect on the past two years' trends.

In 1994 and 1995, corporations wasted no time pioneering new, often insidious methods of on-line interactivity-cum-advertising. Among the most revealing, are cereal-maker's web programming directed at children. Logging on to sites 'hosted' by entertaining animated characters, unwitting (and underage) consumers innocently supply requested information about themselves, including e-mail addresses on their families' accounts. The results? Personalized e-mail greetings, gifts (cyber-games and the like), and a barrage of product-related materials.

This use of e-mail as advertising-medium reminds us that the Internet is not only a Web-ed creature. The World Wide Web is fast becoming the shopping mall of the Internet. Ongoing, interactive communication is better achieved through non-single-direction or push media, that is, less broadcast-like, Internet mediums. (As with television, you still have to choose to visit a web-site.) The more duo-directional, interactive media include bulletin board services with their ongoing postings, real-time conversation in MUDs and MOOs, and e-mail, a highly efficient, low-cost means of transmission. On-line aficionados are familiar with the so-call 'list-serv,' the subscribable, often free, e-mail-delivered postings devoted to a particular subject. Subscribers to such lists – and there are a few about art – receive a daily stream of messages to their electronic mailboxes. The trend is a constant flow of information. It's easy to empathize with a recent message from Armin Medosch, a fellow list-subscriber: 'Today I deleted 500 e-mails,' he wrote. 'And that made me happy.'

How do we slow down this information flow? And how does this relate to publishing an on-line journal? One difference between on- and off-line publishing is that publishing designations like 'daily,' 'weekly,' and 'quarterly,' make little sense in a medium that allows for constant up-dating and obviates former vexations like paper costs and other print-medium considerations. But as a part-time editor with limited financial resources to pay writers, I am unable to commission more (or more frequently postable) content for TalkBack!. Far more important, however, is the cybercultural context in which this publication appears. (The Net, after all, is a social system.) Varied content-producers need to assert their visions of this radically decentralized medium or be content with those of commercializers like AT&T's Robert Allen, or an international class of politicians and apparatchiks intent on regulating on-line information or mandating its commercialization under trade agreements like NAFTA. Despite buzzwords like virtual community – the recent ubiquity of the term is a sure sign of its scarcity – an audience of consumers does not a community make.

Robert Reich aptly defines community as citizenly obligation. (The number of people whose lives have been saved in medical emergencies because they were on-line at the moment of a heart attack or stroke is already legion.) As an editor, however, I am interested in the creation of an intellectual community that might transcend the notion of an audience of site-visitors. How can one distinguish between them? Although it's not difficult to track the number of accesses or 'hits' to a site, a 'visit' may only consist of a ten-second scan of the available material. (Unfortunately these numbers are fetishized by site-operators in search of advertising.) Insightful feedback is another matter entirely. A few dozen postings to TalkBack!'s bulletin board (or to my e-mail) of the 'great site'-variety are simultaneously heartening for their support and disappointing for their lack of criticality. When it comes to reader response, I'm not certain the situation has changed much since Duchamp et al. published their little magazines.

A Post-Script

'The Web as we know it today is dead. It's dead in 2 ways: because it's going to mutate into something else very quickly and be unrecognizable within 12 months, and, secondly, it's dead because all it's got on it is dead information.... It's a big information mausoleum.' (Futurist **Paul Saffo**)

Received as e-mail to the Rhizome list on 8 April 1996.

As an historian in an (amnesiac) American culture, I'm delighted with the capacity of the Web as archive or 'information mausoleum.' What this means is that the first issue of TalkBack! remains accessible to site-visitors at the click of a mouse after the second issue has appeared. Quickly finding an audience for new books or magazines is a daunting and expensive proposition. On-line publishing is more forgiving; it allows a publication to slowly reach an audience through word-of-mouth and publicity.

Saffo's remarks reflect a familiar kind of extremism: a fashionable and contrary nihilism. The claims of both supporters and detractors of on-line publishing are grossly overstated. Although it's clear that on-line (and desktop) publishing offer expanded possibilities, the effects of new telecommunications technologies on reading and writing are anything but clear. Wired's editor **Kevin Kelly** may claim that 'at this point in history, most of the evolution of language, most of the richness in language, is

In 'What Are We Doing On Line? A Forum,' Harper's Magazine (August 1995), pp. 35-46.

happening in this [cyber]space that we are creating,' but I have yet to see it, apart from a tendency for on-line 'writing' to mimic the informality of spoken communication. Likewise for the conventional wisdom that few people have the patience to read long essays on the screen. This supposition is nothing but an intuited prejudice unsupported by any data. Many people I know download on-line essays and articles, then read them off-screen. In any case, such worries seem beside the point at a moment when print publications like Artforum are part of the trend toward tiny articles supplemented with big pictures.

When it comes to art on the Net, something more radical than the nature of reading is up for grabs. The abject unsuitability of the on-line media for doing more with conventional-format paintings and sculptures than reproducing images of them is striking. The Internet tends to call into question the traditional identity of artmakers as a group. Susan Farrell, the creator of the Art Crimes web-site, recently e-mailed me a message thanking me for TalkBack!'s coverage of her international archive of graffiti photographs and noted that 'I know nothing about art; I leave that to the art experts.' Similarly, the creation of web-sites about popular culture by non-artists offers the same deadpan, homage-cum-deconstruction visible in art installations. (A generation ago, the criticality of late-modern/early-post-modern conceptual or media artists might have offered a perceivable distinction, but no longer.) How this will be resolved – if it is resolvable – is unclear right now. As novelist **Robert Coover** has observed about the rush toward judgment of the new, hypernovel form, 'It took 150 years to get from Gutenberg to Don Quixote.'

In 'Hyperfiction: Novels for the Computer,' New York Times Book Review (23 August 1993), p. 1.

Do 150 years in the sixteenth century correspond to fifteen months at the end of the twentieth century? As Museum of Modern Art director **Glenn Lowry** recently commented to me: 'We're living in such a speeded-up world that perhaps the key role of museums in the future is to create ways to slow things down.' In an age of hyper-speed and anxiety, reading and art viewing slow things down by frustrating the split-second glance and

In an interview with the author conducted during October, 1995. An edited version appeared in TalkBack! # 1.

the instant assessment. They are also – despite the untheorized publicness of on-line existence – essentially private experiences. In one sense, the opposite of web surfing is immersion. While immersiveness is a hot topic today in connection with the enveloping quality of so-called virtual reality, immersion is the character of stimulating reading and visual material. It should never be confused with escapism – on-line or off.

'The radios did their job that evening quite satisfactorily. So you see, I sometimes manage to bring about pure processes.' John Cage on the first performance of Imaginary Landscape, no. 4 (1951). Quoted in Daniel Charles, For the Birds (London: Marion Boyars Publishers, 1983), p. 169. Imaginary Landscape no. 4 is an indeterminate score for twelve radios and twelve performers.

Heidi Grundmann

Imaginary Landscapes

'In the beginning there is amazement that all the strange machines and concepts function. But once they start to become widespread and really work, attention shifts to the moments at which the technologies fail ...,' writes Dutch media theorist and activist **Geert Lovink**. And one might add that the moments when the technologies to which we have grown accustomed fail, are the only times we notice them at all. When amazement ceases – and technology works – it becomes transparent/invisible.

In 'Organized Innocence and War in the New Europe,' a lecture given at ISEA 95 in Montreal, published on http://www.thing.desk.nl/bilwet.

In the waning seventies, when European artists were beginning to participate in worldwide network projects and even initiate their own, and for a good part of the eighties, there certainly was much amazement at worldwide networks, at horizontal communication within them, at networks as the place and context for art etc. There was amazement, too, at evident changes in the concept of author or work. Stories were no longer told by a lonely author but 'woven' into the net by an unknown number of authors scattered across the globe, as in 'La Plissure du Texte,' an exemplary project launched by British artist and theorist **Roy Ascott**. Nobody, not even Roy Ascott, has been able to reconstruct the entire global fairy tale – the 'work' – in its ramifications and intersections. It was impossible to document the project. Nobody could claim copyright for what (s)he had put on the Net: everything instantly became material which others could manipulate, place in a different context and pass on in an altered guise.

Participants were located in Vienna, Amsterdam, Pittsburgh, Toronto, Vancouver, San Francisco, Honolulu, and Sydney. The project was a contribution to Electra 1983, an exhibition curated by Frank Popper at the Musée d'Art Moderne de la Ville de Paris.

See, among others: Art+Telecommunication, ed. Heidi Grundmann (Vancouver and Vienna: Western Front and BLIX, 1984).

Some of the **telecommunication projects** of the seventies and eighties made use not only of computer communication but also of Slow Scan TV (a kind of visual telephone), phone sound and fax: the start of (interactive) multimedia art. Interest focused on global communication (it proved possible to involve authors from East-European countries, too); it focused on exploring possibilities of rendering visible modes of horizontal communication and the like as opposed to the verticality of the mass media. It also focused on the question of access to the new communication technologies and finally on the implications of digitization for the availability and manipulability of material.

Part of the Technology & Computer Science section at La XLII Biennale di Venezia (1986) was devoted to multimedia network art (and, in an on-line symposium lasting all that summer, to its theory as well). The Biennial's Laboratorio Ubiqua, which enabled an unascertainable number of artists throughout the world to participate in the Biennial, although their names did not appear in the catalogue, was a kind of swan song to the pioneer phase of telecommunication art – to a phase in which network communication was not yet taken for granted, in which artists regarded weaving networks and making them accessible as their art. As a matter of fact the pioneer phase and some of the pioneers succumbed quite prosaically to the cost of financing their projects and especially to the cost of private phone bills – which (art) institutions did not pay – for accessing the networks. Accessing, however, was one of the main issues (and still is – despite claims to the contrary in computer magazines and from telecom companies).

Another swan song – not to a pioneer phase this time, but to an extremely rich and varied mature development – was performed in 1987 at documenta 8 in Kassel. The documentary and historical acoustic art section, curated by Klaus Schöning, was a remarkable though sparsely registered expansion of the definition of art towards a more comprehensive history of the visual arts. The ideas and traditions of the avant-garde from the beginning of this century to Fluxus and concept art were claimed for radio art, and rightly so. It was a retrospective: the question of the future of the broadcasting media was ignored, as was the question of art's future. There was little overlapping of names of living artists in the Laboratorio

Ubiqua at the 1986 Biennial and the radio art section of documenta 8, although some radio artists were also telecommunication art pioneers and vice versa.

Exploration of radio by telecommunication artists and of the new telecommunication technologies by radio artists took place under varying aspects: it addressed the problem of access, of broadcasting space as sculptural space and part of a larger 'electronic space,' of the appropriation of, for example, archive material or popular media forms, of mixing/sampling material from other artists' 'works,' the collage of different communication systems and technologies ...

Radio/telecommunication artists realized and still realize that radio was and is constantly changing because of digitization. They transfer(red) their perception of the mediascape – a perception changed and honed by practical network experience – to radio, which still preens itself as an autonomous medium and is widely regarded as such by hotshots in the major corporations.

It was striking, after the Laboratorio Ubiqua experience and in particular that of the foregoing telecommunication projects of the seventies and eighties, how intact the concept of work and authorship of works presented at the documenta retrospective remained or had to remain. This is because it would have been difficult to pigeonhole works opposed to the traditional definition of those concepts in this audio library – a kind of handy radio-on-demand system. (This is exactly the closed, retrievable kind of work, the basis of most exhibitions, anthologies, retrospectives and so forth, that is envisaged – although not necessarily as hard-to-sell works of art – by many of those looking to profit from providing on-line services, radio- or video-on-demand and suchlike. They hope this will free them from a situation in which producers and distributors are increasingly losing control over the reception – and further utilization – of broadcast works... But already the first attempts are being made to 'flog' minute-long sections from archived works.)

One of the things that scandalized (and still scandalizes) many – outsider – artists, critics and media people involved in any way at all in artistic network projects and trying to experience them as art, was and is the debunking of the fiction of the author's/producer's control over his or her work. The 'dispersed/distributed authorship' (Roy Ascott) of art in the networks - - practiced daily in, for instance, today's **MUDs and MOOs** – is undermining traditional concepts of radio and TV broadcasts, just as it is undermining the traditional work-concept of theater, film, music, art and literature, once they are put into 'media.' The more channels are available and the greater the increasingly better-trained, practiced user's mastery of them, the less control the author has over the reception of his work. When **Gerhard Ruis** postulates in 1996, in a radio program about new media, that authors still produce 'one-way' works which must be received from beginning to end in the prescribed way, he is forgetting that everyone in our society has long since become, consciously or not, a crystallization point in a permanent, highly personal process of collage. Whether we zap our way through TV channels; make phone calls while watching TV, listening to music, correcting a text on the monitor, scanning an illustration – the combinations are legion – we are in a multimedia environment composed of ever-changing fragments on different levels of perception, selected from an abundance of possible set pieces. Today the collage, the ready-made and a series of related artistic strategies postulated, defined and practiced throughout the twentieth century, not only define art but as a 'sampling culture' or 'recombinant culture' have become our environment/habitat.

MUD = Multi User Dungeon or Domain. MOO = Mud Object Orientated. Text-based role games in the network. MOO users can shape spaces by furnishing them.

Ruis is a member of the Austrian association representing authors' interests

Digitization instantly converts everything into data which can be registered and retrieved in a variety of ways, combined sectionwise with other fragmentary data.

The networks and concepts like cyberspace, the digital highway and equally contestable metaphors cluttering the pages of journals and manuals are making us take a new look at the telephone, radio, live broadcasting, TV, newspapers, answering machines etc. and encouraging us to understand them in a different way. Thereby we discover that what we previously regarded as autonomous broadcasting, communication, mass and distribution media (radio, TV, newspaper, telephone and computer) may be seen as different aspects of a single megamedium.

*

'Razionalnik,' Graz, Ljubljana, Trento, and Budapest, an initiative of Seppo Gründler, Josef Klammer et al.

In 1986 a **MIDI on-line concert** – perhaps the very first one – put an end to the often poor-quality telephone music that featured in early telecommunication projects (and had enabled people without any access to computers to participate in such projects). The cities of Graz, Ljubljana, Budapest and Trento were the respective venues for a group of musicians and an audience in a concert situation. Through the phone lines linking the groups, the musicians sent to each other not musical sounds in poor telephone quality but control data which triggered instruments, samplers and sequencers in each venue, producing top-quality sounds in all of them. The live musicians had no control over which sounds were played and when in their respective concert situations, nor how the performance was shaped by those sounds. In the early nineties artists like Gerfried Stocker or Josef Klammer/Seppo Gründler submitted projects to **'ORF (Austrian Radio) Kunstradio,'** suggesting that the phenomenon of simultaneity be explored under the combined aspects of networks and radio. In one of these projects visitors to Expo in Seville – together with musicians in Seville and Vienna – were involved in **interactive concerts** at the venues and on the radio.

Since 1987 'ORF Kunstradio' has been a weekly platform for radio art. Every Thursday evening at 10.20 p.m. projects specifically conceived and realized for radio by artists, composers, writers and media artists, are introduced in an On Air Gallery. 'Kunstradio' is also a kind of agency for art projects which overstep the framework of the weekly radio gallery, being devised for public urban and/or electronic space. Many of these projects could only be realized with the cooperation of Transit, a non-profit association founded in 1991 in Innsbruck with the aim of promoting art in electronic space with public funding and the knowhow, production and broadcasting facilities of Austrian Radio, ORF. As of April 1995 'Kunstradio On Line' can be reached at http://www/ping.at/thing/orfkunstradio/.

'Puente Telefonico,' a telematic simultaneous live concert, Graz-Seville-'ORF Kunstradio.' A co-production of x-space, Graz, and 'ORF Kunstradio,' 1992.

In international and Austrian projects a steadily growing group of artists (including Mia Zabelka, Andres Bosshard, Roberto Paci Daló) and technicians developed this initiative into complex events in which existing sound, image and data lines connecting three regional ORF studios are activated. The idea

'Chipradio,' a telematic simultaneous concert, Innsbruck, Dornbirn, Salzburg, 'ORF Kunstradio,' Austria 1. A Transit project, 1992. See also Transit # 1 (Innsbruck/Linz: Transit/Prix Ars Electronica, 1993). 'Realtime,' a telematic

simultaneous concert, Innsbruck, Linz, Graz, ORF, Austria 1 and FS 2.
A Transit project, 1993. See also Prix Ars Electronica, Linz, 1994.

was not only that live events in each studio would be influenced by the other two, but that **simultaneous radio and TV events** would be influenced by all three. Eventually, the **Internet** was collaged into this kind of project: on a special home page, surfers triggered top-quality sounds which flowed into simultaneous broadcasts.

'State Of Transition,' a radio and Internet project. Graz, Neue Galerie; Rotterdam, V2–Organisatie; Kunstradio, Austria 1, 1994. A co-production of x-space, V2 and ORF Kunstradio. See also 'Kunstradio On Line.'

'Digital radio, though, means that transmission is control. The data package that is transmitted here and will be processed by a new generation of intelligent receivers contains not only the audio data and parameters of the transmitted music and speech but also any number of parallel control signals which separate music from word, loud from soft, pop from classic, radio drama from feature, news from commentary, in any way you like: every piece of audio information will be codable, meaning that the receivers of this radio will be little programmable computers. This heralds the end of radio, the end of one-way transmission of a source from a transmitter to a receiver.' (**Wolfgang Hagen**)

In 'Über das Radio (hinaus),' Transit # 2 (Innsbruck/Vienna: Transit and Verlag Triton, 1993).

Two complex worldwide projects have taken up the initiatives and developments outlined above: 'Horizontal Radio,' 1995, and 'Rivers & Bridges,' 1996.

'Horizontal Radio' was heard on 22-23 June 1995, for 24 hours on 30 channels of 24 public stations (VHF, MW, SW) and on numerous independent stations. In addition to the Internet, performances, installations, concerts, telephone performances, pirate stations etc., were involved. It was impossible to document the result, for nobody could reconstruct the total event. What remains is the individual recollection of each participant, whether he or she was a round-the-clock artist, technician, organizer involved in the project or a visitor, listener or user who stumbled upon it by chance. And **two sample CDs** which theoretically can be inserted simultaneously in two CD players and played in random mode so as to convey a slight impression of 'Horizontal Radio,' as heard differently by all its different audiences in all its different venues – as a kind of living, ever-changing organism. Incidentally, the intensive preparations at the various participating 'sta-

'Horizontal Radio – Die unmögliche Dokumentation,' 2 CDs, Edition Kunstradio, Vienna, 1996.

tions' yielded a veritable anthology for 'Horizontal Radio' – on the general theme of 'migration' – of what radio art can be, ranging from the simultaneous event to a highly complex sound composition. But once consigned to the (radio and Internet) network, everything became material: retrieved in fragments on line or from the net to be mixed, layered, collaged or processed with other fragments and consigned to the network again ...

'Rivers & Bridges' culminated on 5 September 1996 at 'Ars Electronica' in an international live radio and Internet event, but will continue on the Internet: http://www.ping.at/thing/orfkunstradio/RIV–BR1/.

The **'Rivers & Bridges'** project combined, among other things, acoustic postcards of real bridges and rivers with stories about rivers and bridges told in a wide variety of media by artists and non-artists, young and old. Installations and performances at existing bridges mingled with simultaneous events and compositions or with scientific, informative or traffic radio programs relating to rivers and bridges, with thematic and aesthetic links on the Net and with specific Internet projects and so forth. Close attention was paid to the sound on the radio and the Internet. Sound is not regarded as an autonomous medium here, but as just one (and probably very important) aspect of a hypermedium.

This mega- or hypermedium, a convergence of all the mass and telecommunication media hitherto regarded as individual media, will owe its existence to the computer, which provides – interactive – access to all other media. Hypnotized by their fixation on 'new fields of enterprise,' most public radio corporations still fail to realize that the computer has become the

At the Nuremberg Radio Days, 1995.

'primary medium' (**Wolfgang Hagen**) in our media landscape. Only the promotion of public interest in it, according to this German theorist and radio practitioner, can in the long term legitimize the license and/or radio and television fees so vital to the survival of the public corporations.

Projects like 'Horizontal Radio' and 'Rivers & Bridges' explain some of the effects of digitization on our ideas about mass media: they show, for example, that live events today, immediately transformed into data and instantly retrievable, over and over again, sectionwise or integrally, are nothing but files among a myriad files from different times and places, files in our culture's multimedial, digital data bank. With the aid of the idea of

'The Art of Being Everywhere' was the name of an art project of 1992 organized by the Steierische Kulturinitiative with a diametrically opposite intention. Like previous network projects, it did not focus on passive participation in a spectacle devised by others but on the construction of an easily and cheaply accessible communication network aimed at showing artists, in particular, how to work creatively with networks and also how those possessing network and hypertext know-how could pass on their skills to new users.

simultaneity, 'live radio' or 'live TV' are still regarded and marketed as something 'special.' However, being just one of the worldwide millions watching a spectacle like live football matches or operatic tenors has little in common with what the networks define as your own **'art of being everywhere.'** Even if the witness of a 'live' football goal finds himself still in a state of mind informed by the age of mass media, this will not prevent him at the same time from being turned first and foremost into a potential customer/consumer of the immediate multimedial commercialization of the event characterizing the digital era.

*

In global projects, such as 'Horizontal Radio'and 'Rivers & Bridges,' artists, non-artists and users, within an agreed time-span, adopt a specially active stance towards a common theme, simultaneously calling up data with a common theme and partly processed data which they design, mix, manipulate and then pass on in changed form.

At http://www/thing.or.at/thing/auer

'The Auer Family' is quite a different matter. It is a sitcom with a slightly different twist, that is available on the radio, the Internet, on Voice Mail, on **CD** and in print media. Since 4 January 1996, the cultural channel of Austrian Radio ORF has been broadcasting a weekly 5-minute episode from the life of the Auer family. Each episode is produced by a different team of writers, composers, artists and technicians formed from a group currently numbering more than seventy people and still growing. They are also responsible for updating the Auer Family home page on the Internet with picture stories, games, merchandising, fan club and audio files.

'Auer Power,' CD 1, edition Kunstradio, Vienna, 1996.

This lighthearted year-long project is played out against the serious background of developing new production strategies for the various aspects of the new megamedium made up of mass media, telecommunications and computers. Another aim is to transfer the know-how of computer-literate artists and technicians to people with no previous experience in the field.

And indeed, composers and writers who not long ago were struggling to master their word processors and synthesizers, are now developing picture, sound and text material and stories for the Auer Family home page, for radio, hotline and more recently for chats and a long live radio program in which the actors play scenes supplied via various media by listeners and users, and in which pre-produced module/samples can be triggered by Internet users. It still remains for conclusions to be drawn from this extremely productive situation. At present no one has the energy or time for detached reflection. As a matter of fact, any mention of **'Lindenstrasse'** or other TV soaps which go on-line has both a demotivating and highly motivating effect, for once on the Net, a project like 'The Auer Family' – which operates on a tiny budget and infrastructure – is exposed not only to the judgment of a limited, specialized art scene but is immediately in direct 'competition' with commercial variants of a genre which is being appropriated and varied by artists.

A popular German TV series.

The self-definition of artists, writers, composers and media artists engaged in interdisciplinary collaboration and intermedial work has become a turbulent undertaking in projects like 'The Auer Family.' Cooperation, teamwork, interdisciplinarity, waiving copyright for new ideas or controlling the further development of the project still has to be learned by many of those involved and often leads to conflicts among them.

A few Auer authors have withdrawn from the project because they had problems with losing the control to which they were accustomed, but there are many more who, in the spirit of the intentions of the entire project, deliberately waive the privilege of having their names mentioned in the credits of the radio or Internet episodes to which they have made a major contribution. These authors are aware of the fact that each episode, which after all is only one aspect of a larger entity composed of fragments, is pervaded with ideas from other episodes, from conversations, from technicians' remarks, from monthly conferences, from other teams.

These lines are quoted from a text published on the Internet.

Acoustic space

You hear it rather than see it.

Staring into a flashing screen of a frequency-based machine

receiving and transmitting data through phone lines.

The computer an extension of a radio

Receiving the signals of the new networks.

The digital networks.

In this environment you are everywhere and nowhere...

...

The content is the old media, visually based written word

Leading our linear existence into the new holistic environment...'

In their different ways, projects like 'The Auer Family,' 'Horizontal Radio' or 'Rivers & Bridges' allow radio to come (in difference to itself and thereby) into its own and for the first time to become the content of newer media or a complex of media. The disintegration of traditional narrative structures and their concomitant concept of work and authorship make it clear that even radio drama, radiophonic music, the radio feature etc. still proceed from the premise of a work heard from beginning to end, from the fiction of eagerly receiving a broadcast doled out in exact portions. In these forms radio is thematized as something already of the past.

To understand radio as it was, as it could have been, as it will be, is not only meaningful because - should McLuhan's dictum be true - it will enter the Net as a previously developed medium, but because, as an aspect of the expected megamedium, it reveals, in its own change, a series of major problems in our social dealings with the new technologies - to which the changed, old ones belong. Some of the questions related to this - such as access for all, the guarantee of 'free' exploration of, and reflection on, the current development, its roots and consequences, the aesthetic penetration and conceptual examination of the changing media complex - do crop up in the debate of various scientific disciplines or as a matter of course in speeches and proceedings of conferences on the New Media theme. In practice, though, and in the abundance of theory it generates, these questions are really only asked in the projects of media activists and artists.

'Only those actively integrated in the nets of this **scientific organization** (be it the Internet or the electronic highway à la Al Gore) will track down (and thus influence) the autopoietic rules according to which the military dependencies of the development are hitherto entangled.' (Wolfgang Hagen)

I.e. the scientific organization of the development of the new media, 'which themselves do not represent a process running according to plan either.' Wolfgang Hagen, 'Mediendialektik,' unpublished essay.

The hype surrounding the sectors striving towards a megamedium often makes it look as though the name of the game – even and also in so-called cultural channels – is quotas, or interference-free, bland infotainment, 'attractive' content designed primarily to forestall people's impulses to switch channels or worse, switch off, teleshopping – in short, to turn users into good consumers. Even so, a net is being woven by those who are not fixated on new areas of business and who endeavor – often unpaid – to trace the inner logic of the technologies and to reveal it in the difference to their disappearance in transparency. The 'Small Net in a Big World' that **Geert Lovink** demands from the media activists could benefit from the mistake made by those whom British theorist Richard Barbrook dubs 'corporate cheerleaders' on the way to realizing their ideas of a contemporary media landscape.

In 'A Small Net in a Big World. Or: The Importance of Being Media,' published on 'Nettime,' 2.6.1996. http://www.desk.nl/nettime/.

'... the corporate cheerleaders are trapped within a category mistake: they're trying to impose the form of earlier media onto the new hypermedia ... Above all, interactivity can't be restricted to clicking through a series of menu options. Most people want to meet other people within cyberspace. Unlike the existing electronic media, the Net is not centered on the one-way flow of communications from a limited number of transmitters. On the contrary, hypermedia is a two-way form of communications where everybody is both a receiver and a transmitter. The multimedia corporations will undoubtedly play a leading role in building the infrastructure of the infobahn and selling information commodities over the Net, but they will find it impossible to monopolize the social potential of cyberspace. ... the information superhighway will soon become the basic infrastructure for collaborative work across time and space ...' (**Richard Barbrook**)

In 'Hypermedia Freedom,' 'C-Theory, Theory, Technology and Culture,' vol. 19, no. 1-2 at http://www.ctheory.com/.

Let's hope so, dear Professor Barbrook! As far as many artists/theorists and kindred spirits are concerned, they have indeed been collaborative and interactive across space and time for a long time now – in projects like 'Rivers & Bridges,' for example – but this does not save them, despite all their expertise, from being re-marginalized.

And somewhere, at the very back of our not yet downloaded brains, lurks the suspicion that the converging megamedium might just be part of something which, although there is something in it for human perception and its adequate forms of expression, is not all that interested in human beings after all....

Ground Zero

An e-mail interview

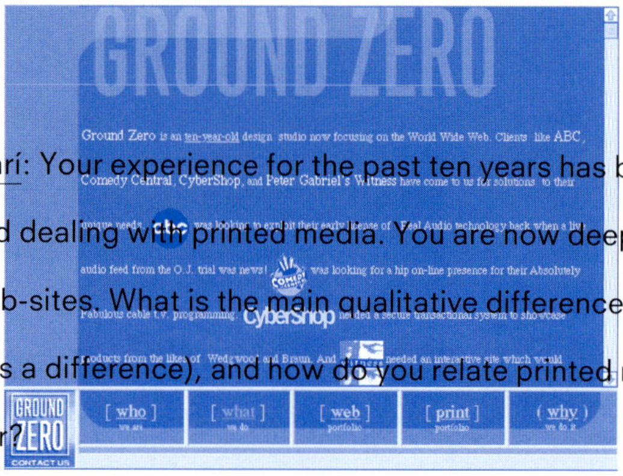

Bartomeu Marí: Your experience for the past ten years has been based on designing and dealing with printed media. You are now deeply involved in designing web-sites. What is the main qualitative difference between the two (if there is a difference), and how do you relate printed matter with on-line matter?

Ground Zero: Years ago, when digital print production was in its infancy, our studio was entirely mobile and exclusively focused on print design. The technology allowed us to set up a shop at a moment's notice and to modem our files to printers virtually anywhere. During that period we made a proposal to design a series of books for the AIR Alexander Manifestation in Rotterdam (1993) using these digital design and production means. Taking inspiration from the modernist approach – we began to look more closely at the aesthetic of the machines we were using to design. We adopted a simple 4x4 grid and resurrected a Van Doesburg typeface – both of which expressed Bauhaus and De Stijl enthusiasm for the technological promise of the machine age. By showing the grid, we exposed our means of construction while creating both a machine-inspired aesthetic and smaller individual digital images (easing our production process). At the same time, we proposed giving the power of the print media to the residents of the Alexanderpolder themselves by allowing them to create a community publication with a mobile studio like our own.

Although the project was never realized, many of our concerns identified in the Air Alexander proposal have resurfaced in our web design work. In our very early web design – months after the World Wide Web was born, allowing information to be viewed graphically on the Internet – we adopted much of the same thinking and techniques. By dividing graphics into smaller elements and reassembling them in a mosaic or grid on screen we both discovered a new aesthetic for the medium and eased the strain on the viewer receiving the digital information.

This new media differs from print in its entirely digital composition, its interactive nature, and its constant availability. Finally, we can not only deliver information to our audience but also collect information from them. This interaction is the greatest quantitative difference between print and web design. We are able to design and provide information not just digitally but dynamically and according to each individual's personal taste. This newfound expression of design and the possibility of collaborating with one's audience has inspired us to create a web-based journal which anyone, anywhere, will be able to contribute to.

Marí: Then you are not only designing but also broadcasting. Putting information on-line as you describe it makes you more publishers than designers.

Ground Zero: Whenever a new medium is born, its earliest practitioners must, of necessity, understand its technical nature. And that understanding leads to the birth of an 'aesthetic.' The earliest photographers were chemists. Bodoni didn't just concern himself with the design of type but created and printed information. The division between those who create and those who disseminate information is new to this century but with the advent of desktop publishing and the World Wide Web, that line is getting blurred every day. Desktop publishing produced a new undisciplined breed of designers – some brilliant, some disastrous. It also allowed individuals to self-publish their work giving birth to the 'zine' which, in turn, is the precursor to the personal home page of the World Wide Web. Internet technology has returned the means of design, production, and distribution back to individuals (an overwhelming number of them).

Marí: How is your audience reacting?

Ground Zero: Our immediate audience is our clients – those that are looking to design and implement Web-sites. Some of our clients are selling smoke-and-mirrors at the moment, some offer sheer entertainment, others are offering very real, tangible informational services that will truly help people in their daily lives. One, The Lawyers Committee for Human Rights, will use their web-site to compel lawyers and laypersons alike to get involved with international asylum issues. Another client, **Witness**, an organization which puts video cameras in the hands of human rights groups to document abuses world wide, is using the medium to self-publish or broadcast very controversial information that the news media shies away from.

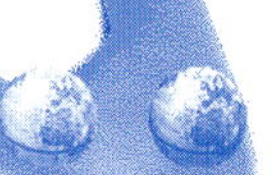

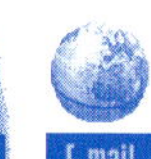

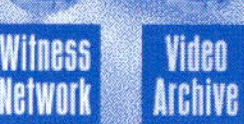

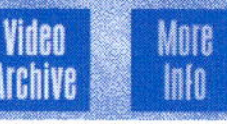

Marí: What kind of feedback are you getting? And, in terms of actual practice, how are you using it?

Ground Zero: The individuals surfing the Net for enlightenment or entertainment are an astoundingly articulate group. With the aid of electronic mail, they voice their opinions liberally. We feel it's our role to push the envelope of the technology and explore new design approaches. Most recently we've been contemplating issues surrounding navigation and are building sites which have everpresent, intuitive navigational systems. The recent redesign of our own Web-site explores this issue and either enthralls or angers people with its more radical use of the technology. We're still weighing their reactions in order to make use of them in our future work.

Marí: You once said that 'In this medium, there hasn't yet been a Marcel Duchamp who has come up with the urinal...' What kind of Duchampian 'revolution' would you expect to happen within this medium?

Ground Zero: In every medium, there are works that expose something so fundamental that all future work will have different meaning – Duchamp's urinal, Rietveld's red & blue chair, Corbusier's modular theories, Godard's shattered narratives. It took years for other media to experience this modernist shattering of convention which the Web must undergo but it's difficult to predict what will expose digital media to that breakdown.

Since its greatest (and as yet untapped) strength is its interactive nature, we expect that the 'revolution' lies there.

Marí: What kind of interaction with other existing media (radio, print, cinema) is now taking place on the Net? How much of this is 'invention' and how much is just 'recycling' or 'alternative use?'

Ground Zero: In working on the Web, it's hard to ignore the precedents set by technologies which fundamentally changed our world such as radio, television and film. While the Web seems to be an extension of these earlier electronic media, the path we hope to see it take is altogether different.

Radio, film and television were initially employed to broaden the scope of what we could see and hear – things that already existed in their own right. The aim of information technology in general, and the Web in particular, is quite different. Through new ways of 'data mining' – looking at raw data with the help of complex computer algorithms – new patterns and relationships are created (often catered to the individual user's preferences) thus approaching an interactivity that has eluded older electronic media.

In terms of the interaction between the Net and existing media, we've built **Web-sites** for print (Random House's Alexander Liberman monograph), radio (ABC RadioNet), television (Comedy Central) and documentary film (Witness). Much of the content used in the Web-incarnations of these projects is recycled but much of it is enhanced by the addition of 'on-demand' interactivity. One can look through Liberman's images, excerpted from his monograph, or listen to Liberman describing his images in a recent interview. One can listen to select ABC radio broadcasts or set up a personalized play list, customizing the site according to the news and information one's most interested in. One can read through the human rights information on the Witness site, or the environmental information on the Mothers

& Others For a Livable Planet site or get involved with current human right or environmental issues directly through these sites.

Marí: What role will art and artists play on the Net?

Ground Zero: Already, the 'plastic' and 'new media' arts have a presence on the Web. Many prestigious art journals and magazines are contributing their illuminating, critical, yet static information while new media-oriented Webzines aspire to create truly interactive dialogues. The best example we've seen of this is Mark Tribe's Rhizome. It is a daily Listserve which sparks a constant dialogue between its members via e-mail.

Marí: How, in your opinion, is the use of the Net evolving, and how will it evolve in the future?

Ground Zero: Today's use of this fledgling media relies too heavily on its precedents, print and broadcast media. Its real strength lies in its malleability, flexibility, custom ability – it's overall dynamism. That's what we **hope**, ultimately, to explore here at Ground Zero.

Biographies

Carl Andre (1935)
is an artist living and working in New York. His work has been shown in solo exhibitions at the Städtisches Museum Mönchengladbach (Monchengladbach, 1968, cat.); the Wide White Space (Antwerp, 1968, 1969, 1971, 1974); the Haags Gemeentemuseum (The Hague, 1987, cat.); the Solomon R. Guggenheim Museum (New York, 1970, cat.); the Museum of Modern Art (New York, 1973); the Kunsthalle Bern (Bern, 1975, cat.); the Clocktower, The Institute for Art and Urban Resources (New York, 1976, 1983); the Kabinett für Aktuelle Kunst (Bremerhaven, 1976); the Whitechapel Art Gallery (London, 1978, cat.); the Musée d'Art Contemporain (Montreal, 1979); the Institute of Contemporary Art (Boston, 1980); the Nouveau Musée (Villeurbanne, 1983); the Westfälischer Kunstverein (Munster, 1984, cat.); the Stedelijk Van Abbemuseum (Eindhoven, 1987, cat.); the Castello di Rivoli (Turin, 1987); the Museum Haus Lange (Krefeld, 1996); the Kunstmuseum Wolfsburg (Wolfsburg, 1996, cat.); and in group exhibitions at the Los Angeles County Museum of Art (Los Angeles, et al., 1967, cat.); *Prospect 68*, Städtische Kunsthalle (Dusseldorf, 1968, cat.); *documenta 4* (Kassel, 1968, cat.); *When Attitudes Become Form*, Kunsthalle Bern (Bern, 1969, cat.); the Whitney Museum of American Art (New York, 1969, 1970, 1973, 1976, 1978, 1982, 1983, 1986, 1989, 1991, cats.); *Sonsbeek* (Arnhem, 1971, cat.); the Rijksmuseum Kröller-Muller (Otterlo, 1972, 1975, cats.); the National Gallery of Victoria (Melbourne, 1973, cat.); the Palais des Beaux Arts (Brussels, 1974, 1994, cats.); the Musée national d'art moderne, Centre Georges Pompidou (Paris, 1977; 1986, cat; 1992); the Stedelijk Museum (Amsterdam, 1978, 1982, cats.); *La XXXVIII Biennale di Venezia* (Venice, 1978, cat.); the Renaissance Society at the University of Chicago (Chicago, 1980); *Westkunst* (Cologne, 1981, cat.); *documenta 7* (Kassel, 1982, cat.); the Museum of Contemporary Art (Los Angeles, 1983, 1986, cats.); the Frankfurter Kunstverein (Frankfurt am Main et al., 1986, cat.); *Münster Skulpturen Projekte* (Munster, 1987, cat.); *Bilderstreit* (Cologne, 1989, cat.); the Städtische Kunsthalle Düsseldorf (Dusseldorf et al., 1990); the Musée d'Art Moderne de la Ville de Paris (Paris, 1990); the National Museum of Art (Osaka, 1990, cat.); the Fundació La Caixa (Barcelona, 1991, 1992); the Malmö Konsthall (Malmo, 1994, cat.); The Museum of Contemporary Art (Tokyo, 1995); the Tel Aviv Museum of Art (Tel Aviv, 1995); and the Centro Galego de Arte Contemporaneo (Santiago de Compostela, 1996).

Rasheen Araeen (1935)
is an artist, curator and writer living and working in London. He is founding editor of the magazine *Third Text: Third World Perspectives on Contemporary Art & Culture*. His artworks have been shown in solo exhibitions at the Ikon Gallery (Birmingham, 1987); The Central Space (London, 1991); the Modern Art Gallery Fukuoka Art Museum (Fukuoka, 1993); and at the *V Habana Bienal* (Havana, 1994, cat.); and in group exhibitions at the Camden Arts Centre (London, 1970); the Whitechapel Art Gallery (London, 1978, 1986); *Magiciens de la terre*, the Musée national d'art moderne Centre Georges Pompidou (Paris, 1989, cat.); the Hayward Gallery (London, 1989); and the Vancouver Art Gallery (Vancouver, 1991). His early writings are published in the collection 'Making Myself Visible' (1984), and his recent writings – mostly published in *Third Text* – have been translated and published in Sweden, the Netherlands, Germany, Austria, France, and Cuba.

Robert Atkins (1951)
is an art historian and writer living and working in New York. He is founder and editor of *TalkBack! A Forum for Critical Discourse*, an on-line journal about on-line art and social issues. Atkins is author of *ArtSpeak; A Guide to Contemporary Ideas, Movements and Buzzwords* (1991) and *ArtSpoke; A Guide to Modern Ideas, Movements and Buzzwords (1848-1944)* (1993). He has written art critism for such publications as *Arena*, *Art + Text*, *Art in America*, *Artforum*, *The New York Times*, the *Village Voice*, and *World Art*. He has written essays on, amongst others, Nancy Burson, Chema Cobo, Hung Liu, and Antoni Muntadas. The exhibitions he has curated include *David Ireland*, The New Museum of Contemporary Art (New York, 1984); and *Between Science and Fiction*, the *XVIII Bienal de São Paulo* (San Paulo, 1985, cat.). He is a visiting professor of art history at San Francisco State University and a co-founder of Visual AIDS, the art-world collective that originated *Day Without Art* and the *Red Ribbon*.

Anke Bangma (1969)
is an art historian living and working in Rotterdam. She is a curator at Witte de With, where she co-curated the exhibitions *Wat eten wij vandaag?* by Jef Geys (1993), *Still/A Novel* (1996) and *Voorwerk 5* (1996). She writes for such art magazines as *Frieze*, and *Metropolis M* as well as the *Witte de With - Cahiers*. She has written essays on James Coleman, Marlene Dumas, Jef Geys, Dan Graham, Maria Roosen, Marijke van Warmerdam, and Jeff Wall.

Marcel Broodthaers (1924-1976)
was an artist who lived and worked in Brussels. During his lifetime, his work was shown in solo exhibitions at the Palais des Beaux Arts (Brussels, 1965, 1967, cat; 1972, 1974); the Wide White Space (Antwerp, 1966, cat; 1968, 1969, 1971, 1972, 1973, 1974); the Städtisches Museum (Monchengladbach, 1971, cat.); the Kunstmuseum (Basel, 1974); the National Galerie (Berlin et al., 1975); the Städtische Kunsthalle (Dusseldorf, 1975); the ICA (London, 1975); and in group exhibitions at the Stedelijk Van Abbemuseum (Eindhoven, 1966); *Prospekt*, Städtische Kunsthalle (Dusseldorf, 1968, 1973); *Konzeption – Conception*, the Städtisches Museum (Leverkusen, 1969); *Information*, the Museum of Modern Art (New York, 1970); *documenta 5* (Kassel, 1972, cat.). Since his death, his work has been shown in solo exhibitions at the Palais des Beaux-Arts (Brussels, 1976); the Tate Gallery (London, 1977, 1980, cats.); the Kunstverein Hamburg (Hamburg, 1979); the Museum Ludwig (Cologne, 1980, cat.); the Museum Boijmans Van Beuningen (Rotterdam, 1981, cat.); the Kunsthalle Bern (Bern, 1982, cat.); the Museum Moderner Kunst (Vienna, 1985); the Bonnefantenmuseum (Maastricht, 1987, cat.); and in group exhibitions *Europe in the Seventies*, the Art Institute of Chicago (Chicago et

al., 1976, cat.); *La Biennale di Venezia* (Venice, 1976, 1978, 1980, 1986, cats.); *documenta 7* (Kassel, 1982, cat.); *Attitudes/Concepts/Images*, the Stedelijk Museum (Amsterdam, 1982); *Reconsidering the Object of Art 1965-1975*, the Museum of Contemporary Art (Los Angeles, 1995, cat.). His films include *Le Corbeau et le Renard* (1967); *La Pluie* (1969); and *Musée d'Art Moderne, Département des Aigles, Section Cinéma* (1971).

Edwin Carels (1964)
is a film and video critic living in Ghent. He teaches film history at the Hogeschool Sint-Lukas in Brussels and conducts seminars at the Film Museum in Antwerp and at the Stuc in Louvain. He contributes film reviews to Belgian Radio (BRTN) and is a film editor for Kunst & Cultuur (associated with the Palais des Beaux Arts, Brussels). He has written essays on, amongst others, Aleksandr Sokurov, Oliver Stone, and Manoel de Oliveira for the film magazine *Andere Sinema*, as well as essays on video art, experimental film, and film in art for the Belgian newspaper *De Morgen*.

Jean-François Chevrier (1954)
is an art historian, art critic and curator living and working in Paris. He teaches history of contemporary art at the École Nationale Supérieure des Beaux-Arts in Paris. He co-curated *Matter of Facts*, the Musée des Beaux Arts (Nantes et al., 1988, cat.); *Une autre objectivité/Another Objectivity*, the Centre National des Arts Plastiques (Paris et al., 1989, cat.); *Photo Kunst*, Staatsgalerie Stuttgart (Stuttgart, 1989, cat.); *Craigie Horsfield*, the ICA (London et al., 1989, cat.); *Lieux communs, figures singulières*, the Musée d'Art Moderne de la Ville de Paris (Paris, 1991, cat.); *Walker Evans & Dan Graham*, Witte de With (Rotterdam et al., 1992, cat.); and *Craigie Horsfield, The City of the People*, the Fundació Antoni Tàpies (Barcelona, 1996, cat.). He has written essays on, amongst others, Jean-Marc Bustamante, John Coplans, Craigie Horsfield, Ken Lum, Michelangelo Pistoletto, and Jeff Wall.

Jan Dibbets (1941)
is an artist living and working in Amsterdam and San Casciano. His work has been shown in solo exhibitions at the Galerie 845 (Amsterdam, 1965); the Galerie Konrad Fischer (Dusseldorf, 1971, 1973, 1976, 1977, 1979, 1986, 1987, 1996); the Museum Haus Lange (Krefeld, 1969, cat.); the Stedelijk Van Abbemuseum (Eindhoven, 1971, 1980, 1988, cats.); *La XXXVI Biennale di Venezia*, Padiglione Olandese (Venice, 1972, cat.); the Stedelijk Museum (Amsterdam, 1972, cat.); the Leo Castelli Gallery (New York, 1973, 1975, 1983, 1990); the Kunsthalle Bern (Bern, 1980, cat.); the Musée d'Art Moderne de la Ville de Paris (Paris, 1980, cat.); the Solomon R. Guggenheim Museum (New York, 1987, cat.); the Walker Art Center (Minneapolis, 1988, cat.); the Fundació Espai Poblenou (Barcelona, 1990, cat.); and in group exhibitions such as *Earth Art*, Cornell University (Ithaca, New York, 1967); *When Attitudes Become Form*, Kunsthalle Bern (Bern, 1969, cat.); *Konzeption – Conception*, the Städtisches Museum (Leverkusen, 1969); *Information*, the Museum of Modern Art (New York, 1970); the *Guggenheim International* (New York, 1971); *Projekt '74 Kunst bleibt Kunst*, Kunsthalle Köln (Cologne, 1974, cat.); *documenta* (Kassel, 1972, 1977, 1982, cats.); *Illusion and Reality* (Canberra, 1977); *Europe in the Seventies*, the Arts Institute of Chicago (Chicago, 1977); *Westkunst* (Cologne, 1981, cat.); *La Grande Parade*, the Stedelijk Museum (Amsterdam, 1984); *Ouverture*, the Castello di Rivoli (Turin, 1985); *Carnegie International* (Pittsburgh, 1985); *La XLIII Biennale di Venezia* (Venice, 1988, cat.); *Bilderstreit* (Cologne, 1989, cat.); *Conceptual Art*, the Musée d'Art Moderne de la Ville de Paris (Paris, 1991); and *Reconsidering the Object of Art 1965-1975*, the Museum of

Contemporary Art (Los Angeles, 1995, cat.).

Yvonne Dröge-Wendel (1961)
is an artist living and working in Amsterdam. Her work has been shown in solo exhibitions at Galerie d'Eendt (Amsterdam, 1994); De Garage (Hoorn, 1995); the Stadsgalerij (Heerlen, 1995); and in group exhibitions at Het Balkon (Ghent, 1991); W 139 (Amsterdam, 1992); the National Museum of Botswana (Gaberone, 1993); *De Kracht van Heden*, Loods 6 (Amsterdam, 1993, cat.); *Prix de Rome*, Arti et Amicitiae (Amsterdam, 1994, cat.); the Ausstellungshalle der Bundesrepublik Deutschland (Bonn, 1995). She has published three artist's books: *Men Wearing* (1992); *Objects Make Our World* (1993); and *La benedizione della macchina* (1995).

Erik Eelbode (1959)
is an art historian living and working in Ghent. He writes essays on photography for the art journal *De Witte Raaf* and the Belgian newspaper *De Morgen*. He programs courses and lectures for the Amarant Foundation, a center for the study and teaching of art, theater and philosophy.

Christoph Fink (1963)
is an artist living and working in Ghent. His work has been shown in solo exhibitions at the Galerij Netwerk (Aalst, 1994); the APP.BXL (Brussels, 1996); and at group exhibitions at the Palais des Beaux Arts (Brussels, 1990, 1992, 1994); the Galerij Bureaux et Magasins (Ostend, 1993); *Prospectus* (Brussels, 1994); the Carre St. Nicolas (Paris, 1994); *Among Others ... Onder Anderen* (Venice, 1995, cat.); and the Galerie des Beaux Arts (Brussels, 1995).

Ground Zero
is a small New York based design studio, specializing in the design of World Wide Web sites for the Internet. Their experience in print media has resulted in a unique and valuable perspective on the need for design and technology to serve content and, ultimately, the viewer. Ground Zero's continous innovations focus on enhancing Web-site flexibility and appeal while seeking out new ways in which to emphasize the media's interactivity.

Heidi Grundmann (1938)
is a radio program producer living and working in Vienna. She works for the Austrian National Radio and Television (ORF) since 20 years. In 1987 she created the radio program 'Kunstradio-Radiokunst' which presents original artworks for radio. She is a founding member and president of Transit, a non-profit association for the production of cultural projects in the public space of the electronic media. She was involved in the realization of 'Horizontal Radio' (1995) and 'Rivers and Bridges' (1996), two international radio and Internet projects. Grundmann lectures and writes on art and the new media and has curated symposia and exhibitions related to art practice in the electronic media, especially radio and television.

Carl Michael von Hausswolff (1964)
is an artist living and working in Stockholm. In 1996 his work was presented in solo exhibitions and projects at the Thomas Nordanstad Gallery (New York); the Bunkder Box 23 (Kaliningrad); Untern Dürchschnitt (Hamburg); Bijster (Amsterdam); and in the groups shows *Interpol*, Färgfabriken (Stockholm, cat.); *(Ut)härda*, Kulturhuset (Stockholm, cat.); and *Manifesta 1* (Rotterdam, cat.). Audio recordings are available through Ash International (London); SubRosa (Brussels); and Silent Records (San Francisco).

Brandt Junceau (1959)
is an artist living and working in Brooklyn, New York. His work has been shown in solo exhibitions at the Galerie Meert-Rihoux (Brussels, 1992, 1994); *Hyde Park*, Witte de With (Rotterdam, 1995, cat.); and in group exhibitions at the Drawing Center (New York, 1982); the Jack Tilton Gallery (New York, 1986); and Witte de With (Rotterdam, 1991).

Sigalit Landau (1969)
is an artist living and working in Jerusalem. Her work has been shown in a solo exhibition at the Israel Museum (Jerusalem, 1995); and in group exhibitions at *Artfocus 94* (Tel Aviv, 1994); the Bograshov Art Gallery (Tel Aviv, 1994); and the Bezalel Academy of Art and Design (Jerusalem, 1994).

Gracia Lebbink (1963)
is a designer living and working in Amsterdam. She studied at the Rietveld Academie in Amsterdam. She designs exhibition catalogues for, amongst others, the Haags Gemeentemuseum; the Stedelijk Museum, Amsterdam; and the Museum Boijmans Van Beuningen, Rotterdam. She was also responsible for the exhibition design of *P. Mondriaan – 1872-1944* (The Hague, 1994).

Jenny Marketou (1956)
is a Greek artist living and working in New York. Her work has been shown in solo exhibitions at the Mailliotis Art Center (Brookline, 1988); The Henry Street Settlement Art Center (New York, 1990); the University of Southern Florida Contemporary Art Museum (Tampa, 1993, cat.); the Western Front Gallery (Vancouver, 1995); the Southeast Museum of Photography (Daytona Beach, 1996); and in group exhibitions at the Maryland Art Place (Baltimore, 1988); the Center for Photography (Woodstock, 1990); the Visual Arts Center of Alaska (Anchorage, 1992); *Expo '92* (Seville, 1992); The Bronx Museum of the Arts (Bronx, 1994, cat.); the Polk Museum of Art (Lakeland, 1995); the Antikenmuseum (Basel, 1996) and *Manifesta 1* (Rotterdam, 1996, cat.).

Rosa Martínez (1955)
is a curator and art critic living and working in Barcelona. She curated such exhibitions as the *Bienal de Barcelona* (1988, 1992, cats.), the Spanish submissions for different editions of the *Mediterranean Biennial* (Bologna, 1988; Marseille, 1990; Tipassa, 1990; cats.); the cycle *5 values for the next millenium* (Sala Montcada, Fundació La Caixa, Barcelona, 1992-93); and *Thinking of You. A Selection of Spanish Contemporary Art*, the Kunsthallen Göteborg (Goteborg, 1996, cat.). She was one of the curators of *Manifesta 1* (Rotterdam, 1996, cat.) and is currently the artistic director of the *5th International Istanbul Biennial*, to be held in September 1997.

Viktor Misiano (1957)
is a curator and art critic living and working in Moscow. Since 1992 he is director of the Contemporary Art Center in Moscow. He curated such exhibitions as *Cultural Differences: Production of a Chef-d'œuvre*, the *3rd International Istanbul Biennial* (Istanbul, 1992); *Identity-Selfhood*, the Museum of Contemporary Art (Helsinki, 1993). He was commissioner for the Russian pavilion at *La XLVI Biennale di Venezia* (Venice, 1995, cat.), and was one of the curators of *Manifesta 1* (Rotterdam, 1996, cat.). He is the founding editor of *Moscow Art Magazine*, and contributes to such art magazines as *Art Press*, *Contemporanea*, *Flash Art*, *Kunstforum*, and *El Pais*.

Eadweard Muybridge
(1830-1904)
was a British photograher who lived and worked in San Francisco. Muybridge is known for his stereoscopic and panoramic photographs of the American landscape, which he published in magazines under the alias Helios. In 1872, Muybridge was the first to photographically record movement. In 1878 Muybridge published his series of motion studies, followed in 1887 by the series *Animal Locomotion*. Muybridge not only assembled the individual images into tableaux, but he also invented the zoopraxiscoop, a projection apparatus with which stills can be synthesized into one flowing movement, creating in a sense the first 'motion pictures.'

Hans-Ulrich Obrist (1968)
is a curator working in Paris and Vienna and living in London. He curated such exhibitions as *The Kitchen Show* (Sankt Gallen, 1991); *Hans-Peter Feldmann*, and *Qui, quoi, où*, Musée d' Art Moderne de la

Ville de Paris (Paris, 1992); *Der Zerbrochene Spiegel* (with Kasper König, Vienna and Hamburg, 1993, cat.); *Migrateurs* (Paris, 1993, 1994, 1995, ongoing); *Cloaca Maxima*, the Museum der Stadtentwässerung (Zurich, 1994); *Do It*, the Ritter Kunsthalle (Klagenfurt et al., 1994, cat.); *Take Me (I'm Yours)*, the Serpentine Gallery (London, 1995); *Vital Use & Traveling Tye*, Museum in Progress (1996); the *Nanomuseum* (traveling); he was one of the curators of *Manifesta 1* (Rotterdam, 1996, cat.). He has edited such publications as *Gerhard Richter, The Daily Practice of Painting* (1996); *Gabriel Orozco, Triunfo della Libertad* (1996); and *Peter Fischli/David Weiss: Börse Zürich* (1996).

Ana Prada (1965)
is a Spanish artist living and working in London. Her work has been shown in solo exhibitions at the Galería Post-Pos (Valencia, 1986); the Galería Temple (Valencia, 1992, cat.); the Centro de Arte Reina Sofia (Madrid, 1995); the Gallery Elba Benitez (Madrid, 1995); and in group exhibitions at the *Mediterranean Biennial* (Thessaloniki, 1987); the Centro Cultural de Mislata (Valencia, 1988), The Mall Gallery (London, 1991); the Casa de America (Madrid, 1993); the *XXII Bienal de São Paulo* (San Paulo, 1994, cat.); and the IVAM, Centre del Carme (Valencia, 1995).

Andrew Renton (1963)
is a curator and art critic living and working in London. He curated the exhibitions *Confrontaciones* (Madrid, 1991) and *Walter Benjamin's Briefcase* (Oporto, 1993). Until 1994, he worked as the British correspondent for *Flash Art* and contributed to numerous books and publications, including editing *Technique Anglaise: Current Trends in British Art* (1991). He is currently the director of Cleveland, a project space in London.

Zeger Reyers (1966)
is an artist living and working in The Hague. His work has been shown in group exhibitions at Maldoror (The Hague, 1995); the Centrum Beeldende Kunst (Rotterdam, 1995); Pictura (Dordrecht, 1995); the Hooghuis (Arnhem, 1995); the Burgvliet (Gouda, 1995); and the Statenhal (The Hague, 1996).

Thomas Sokolowski (1950)
lives in Pittsburgh where he is director of the Andy Warhol Museum. From 1984 until 1996 he was director of the Grey Art Gallery & Study Center, New York University, where he curated such exhibitions as *Morality Tales: History Painting in the 1980s* (1987, cat.); *Success Is a Job in New York ... The Early Art and Business of Andy Warhol* (1989); *Peter Hujar* (1990, cat.); *Interrogating Identity: The Question of Black Art* (1991, cat.); *From Media to Metaphor: Art about AIDS* (1992, cat.); and *Narelle Jubelin 'Soft Shoulder'* (1995).

Hale Tenger (1960)
is an artist living and working in Istanbul. Her work has been shown in solo exhibitions at the Nev Gallery (Istanbul, 1990, and 1992); the Atatürk Library Gallery (Istanbul, 1992); the Women's Library and Research Center (Istanbul, 1993); the Galerie Le Monde de l'Art (Paris, 1995, cat.); and in group exhibitions at the *Istanbul Contemporary Artists Exhibition* (Istanbul, 1986 and 1990, cat.); the *International Istanbul Biennial* (Istanbul, 1992, 1995, cats.); the Stedelijk Museum (Schiedam, 1993, cat.); the *XXII Bienal de São Paulo* (San Paulo, 1994, cat.); the Gallerie Institut für Auslandsbeziehungen (Stuttgart, 1994, cat.); the Museum voor Moderne Kunst (Arnhem, 1995); *Zij Sporen* (Lille et al., 1996, cat.); and *Manifesta 1* (Rotterdam, 1996, cat.).

Nick de Ville (1944)
is an artist and writer on art living and working in London. He is head of visual art at Goldsmiths College, University of London, since 1988. He curated the Arts Council touring exhibition *Refusing to Surface –Art and The Transfiguration of The Ordinary* (London, 1993). His recently published writings include essays on Maria Lalic and Jane Harris.

Colophon

Editor:
Barbera van Kooij

Assistant Editor:
Robin Resch

Editorial Assistants:
Anke Bangma
Ariadne Urlus

Typography:
Gracia Lebbink

Contributors:
Rasheed Araeen, Robert Atkins, Anke Bangma, Edwin Carels, Jean-François Chevrier, Erik Eelbode, Christoph Fink, Ground Zero, Heidi Grundmann, Carl Michael von Hausswolff, Bartomeu Marí, Jenny Marketou, Rosa Martínez, Viktor Misiano, Hans-Ulrich Obrist, Zeger Reyers, Thomas Sokolowski, Hale Tenger, Nick de Ville

Translations:
Brian Holmes (Jean-François Chevrier);
Ruth Koenig (Heidi Grundmann);
Robin Resch (Anke Bangma, Edwin Carels, Zeger Reyers);
John Rudge (Erik Eelbode)

Photography:
Gé Beckman (pp. 8, 9, 12, 13); Bibliothèque Nationale de France, Paris (p. 77); Edwin Carels (pp. 16-23); Konrad Cramer, courtesy of Nadelman Estate, Riverdale-on-Hudson, New York (p. 7); Yvonne Dröge-Wendel (pp. 116, 117, 126-129); Marion Faller (pp. 73, 75); Christoph Fink (pp. 100-107, 111); Bob Goedewaagen (pp. 48-68, 85, 89, 93-99, 108, 109, 114, 120-123, 132-143); Roland Groenenboom (p. 151 [r]); Ground Zero (pp. 180-184); Carl Michael von Hausswolff (p. 144); Brandt Junceau (pp. 4, 6, 10, 11); Jannes Linders (pp. 148-151 [l], 152, 153); Sjoerd v/d Hucht (pp. 112, 131); Bernard Schaub (pp. 45-47); courtesy VPRO, Hilversum (pp.24-39)

Acknowledgements:
Sylvie Amar, Marseilles; Alex Andriaansens, Rotterdam; Ian Christie, London; Chris Dercon, Rotterdam; Ydessa Hendeles Art Foundation, Toronto

Printer:
Heinrich Winterscheidt GmbH, Dusseldorf

Edition:
2000

Publisher:
Witte de With, center for contemporary art, Rotterdam
Richter Verlag, Düsseldorf

Witte de With – Cahier # 6 will be published in March 1997

Witte de With, center for contemporary art
Witte de Withstraat 50
3012 BR Rotterdam
The Netherlands
tel + 31 (0) 10 411 01 44
fax + 31 (0) 10 411 79 24
e-mail wdw@pi.net

Witte de With is an initiative of the Rotterdam Arts Council and is supported by the Dutch Ministry of Culture.

Richter Verlag GmbH
Corneliusstraße 48
D-40215 Düsseldorf
tel + 49 (0) 211 37 02 02
fax + 49 (0) 211 37 70 99

ISBN 3-928762-65-6

The cover was specially designed by Jan Dibbets for Witte de With – Cahier # 5. Work of Jan Dibbets was presented in the exhibition Still/A Novel.

Printed and bound in Germany